Key Thinkers
Past and Present

Social Science Lexicons

Key Topics of Study
Key Thinkers, Past and Present
Political Science and Political Theory
Methods, Ethics and Models
Social Problems and Mental Health

Key Thinkers, Past and Present

Edited by Jessica Kuper

LONDON AND NEW YORK

First published in 1987 by
Routledge & Kegan Paul Limited
11 New Fetter Lane, London EC4P 4EE

Published in the USA by
Routledge & Kegan Paul Inc.
in association with Methuen Inc.
29 West 35th Street, New York, NY 10001

Set in Linotron Baskerville
by Input Typesetting Ltd., London SW19 8DR
and printed in Great Britain
by Cox & Wyman Ltd, Reading, Berks

Library of Congress Cataloging in Publication Data

Social science encyclopedia. Selections.
  Key thinkers, past and present.

  (Social science lexicons)
  Selections from: The Social science
encyclopedia. 1985.
  Includes bibliographies and index.
  1. Social scientists—Biography.
2. Social sciences—Dictionaries.   I. Kuper,
Jessica.   II. Title.   III. Series.
H57.S5825   1987   300'.92'2   [B]   86–33860

British Library CIP Data also available
ISBN 0–7102–1173–2

Contents

Key Thinkers, Past and Present: the entries

Adler
Althusser
Arendt
Aristotle
Aron
Arrow
Barthes
Bateson
Bentham
Blau
Bloch
Boas
Bowlby
Braudel
Bruner
Burke
Chomsky
Comte
Cournot
Dewey
Durkheim
Elias
Engels
Evans-Pritchard
Eysenck
Feyerabend
Foucault
Frazer
Freud, A
Freud, S
Friedman

Goffman
Gouldner
Gramsci
Habermans
Hayek
Hegel
Hobbes
Hull
Hume
Illich
Jakobson
James
Jung
Keynes
Klein, M
Kropotkin
Kuhn
Lacan
Laing
Leontief
Le Play
Lévi-Strauss
Lévy-Bruhl
Locke
Lukács
Luria
Machiavelli
Malinowski
Malthus
Mannheim
Marcuse

Marshall
Marx
Mauss
McLuhan
Mead, G
Mead, M
Merton
Michels
Mill
Montaigne
Montesquieu
Morgan
Mosca
Myrdal
Pareto
Park
Parsons
Pavlov
Peirce
Piaget
Plato
Popper
Radcliffe-Brown
Ricardo
Rogers
Rostow
Rousseau
St Simon
Sartre
Saussure
Schumpeter

Contributor List

General Editor: Jessica Kuper

Bartley, W W III	Dept of Philosophy, California State University at Hayward and The Hoover Institution, Stanford
Baum, Alan	Dept of Social Science, Middlesex Polytechnic, Enfield, Middlesex
Beiner, R S	Dept of Politics, University of Southampton and Dept of Philosophy, Queen's University, Kingston, Ontario
Bem, Sacha	Dept of Psychology, University of Leiden
Birnbaum, Pierre	Dept of Political Science, University of Paris
Black, R D C	Dept of Economics, The Queen's University of Belfast
Bloor, David	Science Studies Unit, University of Edinburgh
Bolen, Jean Shinoda	C G Jung Institute, San Francisco
Bronfenbrenner, Martin	Dept of Economics, Duke University, Durham, N. Carolina and Aoyama Gakuin University, Tokyo
Brown, Barrie	Dept of Psychology, Institute of Psychiatry, University of London
Buckley, Kerry W	Northampton, Massachusetts
Bulmer, Martin	Dept of Social Administration, The London School of Economics and Political Science
Carver, Terrell	Dept of Politics, University of Bristol
Cohen, Brenda	Dept of Philosophy, University of Surrey
Darnell, Regna	Dept of Anthropology, University of Alberta, Edmonton
Elbers, Ed	Dept of Psychology, University of Utrecht

Feiwel, George R	Dept of Economics, University of Tennessee, Knoxville
Femia, Joseph V	Dept of Political Theory, University of Liverpool
Forbes, Duncan	Clare College, and Dept of History, University of Cambridge
Geary, Dick	Dept of German Studies, University of Lancaster
Gibson, H B	Cambridge
Gieryn, Thomas	Dept of Sociology, Vanderbilt University, Nashville Tennessee
Gilgen, Albert R	Dept of Psychology, University of Northern Iowa, Cedar Falls
Green, Jerry	Dept of Economics, Harvard University
Haddock, B A	Dept of Political Theory, University College, Swansea
Hagege, Claude	Dept of Linguistics, Ecole Pratique des Hautes Etudes, Paris
Hansson, Bjorn	Dept of Economics, University of Lund
Hazan, Haim	Dept of Sociology and Anthropology, University of Tel Aviv
Humphreys, Sally	Dept of Anthropology, University of Michigan, Ann Arbor
Ignatieff, Michael	King's College Research Centre, King's College, University of Cambridge
Israel, J	Dept of History, University College London
Johnson, Harry M	Dept of Sociology, University of Illinois at Champaign-Urbana
Kalberg, Stephen	Center for European Studies, Harvard University
Karady, Victor	Centre for European Sociology, CNRS, Paris

Kassiola, Joel	Dept of Political Science, Brooklyn College, City University of New York
Kellner, Douglas	Dept of Philosophy, University of Texas at Austin
Kelly, Aileen	King's College, University of Cambridge
Ketner, Kenneth Laine	Institute for Studies in Pragmatism, Texas Tech University, Lubbock, Texas
Kimmel, H D	Dept of Psychology, University of South Florida
Kraynak, Robert	Dept of Political Science, Colgate University, Hamilton, NY
Kuper, Adam	Dept of Human Sciences, Brunel University, Uxbridge, Middlesex
Lavers, Annette	Dept of French, University College London
Lemert, Charles	Dept of Sociology, Wesleyan University, Middletown, Connecticut
Leonini, Luisa	Dept of Sociology, University of Milan
Lipset, David	Dept of Anthropology, University of Minnesota
Lock, Grahame	Faculty of Social Science, Catholic University of Nijmegen, The Netherlands
Maclean, Ian	Queen's College, University of Oxford
McLellan, David	Eliot College, University of Kent
McQuail, Denis	Dept of Mass Communications, University of Amsterdam
Meja, Volker	Dept of Sociology, Memorial University of Newfoundland, St John's, Newfoundland
Menzies, Kenneth	Dept of Sociology and Anthropology, University of Guelph, Ontario
Minogue, Kenneth	Dept of Government, The London School of Economics and Political Science

Modell, Judith	Dept of Social Sciences, Carnegie-Mellon University
Moggridge, Donald	Royal Economic Society, Toronto
Panoff, Michel	CNRS, Paris
Peach, Terry	Faculty of Economic and Social Studies, University of Manchester
Peel, John	Dept of Sociology, University of Liverpool
Pollack, Alan S, MD	Adult Outpatient Clinic, McLean Hospital, Belmont, Massachusetts
Pollock, George H, MD	President, American Psychoanalytic Association
Pomorska Jakobson, Krystyna	Foreign Languages and Literatures, Massachusetts Institute of Technology
Pouillon, Jean	Editor *L'Homme*, Paris
Prestwich, M C	Dept of History, University of Durham
Prins, Gwyn	Emmanuel College, University of Cambridge
Rangell, Leo, MD	Los Angeles
Rhodes, G F	Dept of Economics, Colorado State University
Richardson, John T E	Dept of Human Sciences, Brunel University, Uxbridge, Middlesex
Rosen, F	Dept of Politics, The London School of Economics and Political Science
Rothschild, Kurt	Dept of Economics, Johannes Kepler University, Linz, Austria
Schnabel, P E	Dept of Sociology, University of Bielefeld, West Germany
Schroder, Peter	Ministry of Education, Leidschendam, The Netherlands
Skinner, Andrew	Dept of Political Economy, University of Glasgow

Smith, N V	Dept of Linguistics, University College London
Stehr, Nico	Dept of Sociology, University of Alberta, Edmonton
Stone, Alan A, MD	Harvard Law School
Tarascio, Vincent J	Dept of Economics, University of North Carolina at Chapel Hill
Tarullo, Louisa B	Cambridge, Massachusetts
Thayer, H S	Dept of Philosophy, City University of New York
Tiryakian, Edward J	Dept of Sociology, Duke University, Durham, North Carolina
Turner, Jonathan H	Dept of Sociology, University of California, Riverside
Whitaker, John K	Dept of Economics, University of Virginia
Whitworth, John	Dept of Sociology, Simon Fraser University, Burnaby, British Columbia
Willis, Roy	University of Edinburgh
Winter, J M	Pembroke College, University of Cambridge
Yolton, John W	Dean, Rutgers, The State University of New Jersey

Introduction

Social scientists typically associate particular theories with individual thinkers, yet in various ways it goes against the grain to do so. Almost by definition, social scientists are averse to any 'great man' theory of history, and as a tribe they are suspicious of claims to unique insight. And certainly, it is true that on inspection virtually any theory, however apparently revolutionary, falls into place once its contemporary context is understood. That being said, individuals have been extremely important in all the social sciences, their political convictions, life experiences, personal fortunes sometimes playing a crucial part in the formulation or dissemination of particular intellectual traditions. Even experts in the field may find it hard to separate a particular explanation from the influential person who first propagated it. The informal history of each discipline is replete with more or less reliable biographical information, and quite rightly so. Intellectual biographies can never be a substitute for a serious history of the social sciences, but they are never irrelevant, and they can provide a valuable orientation. The present volume offers a personalized, sometimes admittedly idiosyncratic view of the history of the social sciences, but at the same time it serves as a stimulating introduction to a great variety of theories, hypotheses, and ways of thinking about the individual in society.

Adler, Alfred (1870–1937)

Born in Vienna in 1870, Alfred Adler trained as an ophthalmologist and first practised general medicine before becoming a psychiatrist and a charter member of Freud's inner circle. An energetic, articulate man and a prolific writer, Adler was soon made the titular president of the first Psychoanalytic Society. Unlike Freud, Adler was a political and social activist; in retrospect it seems that at least some of their conflicts were due to this basic difference. Adler is best known for originating the concept of the inferiority complex and of understanding personality in terms of the compensatory struggle to achieve superiority. Although Adler did in fact formulate these reductionistic and mechanistic theories, he also had other, much more subtle, ideas about human nature.

Adler disagreed with Freud's emphasis on biological and sexual factors; instead he gave primary importance to social, interpersonal, and hierarchical relationships. Adler believed that man is motivated by his expectations of the future: 'The final goal alone can explain man's behaviour.' Human behaviour is not determined by childhood experiences themselves, but by the 'perspective in which these [experiences] are regarded'. The final goal of the individual determines the perspective in which he views these important early experiences. This conception of behaviour, motivated by a particular perspective and by ideas about the future, is described as 'idealistic positivism'. It is compatible with, if not identical to, many strands of contemporary psychological, philosophical and social theory (for example, existential theories). Idealistic positivism de-emphasizes the importance of the unconscious and transforms Freud's conception of psychic determinism.

Adler rejected the idea that a human being is simply a product of environment and heredity. He posited a creative self, which makes something of hereditary abilities and interprets environmental impressions, thus constituting a unique individual personality and life-style. While Adler, the first defector from Freud's circle, is today ignored by most psychologists and psychiatrists, in his Individual Psychology can be found the beginnings of contemporary humanistic psychology. Adler's views suggested the great importance of methods of childrearing and education. According to Adler, physical infirmity, rejection, and pampering were the factors most likely to result in a pathological style of life. He helped establish child-guidance clinics in association with the Viennese school system, and became a major advocate of the child-guidance movement.

Alan A. Stone
Harvard University

Further Reading

Adler, A. (1924 [1920]), *The Practice and Theory of Individual Psychology*, London. (Original German edn, *Praxis und Theorie der Individual-Psychologie*, Munich.)

Ansbacher, H. L. and Ansbacher, R. R. (eds), (1956), *The Individual Psychology of Alfred Adler: A Systematic Presentation in Selections from his Writings*, New York.

Hall, C. S. and Lindzey, G. (1978), *Theories of Personality*, 3rd edn, New York.

Orgler, H. (1973), *Alfred Adler, The Man and His Work*, New York.

Sperber, M. (1970), *Alfred Adler, oder das Elend der Psychologie*, Vienna.

Althusser, Louis (1918 –)

The French Communist philosopher, Louis Althusser, was a prisoner-of-war in Germany throughout the Second World War, thereafter student, lecturer, and finally Secretary of the École Normale Supérieure, rue d'Ulm, Paris.

In 1965 Althusser published a collection of essays under the title of *Pour Marx* (*For Marx*, 1969) in which he opposes new Marxist 'orthodoxies' and in particular 'humanist' and 'Hegelian' interpretations of Marx. In order to designate the form of causality operating in the social and political sphere, he borrows (from Freud) the concept of 'over-determination', which he glosses by reference to Lenin's and Mao's notion of the uneven development of social contradictions. He also rejects the notion of 'alienation', a term found in certain early writings of Marx (and more rarely in the later works), but which is inconsistent with Marx's later explanatory apparatus (class struggle, the dialectic of relations and forces of production, the dictatorship of the proletariat, and so on).

In the same year (1965), Althusser published a collective volume (co-authors Etienne Balibar, Pierre Macherey, Jacques Rancière, Roger Establet), *Lire le Capital* (*Reading Capital*, 1970), where he expounds a supposed opposition between the 'ideological' and 'scientific' domains – an opposition which he was later, in his *Eléments d'auto-critique*, 1974 (*Essays in Self-Criticism*, 1976), to reject as 'rationalist' in inspiration and content. He also borrows another concept from Freud, that of the 'symptomatic reading' of a text (involving the search for the absence of a concept beneath the presence of a word and vice versa). From Gaston Bachelard he takes, in modified form, the notion of the 'epistemological break' to denote the division between the 'problematic' (ideological or theoretical framework) of Marx's earlier and later works.

In the article 'Ideologie et appareils idéologiques d'état' (1969), Althusser adds to the well-known Marxist notion of the (repressive) State apparatus that of the 'ideological State apparatus(es)', these consisting not only of the political parties, the education system, the legal system and other 'public' organisms, but also of 'private' organisms like the family, the Church, the arts, sport and even the trade unions. The distinction between the 'public' and 'private' spheres is itself, he argues, proper to the 'juridical ideology' dominant in bourgeois society;

it is thus the influence of bourgeois, juridical ideology which masks the fact that so-called 'private' institutions can function as State apparatuses, that is, function in the reproduction of capitalist relations of production and of capitalist State power.

In his *Réponse à John Lewis* (1972–73) (*Reply to John Lewis*, 1976) originally published in the journal of the British Communist Party, *Marxism Today*, Althusser maintains his earlier distinction between the early and later Marx (and his preference for the latter), but admits that the break is less clean than he had first suggested. In his *Eléments d'auto-critique* and his Soutenance d'Amiens (1975), entitled 'Est-il simple d'être marxiste en philosophie?' (the answer is 'no'), he attributes his earlier, simplistic account of the break to his adoption of the above-mentioned 'rationalist' distinction between ideology and science. He now believes that these are not opposites, but concepts of different orders (a science may, for example, function as an ideology). There can, he claims, be no *general theory* of science in its opposition to ideology; strictly speaking, there can be no epistemology (or philosophy of science) which is not caught up in the bourgeois juridical practice of adjudging from above the criteria of legitimacy of candidate sciences.

In his *22ème Congrès* – of the French Communist Party – (1977), and his *Ce qui ne peut plus durer dans le parti communiste* (1978), Althusser turns his attention to directly political matters. In the former, he welcomes the opening announced at the Party Congress (the 'Union of the Left', and so on), but criticizes the theoretical arguments used to justify this opening. In the latter, he violently attacks the Party for its organizational forms (half parliamentary, half military – and in any case 'bourgeois') and for its 'fortress' mentality and practices.

From 1965 onwards, when his name became widely known, Althusser was subjected to bitter criticism, both from non-Marxists and from Marxists who had chosen either to defend the old Stalinist line and practices or to attempt to escape from these by adopting humanist positions. Most of these critiques are of little theoretical interest. Notable for its inaccuracies is E. P. Thompson's (1978), which uses *ad personam* invective in order to defame Althusser with the label of 'Stalinist'.

(Althusser had, in the *Réponse à John Lewis*, distinguished between a 'right-wing' and a 'left-wing' critique of Stalin, the former being limited to moral indignation and accusations of violations of legality, the latter attempting 'serious historical research into the causes of the Stalin deviation'.) More interesting, though also of direct political inspiration, is a critical commentary by an ex-pupil, Jacques Rancière (1974).

Althusser's influence on French philosophy, as well as on French Marxism, remains very considerable, though by now it takes mostly indirect forms.

Grahame Lock
Catholic University of Nijmegen

References
Rancière, J. (1974), *La Leçon d'Althusser*, Paris.
Thompson, E. P. (1978), *The Poverty of Theory*, London.

Further Reading
Althusser, L. (1976), *Essays in Self-Criticism*, London. (Contains a bibliography of works by and on Althusser.)
Callinicos, A. (1976), *Althusser's Marxism*, London.
Geras, N. (1972), 'Althusserian Marxism', *New Left Review*, 71.
Kolakowski, L. (1971), 'Althusser's Marx', *The Socialist Register*, London.

Arendt, Hannah (1906–75)

Hannah Arendt was one of the outstanding students of politics of our century, making major contributions both as a political historian and as a political philosopher. Born in Germany in 1906, she attended the universities of Marburg, Freiburg and Heidelberg, where she completed a doctoral thesis on St Augustine under the supervision of Karl Jaspers. After fleeing Germany in the 1930s she worked with Zionist organizations in France, then moved to the United States where she lectured at many universities, principally the University of Chicago and the New School for Social Research in New York. She was the recipient of many distinguished prizes and honours for her contribution to contemporary thought and culture. She died in New York City in 1975.

Arendt first gained prominence as an analyst of the totalitarian form of government, with the publication in 1951 of her monumental three-part study, *The Origins of Totalitarianism*. Her most important philosophical work is *The Human Condition* (1958), in which she argues that there is a 'hierarchy within the *vita activa* itself, where the acting of the statesman occupies the highest position, the making of the craftsman and artist an intermediary, and the labouring which provides the necessities for the functioning of the human organism the lowest'. On the basis of her division of worldly activities into labour, work and action, Arendt affirms that freedom and autonomy can only be fully realized in the context of a politicized existence, and that only by fulfilling the public dimension of life can we give meaning to human affairs. This comprehensive theoretical understanding of politics is further developed in *On Revolution* (1963) and in the essays in *Between Past and Future* (1961; enlarged edition, 1968).

All of Hannah Arendt's works generated intense controversy, from her early writings on Zionism of the 1940s to her essays on the American republic of the 1960s and 1970s. The fiercest of these controversies was provoked by her book *Eichmann in Jerusalem* (1963), in which she argued that the real evil of Eichmann's deeds lay in the bureaucratic shallowness that allowed the monstrous to appear ordinary – Eichmann's mindless banality. This raises the question of whether thoughtlessness is somehow essential to political evil, or whether the active exercise of man's mental abilities actually makes us abstain from evil-doing, and it is to questions such as these that Arendt devoted her last, unfinished work on *The Life of the Mind* (posthumously published in 1978).

Ronald Beiner
University of Southampton
and Queen's University, Kingston, Ontario

Further Reading

Canovan, M. (1974), *The Political Thought of Hannah Arendt*, New York.

Hill, M. A. (ed.) (1979), *Hannah Arendt: The Recovery of the Public World*, New York.

Kateb, G. (1983), *Hannah Arendt: Politics, Conscience, Evil*, Totowa, N.J.

Young-Bruehl, E. (1982), *Hannah Arendt: For Love of the World*, New Haven.

Aristotle (384–322 B.C.)

Aristotle was born in Stagira, a small Greek town on the coast of the Chalcidice peninsula in the northern Aegean, close to the Macedonian kingdom. His father was court physician to Amyntas III of Macedon. He studied with Plato in Athens from 367 to 348 B.C., then moved to the court of Hermias of Atarneus, in the Troad, another pupil of Plato, one of whose relatives became Aristotle's wife. After a period in Lesbos, Aristotle joined Philip of Macedon's court as tutor to Alexander in 342. After Philip's death in 335 he returned to Athens and stayed there until Alexander's death in 323 when the anti-Macedonian reaction forced him to withdraw to Chalcis, the Euboean city from which his mother had come.

Aristotle was thus exposed both socially and intellectually to contradictory influences. Socially, he belonged to the Greek polis in the last generation of its struggle to retain autonomy – a limited local autonomy in the case of Stagira, the claim of a fading imperial power in the case of Athens – but at the same time he had firsthand experience of living in the new form of society which was to succeed the polis. Intellectually, his father was part of the empiricist tradition of Greek medicine with its emphasis on careful reporting and observation as the only basis for accurate prediction of the likely future course of a disease, while his teacher Plato believed that the visible world was merely an imperfect reflection of a reality which could only be apprehended intellectually, and thought it the right and duty of the philosopher to reason out the correct course for man and society and then – if only he could – impose his prescriptions on his fellow-citizens.

This second source of tension in Aristotle's life, between opposing epistemologies, was much more productive than the first. It led him firmly to assert the intellectual satisfactions, as well as the practical utility, of studying apparently low forms of animal life and engaging in the messy activity of dissection (Lloyd, 1968), and to extend the methods of research developed in medicine to the whole field of biology; it also led him to reflect systematically on logic and processes of reasoning, both human and animal. The characteristics which men shared with animals, instead of being seen in a negative way as inescapable defects (mortality) of a 'lower nature' which had to be subdued, became a basis for understanding, a transformation with particularly far-reaching implications for psychology. At the same time the principles of argument which had been worked out piecemeal in law courts, assembly debates, medical practitioners' disputes and treatises (see Lloyd, 1979), mathematical proofs and philosophical dialectic were drawn together in a systematic way which helped to establish methodology or 'second-order thinking, thinking about thinking' (Elkana, 1981) as a problem in its own right. Aristotelian logic eliminated many of the sophistic puzzles that had perplexed earlier philosophers, extended the idea of 'proof' from mathematics to other areas of scientific and philosophical thought, and even, by implication, anticipated modern concern with the relation between logic and language. Aristotle's comprehensive interests and systematic organization of research provided the first foundations for the idea of a university as a place where students are taught how to extend knowledge in all its branches. Discussion and criticism of earlier views was part of the method.

In principle, Aristotle's procedure of taking earlier opinions, particularly those of Plato, and criticizing them on the basis of observation, coupled with his experience of the Macedonian court, might have produced important transformations in political theory. In practice it hardly did so; Aristotle's political and social thought remained enclosed within the frame of the city-state. His view that *chremastiké*, the art of money-making,

was morally wrong prevented him from developing an understanding of the growing importance of trade and commodity
production in the economy, and in general his empirical attitude
tended to lead to a confusion between the statistically normal
and the normative. Since domination of males over females,
parents over children and masters over slaves was so widespread, it must be right. Belief in the superiority of Greeks over
barbarians led Aristotle to assert that some ethnic groups are
naturally fit only for slavery, a view which had a long career
in the service of racism, though Aristotle himself thought of
culturally rather than physically transmitted qualities. The view
that the family, observable in animals as well as humans, is the
basic form of society had already been put forward by Plato in
the *Laws* (earlier Greek thinkers had pictured primitive human
society as a herd rather than a family: Cole, 1967). Aristotle
took it up and extended it, producing the model of development
from family to *gens* and from *gens* to phratry, tribe and city
which was to have such an important influence on anthropological kinship theory in the nineteenth and early twentieth
centuries. Possibly the growing importance of private life in
fourth-century Greece, particularly for those not directly
involved in politics, helped to make attractive this view of
kinship ties as the basic bonds of society (see Humphreys,
1983a-b).

The fact that Aristotle lived an essentially 'private' life (whatever his relations with the ruling Macedonian élite may have
been) is also responsible for his marked interest in the study of
friendship; this plays a large part in his *Ethics*. Friends were
the philosopher's reference-group, the people who assured him
that the philosophical life was indeed the best life; Aristotle's
discussion of friendship supplied the basis for the stoic idea of
the 'cosmopolitan' community of wise men. At the same time
Aristotle's relations with the Macedonians had given him plenty
of experience of patronage and friendship between unequals:
his acute remarks here were to prove useful to later Hellenistic
philosophers grappling with the problems of royal power and
patronage.

There is no doubt that Aristotle was a shrewd observer of

human behaviour. He firmly rejected the Socratic view that virtue is knowledge, on the grounds that people often know what they should do but fail to do it; what we call virtues are consistent patterns of behaviour, though conscious thought must also enter into them. How the habit of virtuous behaviour is to be inculcated Aristotle does not really tell us. He accepted social conflict as inevitable; rich and poor have opposed interests and the best way to achieve stability in society is to have a large middle class of intermediate wealth who will hold the balance between them. This emphasis of the middle class as the key element in society is part of his more general belief that virtue and right action is a mean between two extremes, an adaptation of the Delphic maxim *méden agan*, 'nothing to excess'.

Medical theory helped Aristotle fit a much more liberal attitude than Plato's towards the arts into this framework. Though care must be exercised in choosing music and stories for children, adults can benefit from having their emotions stirred by music and tragedy because this purges them of excess emotion. In an important book, Jones (1962) has argued that Aristotle's remarks on tragedy have been misunderstood in the European tradition and, when correctly interpreted, can throw light on the difference between Greek conceptions of the person and of action and those of the modern Western world.

In a sense Aristotle seems to be a consolidator rather than an innovator, a systematizer and synthesizer of ideas originally raised by others. Nevertheless, the new fields of research he opened up, his contributions to methodology and scientific terminology, and the intelligence of his criticisms of earlier views and proposed solutions to philosophical problems make him a founding figure in many branches of research. The works which survive were written for teaching purposes rather than for the general public: their inelegant, rather jerky style gives an attractive impression of an unpretentious thinker who faced difficulties and objections to his own views honestly.

S. C. Humphreys
University of Michigan

References

Cole, T. (1967), *Democritus and the Sources of Greek Anthropology*, Cleveland.

Elkana, Y. (1981), 'A programmatic attempt at an anthropology of knowledge', in E. Mendelssohn and Y. Elkana (eds), *Sciences and Cultures*, 5.

Humphreys, S. C. (1983a), 'The family in classical Athens', in S. C. Humphreys, *The Family, Women and Death*, London.

Humphreys, S. C. (1983b), 'Fustel de Coulanges and the Greek "genos" ', *Sociologia del diritto*, 9.

Jones, H. J. (1962), *Aristotle and Greek Tragedy*, London.

Lloyd, G. E. R. (1968), *Aristotle: The Growth and Structure of his Thought*, Cambridge.

Lloyd, G. E. R. (1979), *Magic, Science and Religion*, Cambridge.

Further Reading

Guthrie, W. K. C. (1981), *History of Greek Philosophy, VI. Aristotle: An Encounter*, Cambridge.

Wood, E. and Wood, N. (1978), *Class Ideology and Ancient Political Theory. Socrates, Plato and Aristotle in Social Context*, Oxford.

See also. *Plato*.

Aron, Raymond (1905–83)

Raymond Aron was unquestionably the dominant figure in French sociology since World War I. He was born in Paris in 1905 and from 1955 to 1968 was professor of sociology at the Sorbonne. Most contemporary French sociologists were in one way or another his students; his numerous studies have been widely read, and his frequent articles in the press have influenced politicians as well as a broader public. He was a sociological theorist, and an analyst of industrial society, and he re-evaluated the role of politics in society.

In his thesis *Introduction à la philosophie de l'histoire* (1939) (An Introduction to the Philosophy of History) Aron demonstrated the way in which the objective knowledge of history depended on values, and he rejected the pretensions of Christian and Hegelian theories. He introduced to France the German sociology of Dilthey, Tönnies, Simmel and, above all, Weber (*La Sociologie allemande contemporaine* (1936)) (Contemporary German Sociology) which he had studied at source, and he disseminated this relativistic way of thinking in a domestic context often susceptible to deterministic approaches. In *Les Etapes de la pensée sociologique* (1965) (*Main Currents in Sociological Theory*, 1968), Aron argued for the views of a Tocqueville or a Weber in preference to those of a Marx or a Durkheim. Tocqueville had re-evaluated the role of politics in social change, while Weber had based the sociology of action in the recognition of the multiple values of individuals. Aron took issue with the tenets of Marxism, which plays an important role in France, advocating instead a relativistic position and suggesting that the end of the age of ideologies was approaching.

Aron attempted to analyse the novel features of industrial society, the degree of pluralism, the multiplicity of values, the role of social mobility, anticipating studies which were to be developed on the other side of the Atlantic, such as those of Daniel Bell. However, he rejected the view that there would inevitably be a convergence between the societies of the US and the USSR, which some regarded as identical industrial societies, showing that the point at which the political structure intervenes, as an independent variable, has specific effects (*Dix huit leçons sur la société industrielle* (1963) (*18 Lectures on Industrial Society*, 1967); *La Lutte de classes* (1964) (The Class Struggle).

Aron published a great deal on Pareto and on the theory of élites, suggesting a more limited definition of the élite which permitted the differentiation of those situations in which there was an element of pluralism with competing élites, as in France and the US, from those in which a ruling class was formed by the fusion of élites, as in Soviet society. Here again he adopted a comparative approach and insisted, like Weber and Schumpeter, on the specificity of the political élites. He also drew attention to contemporary empirical studies, such as Robert Dahl's, which analysed plural élites.

Given his rediscovery of the weight of the political factor, Aron was logically drawn to the study of international relations, where the political factor was most evident. In *Paix et guerre entre les nations* (1967), (*Peace and War*, 1967), and then in *Penser la guerre, Clausewitz* (1976), (*Clausewitz, Philosopher of War*, 1983), he analysed power politics as a demonstration of the specificity of politics and, in consequence, of the multiple values of the actors themselves.

Pierre Birnbaum
University of Paris

Further Reading
Many books by Aron have appeared in English translation. These include:

(1957) *The Opium of the Intellectuals*
(1968) *Democracy and Totalitarianism*
(1968) *Progress and Disillusion: The Dialectics of Modern Society*
(1969) *The Elusive Revolution: Anatomy of a Student Revolt*

Dahrendorf, R. (1980), 'The achievements of Raymond Aron', *Encounter*.

Arrow, Kenneth (1921–)
Born in 1921 in New York City, Arrow received his education at the City College of New York and Columbia University. In 1947 he went to the Cowles Commission at Chicago as a research associate, and later served as an assistant professor. He was on the faculty at Stanford University from 1949 to 1968, at Harvard University from 1968 to 1979, and is currently Joan Kenney professor of economics and professor of operations research at Stanford. In 1972, he shared the Nobel Prize for economics with John Hicks.

Arrow has been a major innovator in many areas of economic theory. His Ph.D. thesis (published in 1951 as *Social Choice and Individual Values*) was the seminal work in social choice theory. It showed the general impossibility of designing rules for social decision making that are suitably sensitive to the preferences of the members of society and capable of achieving efficient outcomes. Subsequently, he wrote many papers on moral philosophy and applications of social choice theory to welfare economics.

His second major line of work is in the area of general equilibrium theory. Together with Gerard Debreu (who received a Nobel Prize for economics in 1983), he demonstrated the precise circumstances in which a market-clearing price system could be proven to exist. The optimality of this system was also analysed. In the context of this theory, in which the simultaneous and initial interaction among economic agents occurs, Arrow studied the stability of price adjustment processes, the ability of markets to mitigate risks, the departures from optimality when the classical conditions are violated, and the appropriate social policy when these problems arise.

His work has also touched on some applied problems: medical insurance, investment, growth, index numbers and many others. In addition, he has written extensively on the economics of information and uncertainty and has formed some of the central ideas of the subject: measures of risk aversion, the effects of moral hazard, adverse selection and privacy of information on resource allocation in markets and organizations.

Jerry Green
Harvard University

Further Reading
Arrow, K. (1965), *Aspects of the Theory of Risk-Bearing*, New York.
Arrow, K. (1971), *Essays in the Theory of Risk-Bearing*, New York.

Barthes, Roland, (1915–80)

Roland Barthes, after studies in French and Classics interrupted by tuberculosis, started a career as literary critic and researcher in sociology. These pursuits were soon subsumed in his mind under a common theoretical activity which he identified with semiology, the general science of signs (manifested as words, images, gestures, and so on) postulated by the linguist Saussure at the turn of the century. This realization is enshrined in *Mythologies* (1957–72), a brilliant analysis of the myths perpetrated around consumer goods, sporting events or public figures for conservative purposes by cultural institutions and the media. It determined Barthes's image as a censor, casting over contemporary arts and mores the stern eye of a Marxist and existentialist critic, and seeking to account for all symbolic systems, whether observed in everyday life or in innovating, 'difficult' authors like Brecht or the New Novelists, by means of equally new and difficult theories based on linguistics and psychoanalysis. This impression, confirmed by articles reprinted in *Sur Racine* (1963) *(On Racine,* 1964) and *Essais critiques* (1964) *(Critical Essays,* 1972), led to a violent attack by a Sorbonne specialist of Racine; the resulting 'quarrel of the critics' drove Barthes to define, in *Critique et vérité* (1966), an approach to all sign systems, and especially texts, which came to be known as 'structuralism'. This term, largely derived from Lévi-Strauss's application of Jakobson's linguistics to anthropology but also descriptive of recent trends in psychoanalysis, historiography and Marxism, characteristically stressed unconscious structures, as opposed to the self-knowledge and freedom professed by phenomenologists and existentialists, or to the traditional reverence for creators and characters at the expense of critical discourse in literary studies.

Despite rearguard action in academic circles (Barthes always taught in marginal though prestigious establishments, the École Pratique des Hautes Études, then, from 1976, the Collège de France), structuralism soon played a dominant part in all the social sciences. Barthes then set out to develop semiology thanks to a framework supplied by Saussure's study of the linguistic sign. This made linguistics both the method and the object of the prospective new science, a paradox which looms through his structuralist studies: *Eléments de sémiologie* (1967), *Système de la Mode* (1967), and many articles on narrative. Barthes's own overriding concern with language led him to regard science, its methodological constraints and its ideal of truth, as irrelevant in the literary field (this comes out in *S/Z* (1970), a commentary on Balzac which shows his own outstanding gift for formal inventiveness) and even in the social sciences, which depend on ordinary language. Other thinkers had come to the same conclusion, a major factor of this disaffection towards science being the disillusionment of French intellectuals with Marxist rationality, where truth is both intelligible and historical. This left the individual as the sole remaining value, and Barthes's lifelong aspirations towards self-expression came to the fore in the semi-autobiographical works like *Le Plaisir du texte* (1973) *(The Pleasure of the Text,* 1975), *Barthes par Barthes* (1975) *(Roland Barthes by Roland Barthes,* 1977), and *Fragments d'un discours amoureux* (1977) *(A Lover's Discourse: Fragments,* 1978). They even saved him from total theoretical nihilism, since his last work, *La Chambre claire* (1980) *(Camera Lucida,* 1982) unites the scientific and the personal, the observed and the observer; this enquiry into the essence of photography where grief is an actual agent of discovery fittingly sums up a career which epitomized the self-consciousness typical of modern science and modern art.

Annette Lavers
University College London

Further Reading
Culler, J. (1983), *Barthes,* London.
Lavers, A. (1982), *Roland Barthes, Structuralism and After,* London.

Bateson, Gregory (1904–80)

An elusive, Cambridge-trained anthropologist who made his career largely in the United States, Bateson was an interdisciplinary innovator and generalist, with strong interests in philosophy and ecology.

The youngest son of the Cambridge geneticist, William Bateson, his upbringing left him a zoologist by training and marked him as a naturalist by inclination. He was thus well suited to contribute to British social anthropology in the 1920s, when the worth of biological analogies in the social sciences was being debated. Gregory Bateson's awkward classic, *Naven*

(1936), a study of ritual among a New Guinea people, broke ground theoretically: its argument was self-referential and focused explicitly on abstracting patterns of conflict in social relations.

During the New Guinea fieldwork, Bateson met the American cultural anthropologist Margaret Mead, whom he later married. In 1936 they did fieldwork together in Bali, resulting in the publication of a unique photographic ethnography, *Balinese Character* (1942). Influenced by the American subdiscipline of culture-and-personality and by cybernetic theories of self-correcting machinery, Bateson became interested in problems posed by theories of learning. He studied communication and learning among aquatic mammals and families of schizophrenics while based in a Veterans Hospital in Palo Alto, California. Following the failure of dolphin research in the 1960s, he turned his attention to global ecological crises and the bearing of cybernetic theory upon Western thinking.

Bateson's most influential post-war work came in 1956. Seeking a theory of communication, he developed an interpretation of schizophrenia in which the concept of a 'double bind' played a central role. Double binds were patterns of paradoxical love/hate messages exchanged in families leading to the psychosis of one of the members. Bateson regarded this theory as an attack upon reductionist learning theory. He was dismayed when his notion and the holistic focus on the family as an integrated unit was taken up for therapeutic purposes by psychiatrists.

It is, as yet, too early to assess Bateson's unique career and his various contributions to the social sciences. His diverse enterprise can be approached best in the anthology *Steps to an Ecology of Mind* (1973). His final book, *Mind and Nature* (1978), returned to an early interest in the analogy between evolutionary change and the structure of mind.

David Lipset
University of Minnesota

Further Reading
Lipset, D. (1982), *Gregory Bateson: The Legacy of a Scientist*,
 Boston.

Bentham, Jeremy (1748–1832)

Jeremy Bentham was undoubtedly one of the most important
and influential figures in the development of modern social
science. His numerous writings are major contributions to the
development of philosophy, law, government, economics, social
administration and public policy, and many have become
classic texts in these fields. To these subjects he brought an
analytical precision and careful attention to detail which,
especially in matters of legal organization and jurisprudence,
had not been attempted since Aristotle, and he transformed in
method and substance the way these subjects were conceived.
He combined a critical rationalism and empiricism with a vision
of reform and, latterly, radical reform, which gave unity and
direction to what became Philosophic Radicalism. Although he
was not the first philosopher to use the greatest happiness
principle as the standard of right and wrong, he is rightly
remembered as the founder of modern utilitarianism. Many of
Bentham's writings were never published in his lifetime or were
completed by various editors. The new edition of the *Collected
Works* (1968 — in progress) will replace in approximately sixty-
five volumes the inadequate *Works of Jeremy Bentham* (1838–43),
edited by John Bowring, and will reveal for the first time the
full extent and scope of Bentham's work.

Bentham is best known for some of his earliest writings. *An
Introduction to the Principles of Morals and Legislation* (printed in
1780 and published in 1789) and *Of Laws in General* (not
published until 1945) are important texts in legal philosophy
and, together with his critique of William Blackstone's *Commentaries on the Laws of England* in the *Comment on the Commentaries*
(published first in 1928) and *A Fragment on Government* (1776),
represent major landmarks in the development of jurisprudence.
The *Introduction to the Principles of Morals and Legislation* was also
intended to serve as an introduction to a penal code, which was
an important part of a lifelong ambition, never fully realized,

of constructing a complete code of laws (latterly called the Pannomion). At this time Bentham also turned to economic questions which were to occupy him in various forms throughout his life. His first publication was the *Defence of Usury* (1787), a critique of Adam Smith's treatment of this subject in *The Wealth of Nations*.

From the outset of his career, Bentham was devoted to reform and especially to the reform of legal institutions. His attitude towards fundamental political reform developed more slowly. Although at the time of the French Revolution he was not part of the radical movement in England, he wrote numerous manuscripts in support of democratic institutions in France. He eventually reacted strongly against the excesses of the revolution, but earlier contacts, largely developed through Lord Lansdowne, and the publication of his *Draught of a New Plan for the Organisation of the Judicial Establishment of France,* led to his being made an honorary citizen of France. One important development of this period was his friendship with Etienne Dumont, the Swiss reformer and scholar, whose French versions of Bentham's works, especially the *Traités de législation, civile et pénale* (1802), were read throughout Europe and Latin America and earned for Bentham a considerable international reputation. Following the French Revolution much of Bentham's practical energies were devoted, in conjunction with his brother Samuel, to establishing model prisons, called Panopticons, in various countries. His main effort in England failed, and this failure, though ultimately compensated by the government, was one factor leading him to take up the cause of radical political reform. The influence of James Mill was perhaps the most important factor (there were many) in his 'conversion' to radicalism in 1809–10, and the publication of *A Plan of Parliamentary Reform* in 1817 launched the Philosophic Radicals in their quest for parliamentary reform. In the 1820s, though now in his seventies, Bentham resumed the task of codification and the construction of the *Pannomion* in response to requests from governments and disciples in Spain, Portugal, Greece and Latin America. In his massive, unfinished *Constitutional Code* (1822–), he set forth a theory of representative democracy which was a grand synthesis of many of his ideas and a classic of liberal political thought.

Frederick Rosen
The London School of Economics
and Political Science

Further Reading
Halévy, E. (1901–4), *La Formation du Radicalisme Philosophique,* 3 vols, Paris.
Hart, H. L. A. (1982), *Essays on Bentham: Jurisprudence and Political Theory,* Oxford.
Hume, L. J. (1981), *Bentham and Bureaucracy,* Cambridge.
Rosen, F. (1983), *Jeremy Bentham and Representative Democracy,* Oxford.
See also: *Mill.*

Blau, Peter M. (1918–)

Peter Blau has contributed substantially, both theoretically and empirically, to the scientific analysis of social structure. He was a graduate student in sociology at Colombia University during a revival of Max Weber's theories of bureaucracy. Blau's dissertation, published as *The Dynamics of Bureaucracy* (1952), combined with those by Columbia graduates Philip Selznick and Alvin Gouldner to establish a foundation for the systematic study of formal organizations. His interest in bureaucracies continued for over two decades, although a collection of essays *On the Nature of Organizations* (1974) shows important shifts in theoretical orientation.

Initially, Blau adopted a social psychological perspective focusing on interpersonal relations among workers in bureaucracies. His exploration of how *formal* structures of organizations constrain *informal* social relations of bureaucrats remains a classic of sociological analysis. Blau's early social psychological perspective led to his first contribution to general social theory, *Exchange and Power in Social Life* (1964). Along with work by George Homans, Blau established 'exchange theory' in sociology, which tries to derive theories of social structure from simple processes of social association such as reciprocity and obligation, differentiation of power, bonds of attraction and competition for status.

In the late 1960s, Blau's orientation shifted from social psychological to social structural, from 'micro' to 'macro'. While making this transition, Blau stepped outside the specialty of formal organizations to collaborate with Otis Dudley Duncan on *The American Occupational Structure* (1967), an examination of inter-generational mobility and occupational achievement that initiated sophisticated statistical studies of social stratification and processes of 'status attainment'. His work on bureaucracies went on, but he focused on structural features of organizations, for example, how the size of a bureaucracy affected the proportion of its workers in administrative positions. The social structural perspective led to a second contribution to general social theory, *Inequality and Heterogeneity* (1977). With the elegantly simple definition of 'social structure' as 'the distribution of people among social positions', Blau has offered several (now empirically confirmed) predictions, among them the idea that as a social group increases in size, the proportion of its members who marry outside the group declines.

Blau's theorizing has been consistently rigorous: he defines his terms precisely, announces clearly his assumptions, and states his principles in a way that yields empirical deductions. He once wrote, 'The theorist's aim is to discover a few theoretical generalizations from which many different empirical propositions can be derived.' Few sociologists have done this as often and with as much success.

Thomas F. Gieryn
Indiana University

Bloch, Marc (1886–1944)

One of the most influential medieval historians of the twentieth century, Marc Bloch was a pioneer in broadening the range of historical inquiry. He firmly believed that history was a science, and was a powerful advocate of the value of comparative methods in studying past societies. He was skilled in the use of a wide range of evidence, from chronicles and charters to folk-lore, and he never lost a keen sense of the value of precise detail even when presenting the most general arguments. His initial work on serfdom in the Ile-de-France led on to his classic study of *Les charactères originaux de l'histoire rurale française* (1931) (*French Rural History: An Essay on its Basic Characteristics,* London, 1966). By the time that was written, he had already displayed the width of his interests with *Les rois thaumaturges* (*The Royal Touch,* London, 1973), a remarkable study of healing powers claimed by the French and English monarchies, which showed his ability to take an apparently limited problem and develop its implications extensively. His aim, above all, was to present a total study of medieval society, and he came nearest to achieving this in his great work *La société féodale* (1939, 1940) (*Feudal Society,* 1961). His work focused not upon individuals and their role, but upon society as a whole, and he laid little stress upon political developments. In 1931 Marc Bloch was, with Lucien Febvre, a founder of the influential *Annales d'histoire économique et sociale,* a journal which did much to popularize his novel conception of history. He taught for many years at Strasbourg, and moved to the Sorbonne in 1936. He was an ardent, though not uncritical, patriot, and volunteered for active service in 1939. In 1944 he was executed by the Gestapo because of his activities in the Resistance.

Michael Prestwich
University of Durham

Further Reading
Perrin, Ch.–E. (1948), 'L'oeuvre historique de Marc Bloch', *Revue Historique,* 199.
See also: *Braudel.*

Boas, Franz (1858–1942)

Franz Boas, born in Germany in 1858, naturalized American citizen in 1892, unquestionably dominated both the intellectual paradigm and institutional development of twentieth-century American anthropology until the Second World War, presiding over the emergence of anthropology as a professional discipline based on the concept of culture, and establishing a subdisciplinary scope including cultural, physical and linguistic anthropology as well as prehistoric archaeology.

In spite of his focus on professionalism in science, Boas himself was trained in (psycho) physics in his native Germany, thereby coming into contact with the folk psychology of Wundt and the anthropology of Bastian (European folk cultures) and Virchow (anthropometry). Boas's dissertation at the University of Kiel in 1881 on the colour of sea water led to concern with the inherent subjectivity of observer perception. His work in geography with Fischer initially supported environmental determinism, but his expedition to the Eskimo of Baffin Land in 1882–3 led to a more flexible argument stressing the interaction of culture and environment.

Boas settled permanently in North America only in 1887, recognizing greater opportunities there for an ambitious young Jewish scholar. In the ensuing years, he was crucially involved in the development of American anthropology in all of its early major centres. The institutional framework for the emerging Boasian anthropology was usually collaboration between a university, ensuring the academic training of professional anthropologists, and a museum to sponsor field research and publication. Boas himself settled in New York, teaching at Columbia from 1896 until 1936. He had previously served as Honorary Philologist of the Bureau of American Ethnology, which dominated Washington and government anthropology. Through F. W. Putnam of Harvard, he organized anthropology at the Chicago World's Fair of 1892 and acquired ties to archaeological work centring at Harvard. Boas's own students established programmes elsewhere, particularly Kroeber at Berkeley, Speck at Pennsylvania, and Sapir in Ottawa. By about 1920, Boasian anthropology was firmly established as the dominant paradigm of the North American discipline.

Boas's theoretical position, often characterized as historical particularism, claimed that unilinear evolution was an inadequate model for the known diversity of human cultures. Human nature was defined as variable and learned tradition.

Although he was extremely interested in particular historical developments, Boas argued that progress did not necessarily follow a fixed sequence, nor was it always unidirectional from simple to complex. He further parted from evolutionary theorists like E. B. Tylor in his contention that cultural learning is basically unconscious rather than rational. Boas produced particular ethnographic examples to argue the limits of theoretical generalization in anthropology, indeed in social science generally. 'Laws' comparable to those of the natural sciences were possible in principle though usually premature in practice. The ultimate generalizations of anthropology would be psychological (1911b), but Boas's own studies rarely transcended the prior level of ethnographic description. Later students, especially Margaret Mead and Benedict, elaborated these ideas in what came to be called 'culture and personality'.

Particular histories could not be reconstructed in detail for societies without written records. In contrast, Boas stressed the historical dimensions of synchronically observable, particular cultural phenomena. For example, distribution was the primary reconstructive method to trace the diffusion (borrowing) of folklore motifs and combinations on the Northwest Coast. Elements in a single culture had diverse sources rather than a single common origin. Boas applied this same argument to linguistic work, assuming that language was a part of culture. His scepticism about distant genetic relationships of American Indian languages was consistent with his lack of training in Indo-European philology, and brought him into frequent disagreement with his former student Edward Sapir whose linguistic work was far more sophisticated.

On the other hand, Boas made important contributions to linguistics, being the first to establish the theoretical independence of race, language and culture as classificatory variables for human diversity (1911a). He broke with the Indo-European tradition in insisting on the 'inner form' (Steinthal) of each language in its grammatical patterning, developing new analytic categories appropriate to American Indian languages.

Boas insisted on the importance of firsthand fieldwork in living cultures, and he returned again and again to the Kwakiutl and other Northwest Coast tribes. He trained native informants to record their own cultures, and collected native language texts for folklore as well as linguistics. He was particularly concerned to record the symbolic culture of these tribes, focusing on art, mythology, religion and language, and was influential in the development of the disciplines of folklore and linguistics as well as anthropology.

Boas's own research spanned the scope of anthropology in its North American definition. In archaeology, he pioneered in Mexico and the Southwest in developing research programmes to reconstruct the history of particular cultures. In physical anthropology, he demonstrated that the head-form of descendants of immigrants can change in a single generation, thereby illustrating the essential variability and plasticity of the human form. He further developed important statistical methods for human growth studies, using longitudinal studies and family-line variation to show the role of environment in modifying heredity. Moreover, Boas was dedicated to the idea that anthropology had practical consequences for society generally, arguing, particularly in response to events in Nazi Germany at the end of his life, for the essential equality of races (defined in terms of statistical variability) and the validity of each cultural pattern.

Boas is, then, more than any other individual, responsible for the characteristic form which the discipline of anthropology has taken in North America. During his long career, he and several successive generations of students stood for a particular scope, method and theory, applied largely to the study of the American Indians. The increasing diversity of North American anthropology since World War II still has Boasian roots.

Regna Darnell
University of Alberta

References
Boas, F. (1888 [1964]), *The Central Eskimo,* Lincoln, Nebraska.
Boas, F. (1911a), 'Introduction', in *Handbook of American Indian Languages,* Washington, D.C.

Boas, F. (1911b), *The Mind of Primitive Man*, New York.
Boas, F. (1940), *Race, Language and Culture*, New York.

Further Reading
Goldschmidt, W. (ed.) (1959), *The Anthropology of Franz Boas.
Memoir of the American Anthropological Association*, 89.
Harris, M. (1968), *The Rise of Anthropological Theory*, New York.
Stocking, G. (1968), *Race, Culture and Evolution*, New York.
See also: *Mead, M.*

Bowlby, John E. (1907–)

John Bowlby is best known for his pioneering research on the development and nature of mother-child attachment and for his long association with the child family psychiatry service at the Tavistock Clinic in London. Born on 26 February 1907 in London into a medical family, he was educated at Dartmouth and Trinity College, Cambridge. In 1937, he was appointed staff psychiatrist at the London Child Guidance Clinic. Later during the Second World War he served as consultant psychiatrist in the RAMC (1940–5) in the rank of Lieutenant Colonel. In 1946 he joined the Tavistock Clinic as chairman of the Department for Children and Parents, where he remained until his retirement in 1972.

Bowlby is both a prolific writer and controversial figure. His many publications include *Personal Aggressiveness and War* in 1938, *Forty Four Juvenile Thieves* in 1946, *Maternal Care and Mental Health* (written for the World Health Organization) in 1951, *Child Care and the Growth of Love* in 1953 and, perhaps most extensive and authoritative, his three volumes in the series *Attachment and Loss* published between 1969 and 1980.

Bowlby received many academic and national honours in his years of work with disturbed children and their families including an honorary D.Sc at Cambridge in 1977 and the Distinguished Scientific Contribution Award for research into child development in 1981. Well before this latter honour, however, Bowlby's research and clinical work into early separation, mother-child attachment, and childhood disturbance had had a widespread impact on all the mental health and welfare professions, in particular child psychiatry and social work, although in later years the methodological basis for Bowlby's theory of maternal deprivation was subjected to criticism and debate, with new evidence and more thorough analysis suggesting alternative explanations for his earlier work. His influence on professionals of all kinds working with disturbed children and their families has been acknowledged world-wide.

Barrie J. Brown
Institute of Psychiatry
University of London

Braudel, Fernand (1902–1985)

Fernand Braudel is one of the most influential historians of this century. The third of the founding fathers of the so-called Annales School of French historians, he followed the lead of such pre-World War II historians as Lucien Fèbvre and Marc Bloch in seeking to revitalize the study of history in the light of the methods and concerns of the social sciences. However, Braudel went considerably further along this path than his predecessors, developing an entirely new concept of, and approach to, historical studies. In a more systematic way than his precursors, Braudel sought to emancipate history from its traditional division into political, economic and cultural history and to achieve a 'total' history of society. The objective was to integrate all aspects of man's past, placing the chief emphasis on the changing environment and life-style of the common man and of society as a whole. Inevitably, the new approach involved a marked de-emphasizing and distancing from the political and constitutional history, which had always been the central preoccupation of historians and which Braudel and his followers term 'histoire événementielle'.

Braudel's most famous and important work, on the Mediterranean world in the age of Philip II, was first published in 1949 and was greeted with widespread and eventually almost universal acclaim. A revised and considerably expanded second edition was published in 1966. In this vast undertaking, Braudel transcended all political and cultural borders, as he did in all historical practice and procedure. He sought to reveal the immense scope and implications of the decline of Mediterranean society in the sixteenth century, achieving a majestic and often elegant synthesis of economic, demographic, cultural and political data and interpretation. It was by no means Braudel's intention to disregard political phenomena; rather he wished to tackle these in a new way, within the context of long- and medium-term socioeconomic trends. Thus one of his principal objectives was to throw new light on the shift in the policy concerns of Philip II of Spain away from the Mediterranean and towards the Atlantic, a change in the direction of Spanish policy making which dates from the 1580s.

Basic to Braudel's approach was his novel categorization of history into simultaneous processes proceeding on different levels at quite different speeds. He envisaged these various trends as taking place on three main levels and, on occasion, compared the processes of historical change to an edifice consisting of three storeys. On the lowest level, he placed the slow, long-term changes in mankind's agrarian, maritime and demographic environment. On the middle level, Braudel placed the medium-term economic and cultural shifts which take place over one or two centuries rather than millenniums. Finally, on his uppermost storey, he located all short-term fluctuations and 'events' in the traditional sense.

This novel approach to history is further developed in Braudel's second major work, an ambitious trilogy entitled *Civilisation matérielle et capitalisme* (1967), (English trans., 1973–82, *Civilization and Capitalism*) which deals with the evolution of the world economy and of society generally from the end of the Middle Ages down to the Industrial Revolution. Despite Braudel's insistence on material factors as the determinants of social change, and his readiness to borrow concepts from Marx, including the term 'Capitalism' which figures prominently in his later work, Braudel's system, like the work of the Annales School more generally, is in essence quite outside the Marxist tradition in that it allocates no central role to class conflict. In the view of some scholars, certain weaknesses evident in the earlier work are much more pronounced in the later study. A less secure grasp of detail, frequent errors both of fact and interpretation of data and, generally, much less convincing evaluations detract considerably from the value of the later work. Certain historians now also see serious defects in Braudel's overall approach, running through his entire *oeuvre* which, besides the two major works, includes a number of noteworthy short books and essays. In particular it is felt that Braudel's method of handling the interaction between socioeconomic and political history is unconvincing and unsatisfactory. Thus, his radical de-emphasizing of political and military power, and the impact of 'events' on socioeconomic development, gives rise in his writing to numerous, often major, distortions.

The influence of Braudel's ideas and the extent to which they have been adopted as the 'modern' approach to historical studies varies from country to country, but is pervasive in several European and many Latin American countries as well as in North America. It was repeatedly asserted that he was 'indisputably the greatest of living historians', but it must also be said that a tendency towards uncritical adulation of his work has become fashionable in many quarters on both sides of the Atlantic. Some history departments in universities, and a number of collaborative historical research projects and publications, have professed Braudel and his approach as the guiding principle directing their studies.

Jonathan I. Israel
University College London

References

Braudel, F. (1966), *La Méditerranée et le monde méditerranéan à l'époque de Philippe II* (2nd enlarged edn, 2 vols), Paris. (English translation of this edn, *The Mediterranean and the Mediterranean World in the Age of Philip II*, 2 vols, New York.)

Braudel, F. (1967–79), *Civilisation matérielle et capitalisme*, Paris. (English translation, *Material Civilization and Capitalism, 15th–18th Century*, Vol. 1: *The Structure of Everyday Life*,

London, 1982; Vol. II: *The Wheels of Commerce*, London, 1983; Vol. III: *The Perspective of the World*, London, 1984.)

Further Reading
Journal of Modern History (1972), Vol. 44: special issue on Braudel with articles by H. R. Trevor-Roper and J. H. Hexter, and Braudel's own 'Personal testimony'.
Israel, J. I. (1983), 'Fernand Braudel – a reassessment', *The Times Literary Supplement*, no. 4, 164.
See also: *Bloch*.

Bruner, Jerome Seymour (1915–)

Jerome Seymour Bruner was educated at Duke University and Harvard, where he received his doctorate in psychology in 1941. During the Second World War, he studied public attitudes and the effects of propaganda in the US Office of War Information and, later, in the Psychological Warfare Division of the Supreme Headquarters of the Allied Expeditionary Forces. After the war he returned to Harvard and became professor of Psychology in 1952.

At Harvard, he and George Miller founded the Center for Cognitive Studies in 1960. Between 1972 and 1980, Bruner was professor of psychology at the University of Oxford. He returned to the United States in 1980 as Director of the New York Institute for the Humanities, New York University.

Much of Bruner's work deals with the nature and function of human cognition. His early work with Leo Postman on visual perception and recognition led to a major research programme concerned with categorization, identification, and concept formation (Bruner, Goodnow, & Austin, 1956). In explicit contrast to the dominant behaviourist ethos of North American psychology at the time, Bruner and his colleagues emphasized the strategic, goal-driven nature of much of human thinking, and the fact that human beings systematically select or abstract from the potential information contained within their environment. Inevitably, Bruner became interested in the differences between people in their strategies for acquiring concepts and their subsequent performance in cognitive tasks. This work represents an early but significant landmark in the development of 'cognitive psychology': the systematic investigation through laboratory experimentation of human thinking, reasoning, and remembering, and of the different types of mental processes and representations which underlie such faculties.

Most of Bruner's subsequent work has applied cognitive psychology to the study of human development, and has moved from laboratory-based research to more naturalistic methods of inquiry. In 1959 he chaired an interdisciplinary meeting on science education in primary and secondary schools in which he and other psychologists considered a wide range of serious pedagogical issues concerning curriculum development and teaching skills, as well as more general questions of human learning and the growth of knowledge. His report of the meeting (Bruner, 1960) is very much a personal account of the potential contribution of research in cognitive psychology to the practical problems of schoolroom learning.

Bruner took up many of these issues during the 1960s in essays about the biological, developmental, and cultural constraints upon the growth of human knowledge and intelligence. He emphasized that course design and instructional practice should be based on a proper understanding of the nature of cognitive development and should exploit the learners' active participation in the educational process (Bruner, 1966, 1971, 1973). He also explored the origins of intellectual capabilities in infancy and early childhood, stressed the role of organization and discovery in the acquisition of complex skills, and considered the role of language and culture in mediating the development of children's thought.

However, the political events of that decade, particularly the student protest in the United States and Europe, caused Bruner to consider whether educational reform was inhibited by deeper, structural characteristics of Western society and especially by the preschool impact of social class divisions upon children's goals and aspirations. He was involved in establishing the Head Start programme in the 1960s and with other efforts to explore and improve the quality of children's preschool care in the United States. In the United Kingdom, Bruner undertook a commissioned study of the provision of care for preschool children through nursery schools, play-groups, day-care centres, and child-minders. Here, too, he was concerned both with the research findings themselves and then practical applications: how they might be effectively disseminated to those responsible for the provision of preschool care and also to the practitioners themselves (Bruner, 1980).

While in Oxford, Bruner carried out several experimental studies of prelinguistic communication in infants as well as a longitudinal investigation of the acquisition of language in young children. In other respects, however, Bruner's time in Oxford seems to have been less successful. His colleagues were unsympathetic to his suggestions that empirical psychology should not restrict itself solely to the study of problems which were open to formal experimental investigation.

Bruner has not only been concerned with the intellect but also with the artistic or intuitive side of human nature. He sought to link the growth of knowledge through science and education to its expression in art and literature (Bruner, 1962). He has tried to provide an integrated account, which incorporates both the scientific and the humanistic conceptions of human intelligence. This is a major theme of his most recent books (Bruner, 1984, 1986).

John T. E. Richardson
Brunel University, Uxbridge

References

Bruner, J. S. (1960), *The Process of Education*, Cambridge, Mass.

Bruner, J. S. (1962), *On Knowing: Essays for the Left Hand*, Cambridge, Mass.

Bruner, J. S. (1966), *Toward a Theory of Instruction*, Cambridge, Mass.

Bruner, J. S. (1971), *The Relevance of Education*, New York.

Bruner, J. S. (1973), *Beyond the Information Given*, New York.

Bruner, J. S. (1980), *Under Five in Britain*, London.

Bruner, J. S. (1983), *Child's Talk: Learning to Use Language*, New York.

Bruner, J. S. (1984), *In Search of Mind: Essays in Autobiography*, New York.

Bruner, J. S. (1986), *Actual Minds, Possible Worlds*, Cambridge, Mass.

Bruner, J. S., Goodnow, J. J. and Austin, G. A. (1956), *A Study of Thinking*, New York.

Burke, Edmund (1729–97)

Edmund Burke, the British statesman and political theorist, was born in Dublin in 1729. He came to London in 1750 and soon acquired a reputation as a philosopher and man of letters. In 1765, he was elected to the House of Commons, acting as party secretary and chief man of ideas to the Whig connection led by the Marquis of Rockingham. He wrote voluminously, and the eloquence he brought to expressing a high-minded but by no means unrealistic view of political possibilities has never been surpassed. He could bring out the universal element in the most parochial of issues.

Burke's enduring importance in articulating a political tendency is particularly evident in the *Reflections on the Revolution in France* (1790) and subsequent late works in which he defended his criticism of the Revolution against fellow Whigs who had welcomed it as an act of liberation from an odious Bourbon absolutism. Attacked as one who had betrayed the cause of liberty, Burke agreed (in the *Appeal from the Old to the New Whigs*) that consistency was the highest virtue in politics, but proceeded to theorize its complex nature. In supporting the American colonists, he argued, he was in no way committed to support every movement which raised the banner of liberty, for in his view the Americans 'had taken up arms from one motive only; that is, our attempting to tax them without their consent . . .' (Burke, *Appeal*, Vol. III). Real political consistency must take account of circumstances, and cannot be deduced from principles. And it was in terms of the contrast between historical concreteness and abstract principle that Burke interpreted the challenge posed by the revolutionaries in France.

The revolutionaries were, Burke argued, amateur politicians attempting to solve the complex problems of French society with a set of theories or what he called 'metaphysic rights'. They believed that an ideal rational constitution, in which a republic guaranteed the rights of man, was suitable for all societies. This belief constituted a revelation which stigmatized most existing beliefs as prejudice and superstition, and all existing forms of government as corrupt and unjust. On Burke's historical understanding of the specificity of different societies, the beliefs and practices of any society revealed their character; indeed, properly understood, they revealed a kind of rationality much more profound than the propositional fantasies of revolutionaries. To condemn what whole societies had long believed as merely mistaken was in the highest degree superficial. Society is a delicate fabric of sentiments and understandings which would be irreparably damaged if subjected to the butchery of abstract ideas. Burke judged that as the revolutionaries discovered that the people were not behaving according to the rationalist prescriptions, they would have increasing recourse to violence and terror. At the end of every prospect would be found a gallows. He predicted that the outcome would be a military dictatorship.

Burke's genius lay in breaking up the conventional antitheses through which politics was then understood. He had never been, he wrote, 'a friend or an enemy to republics or to monarchies in the abstract' (Burke, 1855, *Appeal*, Vol.III), and this refusal to take sides on an abstractly specified principle became a dominant strain in conservatism. The real clue to wisdom in politics lay not at the level of high principle but of low and humble circumstance. This was the level of actual human experience, and at this level, there was not a great deal that governments could achieve, and most of what they could was to prevent evils rather than promote goods. No stranger to paradox, Burke insisted that one of the most important of the rights of man is the right to be restrained by suitable laws. Again, Burke was prepared to agree that society was indeed a contract, but he instantly qualified this conventional judgement by insisting that it was a contract of a quite sublime kind, linking the living, the dead and those yet to be born. It is in these hesitations and qualifications of conventional wisdom to which he was impelled by the excitements of his time that Burke's contribution to political understanding lies.

More philosophically, Burke adapted to political use the empiricist doctrine that the passions, especially as entrenched in and shaped by social institutions, are closer to reality than the speculations of philosophers, and especially of *philosophes*. His defence of prejudice threw down a gauntlet to the superficial rationalism of his opponents, and has sometimes been seen as expressing an irrationalism endemic to conservative thought. It is, however, an argument about the relations between reason and passion similar to that of Hegel, though in a quite different idiom.

Burke's political judgement is a conservative modification of the English political tradition and covers many areas. On the nature of representation, for example, he argued that the House of Commons was not a congress of ambassadors from the constituencies. His defence of the place of parties in British politics contributed to the acceptance and development of party government, however limited in intention it may have been (Brewer, 1971). In the indictment of Warren Hastings, he stressed the trusteeship of power and property which was never far from his thoughts. But in all his political writings, Burke wrote to the occasion, and it is perilous to generalize about him too far. His personal ambitions required manoeuvring in the complex world of late eighteenth-century politics which have led some writers (for example, Namier, 1929, and Young, 1943) to regard him as little more than a silver-tongued opportunist. This is to do less than justice to the suggestiveness of his prose and the momentousness of the occasions to which he so brilliantly responded.

Kenneth Minogue
The London School of Economics
and Political Science

References

Burke, E. (1855), *Works*, London.

Brewer, J. (1971), 'Party and the double cabinet: two facets of Burke's thoughts', *The Historical Journal*, XIV.

Namier, L. (1929), *The Structure of Politics at the Accession of George III*, London.

Young, G.M. (1943), *Burke* (British Academy Lecture on a Mastermind), London.

Further Reading

Canovan, F. P. (1960), *The Political Reason of Edmund Burke*, North Carolina.

Cone, C. (1964), *Burke and the Nature of Politics: The Age of the French Revolution*, Lexington, Mass.

Macpherson, C. B. (1980), *Burke*, Oxford.

O'Gorman, F. (1973), *Edmund Burke*, London.

Parkin, C. (1956), *The Moral Basis of Burke's Political Thought*, Cambridge.

Stanlis, P. J. (1958), *Edmund Burke and the Natural Law*, Ann Arbor.

Chomsky, Noam (1928–)

Noam Chomsky, born 1928 in Philadelphia, the son of a Hebrew scholar, has achieved eminence both as a linguist and as a political activist and writer. His linguistic research, conducted for the last 30 years at MIT, has revolutionized the study of language, has been profoundly influential in psychology and philosophy, and has had repercussions in mathematics, anthropology, sociology and the study of literature. His political work is less original but, in reflecting his adopted role of conscience of the West, has been important in focusing attention on the perceived injustices of the American social and political system.

Twentieth-century linguistics prior to Chomsky (e.g. Bloomfield) was preoccupied with cataloguing and describing the facts of language, and was largely limited to phonology (sound structure) and morphology (word structure). Chomsky reoriented the discipline in two ways: on the one hand he initiated a technical breakthrough which for the first time made possible a rigorous account of syntax; on the other he moved beyond the description of data to concentrate on those human mental properties which underlie our observable linguistic abilities. The ability to speak and understand a language entails having a certain body of linguistic knowledge, usually referred to as our *competence*. This knowledge is conceived as being embodied in a set of mentally represented rules which interact with other cognitive systems (memory, logic) to determine our linguistic behaviour or *performance*. Chomsky's claim that these rules and the principles which govern their operation are in part innate rather than learned has been instrumental in reopening the philosophical debate on innate ideas.

That our use of language is rule-governed is clear from the infinite *creativity* of language (our ability to produce and understand any of an indefinitely large number of sentences we have never heard before); from *over-generalization* of the sort indulged in by children who remark that 'the sheeps comed'; and from the identifiability of *mistakes* in speaking (how else would you know that this sentence wrong was?). Part of Chomsky's contribution has been to provide a *formalism* in which many of these rules (phonological, syntactic and semantic) can be satisfactorily couched. The best known of these rule types is the *transformation*, a device which has given its name to the theory of Transformational Grammar, and which encodes the claim that the syntax of human languages is optimally described by reference to (at least) two levels of representation: deep structure and surface structure. One of the hallmarks of Chomsky's formal work, however, has been its continual unpredictability and innovativeness. As descriptive problems arise, theoretical constructs of a novel kind are drawn in to deal with them. The status of such constructs is a matter of endless and fruitful debate within linguistics, but whether the grammars of all human languages necessarily contain transformations is of secondary importance, as even a demonstration that they were not the optimal descriptive device would leave untouched the philosophical and psychological speculations that are his prime concern. Part of Chomsky's argument is that the complexity of our linguistic knowledge and the relative poverty of the data we are exposed to as children make implausible any form of inductive learning of the rules involved. Hence, whatever formal properties the rules may have, we must postulate a rich innate component to our linguistic knowledge if we are to explain our mastery of them. It follows, moreover, that if our knowledge is in part innately determined, then universal properties of language can be investigated by tapping the linguistic intuitions of the speakers of just one language, for example, English. Claims of universality must obviously then be tested against other languages, but it is both unnecessary (and impossible) to document the totality of facts about all languages first.

In this desire to *explain* (some of) the data, rather than describe all of them, Chomsky has devoted much of his recent work to developing a theory with a deductive structure rich enough to provide explanatory principles showing *why* linguistic phenomena have the form they do, and not merely that they have this form. For instance, the possibility of construing *themselves* as referring to *the girls* but not *the boys* in 'the boys think the girls admire themselves', and of construing *them* as referring to *the boys* but not *the girls* in 'the boys think the girls admire them) follows from principles of considerable abstractness: principles which are so general that the child has only to learn that *them* is a pronoun and *themselves* a reflexive pronoun for these and a number of other facts to follow without further stipulation. The conclusion Chomsky draws is that these principles can be neither learnt piecemeal nor motivated by considerations of the communicative function of language, but are part of Universal Grammar: the innate endowment which controls the growth of language in each individual.

Chomsky's contribution to philosophy and his impact on psychology – both by his demolition of Skinner's behaviourism and by his emphasis on linguistics as a branch of cognitive psychology – are incontestable. His influence on other fields is less direct, but it is a measure of his stature and pre-eminence in linguistics that even those who disagree with him are forced to argue in terms of the concepts and idealizations he has propounded.

Chomsky's linguistics and politics are intellectually unconnected. He brings the same devastating analytic ability to both; he displays the same unflagging persistence in putting forth his ideas and correcting his opponents in both, but only his linguistic ideas with their philosophical and psychological ramifications have the originality of genius, and it is these which will still be discussed in future centuries.

N. V. Smith
University College London

Further Reading
D'Agostino, F. (1985), *Chomsky's System of Ideas*, Oxford.

Chomsky, N. (1957), *Syntactic Structures*, The Hague.

Chomsky, N. (1969), *American Power and the New Mandarins*, Harmondsworth.

Chomsky, N. (1973), *For Reasons of State*, London.

Chomsky, N. (1975), *The Logical Structure of Linguistic Theory*, New York.

Chomsky, N. (1980), *Rules and Representations*, Oxford.

Smith, N. and Wilson, D. (1979), *Modern Linguistics: The Results of Chomsky's Revolution*, Harmondsworth.

Comte, Auguste (1798–1857)

Auguste Comte, philosopher of science and social visionary, is perhaps best known for giving a name to a subject he outlined rather than practised: sociology. As the Comtist motto 'Order and Progress' suggests, the keynote of his thought is his search, in chaotic times, for principles of cultural and political order that were consistent with the forward march of society. Born at Montpellier in southern France of a conservative, middle-class family, Comte received a good scientific education at the École Polytechnique in Paris, a centre of advanced liberal thought. From 1817 to 1824 he was closely associated with the radical prophet of a new industrial order, Henri de Saint-Simon, to whom he owed a considerable (and largely disavowed) intellectual debt. At the same time, despite the loss of his Catholic faith, he was drawn to some of the ideas of the conservative thinker, Joseph de Maistre, and eventually based much of the 'religion of humanity' on medieval, Catholic models.

Comte's writings fall into two main phases, which express different aspects of a single, unified vision of knowledge and society, rather than a change in fundamental emphasis. Of the first, the major work is the six-volume *Cours de philosophie positive* (1830–42) (*The Positive Philosophy of Auguste Comte*, 1896), which sets forth a developmental epistemology of science. In his later writings, especially the *Discours sur l'esprit positif*, (1844) (*Discourse on the Positive Spirit*), the *Système de politique positive* (1848–54) (*System of Positive Polity*, 1875–77), and the *Catechism of Positive Religion* (l858), Comte gives the blueprint of a new social order, including the 'religion of humanity' which was to provide its ethical underpinning. For Comte, 'positivism' was not merely the doctrine that the methods of the natural sciences provide the only route to a knowledge of human nature and society (as it has latterly come to mean), but also a source of value for social reorganization. 'Sociology' is, in fact, the specific knowledge requisite to this task.

In the *Cours* Comte sets forth the famous 'Law of the three stages'. In its origins, human thought is 'theological', making use of an idiom of spiritual forces; later, in a phase which culminates in the Enlightenment, it moves to a 'metaphysical' stage, which is conjectural and largely negative; finally, when it is able to grasp real causal relations between phenomena, it achieves the scientific or 'positive' stage. To these stages there also correspond characteristic social and political institutions. Individual sciences develop in the same manner, emerging at the positive stage in the order of their complexity: mathematics, astronomy, physics, chemistry, biology and, finally, sociology. Comte's view of sociology is highly programmatic: he argues for an analytic distinction between social 'statics' and 'dynamics', and for society to be analysed as a system of interdependent parts, based upon a consensus.

Despite his religious eccentricities, Comte exercised an immediate influence on his contemporaries. J. S. Mill introduced his work to the English-speaking world, where the positive philosophy appealed as a check to the extremes of liberal individualism, and even Spencer adopted the name 'sociology'. Though he is little read today, the functionalist and natural scientific paradigms which Comte advocated have remained in sociology's mainstream.

J. D. Y. Peel
University of Liverpool

Further Reading

Lenzer, J. (ed.) (1975), *Auguste Comte and Positivism: The Essential Writings*, New York.

Thompson, K. (1975), *Auguste Comte: The Foundation of Sociology*, London.

See also: *Saint-Simon*.

Cournot, Antoine Augustin (1801–77)

During a prosperous career in the French civil service and academic establishment, Cournot contributed to three related branches of knowledge: probability theory, foundations of knowledge (broadly, epistemology), and economics. Of these, his contributions to economics (recorded in *Recherches sur les principes mathématiques de la théorie des richesses*, 1838) have been most enduring, even though his works in probability theory and philosophy of science met with more immediate acclaim. Cournot himself apparently regarded the works in probability theory and epistemology more favourably, despite the fact that they do not adduce new results still bearing his name, as do his essays in economics.

Cournot's application of mathematics to economic reasoning was both novel and elegant. Indeed, his main success consisted in giving rigorous mathematical statement to economic concepts and propositions that already existed, but only in confusing and fuzzy form. Cournot's analysis is one of the mainsprings that turned economics from literary discourse to formal logic and mathematical exposition.

Cournot provided a rigorous formulation of the Law of Demand. Prior to his performance, literary economists had experienced considerable difficulty in formulating this simple relationship between price and quantity demanded. After the appearance of *Recherches*, the debate, which still continues today, focused on whether Cournot regarded the price-quantity schedule as primarily empirical or mainly theoretical. Cournot's exposition of the Law of Demand was apparently used as foundation by Alfred Marshall in his famous *Principles of Economics* (1890).

The theory of the monopoly firm attributed to Cournot also found its way into Marshall's *Principles*. To this original contribution Cournot added works on bilateral monopoly, competitive and oligopolistic markets, and the theory of costs. His theories of bilateral monopoly and oligopoly have often provided either target straw men or gambit points for the extensive literature on market behaviour, including game theory. While the ideas in *Recherches* were not novel, the precise formulation, together with extensive deductive exploration that Cournot offered, showed the way to improved clarity and precision in an infant social science. In all of his writing Cournot urged a marriage between theoretical formulation and empirical testing that has become popular in many of the sciences.

G. F. Rhodes, Jr
Colorado State University

Further Reading

Cournot, A. A. (1960 [1838]), *Researches into the Mathematical Principles of the Theory of Wealth*, New York. (Original French edn, *Recherches sur les principes mathématiques de la théorie des richesses*, Paris.)

Cournot, A. A. (1956 [1851], *An Essay on the Foundations of Our Knowledge*, New York. (Original French edn, *Essai sur les fondements de nos connaissances*, 2 vols, Paris.)

Dewey, John (1859–1952)

One of America's greatest philosophers and educators, John Dewey was born in Burlington, Vermont, in 1859. He was educated at the University of Vermont and Johns Hopkins University. After teaching for some years at the Universities of Minnesota and Michigan, Dewey moved to Chicago University where he founded the Laboratory School, an experimental elementary school that rapidly received wide attention for its innovative curriculum and methods. One of his most influential books, *The School and Society* (1900), presented the philosophy of the school, a model for what later became known as 'progressive education' in the United States. Dewey's writings at the time on education as well as philosophy, and his advocacy of his version of pragmatism called 'Instrumentalism', established him as a noted figure in academic and intellectual circles. He moved to Columbia University in 1904 where he remained for the rest of his professional life. There he produced his major philosophical books while also writing extensively on political, social, and educational matters. He was always a remarkably prolific author. His collected published writings will consist of thirty-three volumes.

Dewey suffered kindly the demands that are made on famous men. He was active in a variety of liberal and progressive organizations, often serving as a speaker. He visited Europe and Russia and in 1918 was invited to give a series of lectures in China and one year later in Japan. The latter formed the popular book *Reconstruction in Philosophy* (1920). To the very end of his long lifetime he also succeeded in carrying on his more technical work in philosophy.

Dewey's early thought was animated by means of a novel synthesis of physiological psychology – in which he had been thoroughly trained – and Hegelian Idealism – in which he found both religious solace and methodological insights. A lasting influence on Dewey was the Hegelian treatment of subject matters as exhibiting temporal phases and developments within which conflicts and tensions among elements eventuated in unification and growth. Two of his first books were on psychology (1887) and on ethics (1891); the pair of subjects foreshadows concerns of permanent interest to him. In the 1890s there occurred a gradual but notable shift in Dewey's outlook and style from idealism to philosophic naturalism. The change was due both to his increasing appreciation of the implications of Darwinian evolution for the interpretation of thought and behaviour as adaptive functions, and to the appearance of William James's *Principles of Psychology* (1890) with its view of conscious processes as biologically conditioned purposive activities. In a now classic paper, 'The reflex arc concept in psychology' (1898), Dewey advanced a penetrating criticism of the received doctrine of stimulus events and reflexive response and developed a remarkable theory of how the process of behaviour involves a continuous integration of reciprocal forces of stimulus and response directed to organic equilibrium. The paper was a precursor of the schools of 'functional psychology' and 'behaviourism' in America. It also contains in germinal form the main ideas of Dewey's later pragmatism.

Throughout his career Dewey was especially critical of the widely accepted dichotomy of fact and value and the division between scientific beliefs about the world and beliefs about values. The dualism generates others such as mind-body, spiritual-material, individual-social, theory-practice, and it constitutes the deepest and most far-reaching intellectual problem of Western culture. The urgent task of philosophy, Dewey argued, was to provide a coherent relationship between these otherwise disparate subject matters. To this end, in a number of works he carefully analysed the conditions under which knowing and evaluation actually occur. He showed how the pattern and direction of reflective inquiry is the same whether the problem is one whose resolution consists in the ascertainment of factual information or one requiring moral appraisal and effort. In either case, knowing and evaluation are interdependent functions of the same intellectual process. The primary vocation of knowledge is to enable us to clarify and modify present experience in order to control and enrich future experience. Dewey's book *Logic: The Theory of Inquiry* (1938) contains his most complete statement of the regulative norms of intelligent behaviour, of the concepts, propositions, and inferences that serve as instruments to warranted judgement, and his view of truth and good as complementary features of completed inquiries. This work is described as the most comprehensive attempt to determine the meaning as well as the moral significance of experimental method.

It has been a venerable aspiration of philosophers to secure knowledge on a foundation of indubitable truths. Dewey, however, maintained that the continuous use of inquiry for appraising beliefs in the light of their consequences and bearing on future thought and action establishes the decisive measure of their reliability. The transforming and liberating power of experimental inquiry is central to Dewey's many writings on educational and social theory. These themes coalesce in a book that is also one of the best introductions to his philosophy, *Democracy and Education* (1916).

While we are changed by thinking, and inquiry produces changes in the world, some of the most basic conditions vitally shaping human conduct have a nonhuman origin. There are certain 'generic traits of existence' which become the subject of metaphysical inquiry for Dewey. Change and the passage of events from future to past are among such ultimate traits. Change also breeds variety, stability, instability and recovery permeate all nature. These tropes and rhythms of the precarious and stable enter in to qualify human existence; they infuse the course of living and are appropriated into the institutions of culture and the arts of communication and enjoyment. *Experience and Nature* (1925) is the major expression of Dewey's metaphysical views. The subject of *Art as Experience* (1934) is how the energies and rhythms of nature become transmuted into aesthetic objects of perceptual delight, criticism, and value.

Dewey's thought covers the entire range of philosophic speculation. His vision is coherent, often highly original, and scrupulously articulated in detail. His work is a fertile source of ideas and suggestions that have inspired and merit further study.

H. S. Thayer
The City College of the University
of New York, New York.

Further Reading

Dewey, J. (1969–), *Collected Works of John Dewey*, ed. J. A. Boydston, Carbondale, Ill.

Dykhuizen, G. (1973), *The Life and Mind of John Dewey*, Carbondale, Ill.

McDermott, J. (1973), *The Philosophy of John Dewey*, 2 vols, New York.

Thayer, H. S. (1984), *Meaning and Action: A Critical History of Pragmatism*, Indianapolis, Ind.

Durkheim, Émile (1858–1917)

Émile Durkheim was the founding father of academic sociology in France and the most influential early theoretician of archaic or primitive societies. A Jew from north-east France, Durkheim followed the educational and ideological path of the positivist generation of great Republican academics. He was educated at the École Normale Supérieure, taking a teacher's degree in philosophy and a doctorate (1893). After a short period as a *lycée* teacher, he spent a year in German universities studying social theory. On his return, he was appointed the first ever lecturer in 'social science and pedagogy' in a French university, at Bordeaux (1887). In 1902 he transferred to the Sorbonne, where he held a chair for the rest of his life.

Durkheim's seminal teaching and publications, included *De la Division du travail social* (1893) (*The Division of Labor in Society*, 1933), *Les Règles de la méthode sociologique* (1894) (*The Rules of Sociological Method*, 1938), *Le Suicide* (1897) (*Suicide*, 1952), and work on socialism, family organization, the scope and development of German social theories. He attracted a cluster of gifted young scholars – mostly philosophers but also historians, economists and jurists (including Mauss, Hubert, Simiand, Fauconnet, Richard and Bouglé) – with whom he founded the *Année sociologique* (1898). This was an essentially critical journal intended to cover the whole range of emerging social disciplines (social geography, demography, collective psychology, social and economic history, history of religion, ethnology and sociology proper). It was to become instrumental in developing and promoting a synthetic theory of social facts which overrode earlier disciplinary divisions.

Durkheim's later work included studies and lecture courses on the sociology of education, morality and moral science, pragmatism, family sociology, history of the social sciences, vital statistics and several other topics, but after the birth of the *Année* he was primarily concerned with the study of archaic societies, and especially with primitive religion and social organization. The problem of social cohesion in so-called polysegmentary societies which, according to Durkheim, were based on mechanical solidarity (as against the organic solidarity of modern societies, based on a division of labour) had been a major theme in his doctoral thesis (1893), but there it lacked any significant ethnological underpinning. Durkheim developed an intense interest in primitive society much later, after reading contemporary British 'religious anthropologists', above all Robertson Smith and Frazer. This resulted in a reorientation of his work towards the study of 'collective representations' and, more specifically, of religion, from 1896 onwards.

There were two sets of reasons, theoretical and methodological, for this shift: (1) Religion was considered to serve an essential social 'function', creating a strong community of beliefs and providing a basis for social cohesion. The 'sacred' and the 'profane' became the two essential categories in Durkheim's sociology, which ordered the system of social facts. (2) Primitive religion, either because it was believed to be more simple and consequently easier to study, or because it appeared to be functionally interconnected with most other 'social facts' (like economy, law, technology and so on, which had gained a measure of functional autonomy in the course of later development) seemed to provide the key to a theory of social order. The religious system of archaic societies thus became a privileged topic of research for Durkheim and some of the most gifted scholars of his cluster, notably Mauss, Hubert and Hertz. One out of four review articles published in the *Année* was dedicated to social anthropology, and primitive societies now supplied, for the first time in French intellectual history, a central topic in public philosophical debate, which soon engaged other leading academics (like Bergson and Lévy-Bruhl) as well.

In his anthropological work, Durkheim never surmounted the basic ambiguity of his approach to 'primitives', who were regarded either as prototypes, or as exemplifying the simplest imaginable occurrences of observable social types, or both at the same time. Moreover, he was initially sceptical about the heuristic utility of ethnographic data, and believed that preference should be given to historical documents over ethnographic information. His attitude changed, however, especially with the publication of more 'professional' ethnographies, like Spencer and Gillen (on the Australian aborigines), Boas (on the Kwakiutl Indians), and the Cambridge scholars of the expedition to Torres Straits. He discussed all these new studies in painstakingly detailed critical reviews. They also supplied the data for his own contributions in the contemporary international debate concerning archaic societies. These fall broadly under two thematic headings: social organization and belief systems (and various combinations of the two).

The essay on 'La Prohibition de l'inceste et ses origines' (1898) (*Incest: The Nature and Origin of the Taboo*, 1963) obeyed to the letter his own prescription, 'Explain the social fact by other social facts.' Social institutions could not be explained by invoking instinctive behaviour. They must be accounted for purely in terms of social causes. Incest and exogamy derived from the nature of the elementary, that is, uterine, clan. Respect for the clan's totem manifested itself by a religious aversion to the blood of fellow clanspeople and, by extension, to sexual contact with the clan's women. The prohibition of incest was accompanied by prescriptions concerning interclan marriage. Some modern writers on kinship (for example, Lévi-Strauss, 1949) recognize their debt to Durkheim, though they have submitted his theory to substantial criticism. Similarly, in his essays on totemism (1902) and Australian kinship (1905a), Durkheim seemed clearly to anticipate much later structuralist approaches. He identified, beyond the social categories of kinship, truly logical categories which, he suggested, could be understood as 'mathematical problems' (Durkheim, 1905a). He went further in the exploration of such logical categories in a famous study, written together with Mauss, 'De quelques formes primitives de classification: contribution à l'étude des représentations collectives' (1903) (*Primitive Classification*, 1963). This essay related ideas about space among some Australian and North-American tribesmen to their social organizations. Durkheim and Mauss argued that men 'classified things because they were divided into clans'. The model of all classification (especially of spatial orientation) is the society, because it is the unique whole (or totality) to which everything is related, so that 'the classification of things reproduces the classification of men'. Primitive classifications generated the first concepts or categories, enabling men to unify their knowledge. They constituted the first 'philosophy of nature'. Durkheim and Mauss suggested that in these classifications could be discerned 'the origins of logical procedure which is the basis of scientific classifications'. Durkheim would systematize these intimations in his last great work which focused on the social functions of religion proper.

Les Formes élémentaires de la vie religieuse (1912) (*The Elementary Forms of Religious Life*, 1915) was the culmination of Durkheim's anthropological studies. His focus upon Australians (and to some extent on American Indians) was grounded on the methodologically essential (and still ambiguous) assumption that their clan system was the most 'elementary' observable. The 'elementary' religion is that of totemic clans. It contains the germ of all essential elements of religious thought and life.

Durkheim starts from the proposition that religious experience cannot be purely illusory and must refer to some reality. The reality underlying religious practice is society itself. Religion is 'above all a system of ideas by which individuals represent the society they belong to'. Moreover, 'metaphorical and symbolic as it may be, this representation is not unfaithful'. Certain types of 'collective effervescence' produce religious beliefs, or help to reconfirm beliefs and values of religious relevance. The type of religion is also determined by social structure. For example, the cult of the 'great god' corresponds to the synthesis of all totems and to the unification of the tribe.

Religion also helps to interpret or 'represent' social realities by means of their projection in a special symbolic language. Thus, mythologies 'connect things in order to fix their internal relations, to classify and to systematize them'. They represent reality, as does science. The function of religion is ultimately social integration, which is effected by 'constantly producing and reproducing the soul of the collectivity and of individuals'. Symbolism is the very condition of social life, since it helps social communication to become communion, that is, 'the fusion of all particular sentiments into one common sentiment'.

Durkheim's religious anthropology has been severely criticized by field researchers, yet without ceasing to inspire scholars concerned with archaic religions. At the time, his sociology of religion had an immediate public appeal in consequence of the conflict then raging between the Church and the Republican State. The study of primitive religion allowed Durkheim to adopt a purely scientific posture, while offering an historical criticism and a sociological evaluation of contemporary religious institutions. (He once described the Catholic Church as a 'sociological monster' (1905b).)

Ethnographic evidence drawn from primitive societies also led to heuristic generalizations concerning the nature of social cohesion, its agents and conditions. Ethnology, moreover, lent itself more easily than other established disciplines (like history or geography) to Durkheimian theorizing, because it was an intellectually weak and institutionally marginal branch of study (see Karady, 1981). Durkheim's theoretical anthropology, together with the work of his followers and debating partners (such as Lévy-Bruhl, Mauss, Hubert and Hertz) contributed decisively to the birth of French academic field anthropology between the two world wars. A later generation of French anthropologists, including Griaule, Métraux, Dumont and Lévi-Strauss, continued to exploit Durkheim's heritage, while critically re-evaluating it. As a consequence of its Durkheimian roots, French social anthropology never broke with the other social sciences, and retained a penchant for high-level generalization.

Victor Karady
Centre National de la Recherche Scientifique
Paris

References
Durkheim, E. (1902), 'Sur le totémism', *L'Année Sociologique*, 5.
Durkheim, E. (1905a), 'Sur l'organisation matrimoniale des sociétés australiennes', *L'Année Sociologique*, 8.
Durkheim, E. (1905b), 'Conséquences religieuses de la séparation de l'Eglise et de l'Etat', republished in E. Durkheim (1975), *Textes*, Paris.
Karady, V. (1981), 'French ethnology and the Durkheimian breakthrough', *Journal of the Anthropological Society of Oxford*, XII.
Lévi-Strauss, C. (1949), *Les Structures élémentaires de la parenté*, Paris. (English edn, *The Elementary Structures of Kinship*, London, 1969.)

Further Reading
Besnard, P. (ed.) (1983), *The Sociological Domain: The Durkheimians and the Founding of French Sociology*, Cambridge.
Lukes, S. (1972), *Émile Durkheim: His Life and Work. A Historical and Critical Study*, London.
Pickering, W. S. F. (ed.) (1975), *Durkheim on Religion. A Selection of Readings with Bibliographies and Introductory Remarks*, London.
See also: *Lévi-Strauss; Lévy-Bruhl; Mauss*.

Elias, Norbert (1897–)

The sociologist Norbert Elias was born in Wroclaw, in 1897. He studied medicine, philosophy and psychology at the universities of Wroclaw and Heidelberg, and later worked with Karl Mannheim in Frankfurt. In 1933 he fled Germany, going first to Paris and then to London. After the Second World War, Elias was appointed to a lectureship at the University of Leicester (1954–1962), then became professor at the University of Ghana (1962–1964), and finally returned to Germany as visiting professor at Zentrum für Interdisziplinare Forschung in Bielefeld. He now lives in Amsterdam.

Elias's *magnum opus*, *Ueber der Prozesz der Zivilisation* (1939) (*The Civilizing Process*, 2 vols, 1978–1982), is a historical sociological study of European civilization between the end of the Middle Ages and the nineteenth century. It shows the interdependence of the developments in the structure of European societies and in the personality of their citizens. Processes of state-formation, characterized by ever-increasing state control of violence and taxation, are accompanied by increasing self-restraint on the part of their citizens. The progressive stylization of the elementary (corporal, emotional) activities of life is vividly illustrated, successive contemporary guides to etiquette serving as sources. In *Die Höfische Gesellschaft* (1969) (*The Court Society*, 1984), Elias deals specifically with the transformation of France from a regional system governed by a warrior aristocracy, to a centralized state under the court nobility of Louis XIV.

In these two works, Elias succeeds in integrating macrosociological conceptualizations of command structures, reminiscent of Max Weber, with Freudian ideas of self-control on the individual level. He argues that man's deepest feelings are social, and that individuals have no nonsocial identity. The theoretical implications of this interpenetration of individuals and their society, which is called figurational sociology, are worked out in *Was ist Soziologie?* (1970) (*What is Sociology?* 1978).

Goudsblom has formulated the basic principles of figurational sociology as follows:

(1) Human beings are interdependent, in a variety of ways: their lives evolve in, and are significantly shaped by, the social figurations they form with each other. (2) These figurations are continually in flux, undergoing changes of different orders – some quick and ephemeral, others slower but perhaps more lasting. (3) The long-term developments

taking place in human social figurations have been and continue to be largely unplanned and unforeseen. (4) Development of human knowledge takes place within human figurations, and forms one important aspect of their overall development: as an aspect of the largely unplanned and unforeseen development of industrial state societies.

The publication of *Ueber der Prozesz der Zivilisation* just before the outbreak of the Second World War went almost unnoticed by the profession, and Elias's English publications of the 1950s met with the same fate. Only after his retirement, with the support of Goudsblom, did he found something of a school, starting in Amsterdam and spreading first to Germany and France, where he met a favourable reception from the *Annales* historians, and then to England and the United States.

Peter Schröder
Ministry of Education, The Netherlands

Reference
Goudsblom, J. (1977), *Sociology in the Balance*, Oxford.

Engels, Friedrich (1820–95)

Friedrich Engels was born into a family of mill-owners in the Rhineland with business interests in Manchester. He took employment in the family firm at sixteen and never formally attended university. When he was eighteen, he published an attack on industrial poverty and middle-class philistinism in his home town, launching a career for himself as social critic. While on national service in Berlin the young Engels joined liberal and radical Young Hegelians in attacking the conservatism encouraged by the Prussian state. His first meeting in November 1842 with Karl Marx, then editor of a liberal newspaper in Cologne, was cool because Marx found the Young Hegelians amateurish. In August 1844 they met again in Paris and established a lifelong partnership.

The works produced by Engels during the intervening two years' residence in England were his most substantial independent efforts: *Umrisse zu einer Kritik der Nationalökonomie* (1844) (*Outlines of a Critique of Political Economy*, 1930), and *Die Lage der arbeitenden Klasse in England* (1845) (*The Condition of the Working Class in England*, 1958). Both were praised by Marx, the former as an anticipation of his own critique of political economy and the latter for its adumbration of the proletarian revolution which he considered inevitable. In partnership, Marx and Engels produced only three major works: *Die heilige Familie* (1845) (*The Holy Family*, 1956) with separately signed contributions; *Die deutsche Ideologie* (1845–46) (*The German Ideology*, 1939), and *Manifest der Kommunistischen Partei* (1848) (*The Communist Manifesto*, 1963), where Engels's analysis of industrialization and Marx's rhetorical gifts contributed equally to a masterpiece.

Engels's later career as Marx's chief interpreter began with his 1859 review of Marx's *Zur Kritik der politischen Ökonomie* (1859) (*A Contribution to the Critique of Political Economy*, 1971), in which he set the standard canons of interpretation for Marx: a similarity with Hegel as a systematic theorist, an inversion of Hegel's idealist premisses, a demystification of Hegel's dialectical method, and the discovery of laws within a unified and comprehensive materialist science. These themes were developed subsequently in *Herrn Eugen Dührings Umwälzung der Wissenschaft* (1878) (*Anti-Dühring*, 1959) and in *Socialism: Utopian and Scientific* (1880) (first published in French) which were powerfully influential in attracting adherents to socialism.

The mature Engels was the first Marxist historian ('Der deutsche Bauernkrieg', 1850) (*The Peasant War in Germany*, 1956), and *Germany: Revolution and Counterrevolution* (1851–52) (first published as newspaper articles in English), anthropologist (*Der Ursprung der Familie, des Privateigentums und des Staats*, 1884) (*The Origin of the Family, Private Property and the State*, 1942) and philosopher (*Ludwig Feuerbach und der Ausgang der klassischen deutschen Philosophie*, 1886), (*Ludwig Feuerbach and the Outcome of Classical German Philosophy*, 1941 [1886]), and the posthumously published *Dialektik und Natur* (1935) (*Dialectics of Nature*, 1954). He was the first commentator on the early Marx, became his first biographer, and after Marx's death, his literary executor, editor of Volumes 2 and 3 of *Das Kapital* and the author of more than twenty introductions to Marx's works. He also coined the phrases 'materialist interpretation of history' and 'false consciousness', and formulated three dialectical laws: the transformation of quality into quantity and *vice versa*, the interpenetration of opposites, and the negation of the negation. Throughout his life Engels was in no doubt that his own writings agreed exactly with Marx's and even expanded their scope, but it is now widely accepted that discrepancies between the two men's works are at the root of many of the debates in contemporary Marxist theory and practice.

Terrell Carver
University of Bristol

Further Reading
Carver, T. (1981), *Engels*, Oxford.
Carver, T. (1983), *Marx and Engels: The Intellectual Relationship*, Brighton.
Henderson, W. O. (1976), *The Life of Friedrich Engels*, 2 vols, London.
Lichtheim, G. (1964), *Marxism: An Historical and Critical Study*, London.
McLellan, D. (1977), *Engels*, Glasgow.
Marcus, S. (1974), *Engels, Manchester and the Working Class*, New York.
See also: *Marx*.

Evans-Pritchard, Edward Evan (1902–73)

Edward Evan Evans-Pritchard was the most eminent social anthropologist in the English tradition since Malinowski and Frazer. In 1946 he succeeded his distinguished teacher A. R. Radcliffe-Brown as professor of social anthropology at Oxford University, a post he held until his retirement in 1970. Evans-Pritchard's abundant writings reflect a fruitful tension between a native tradition of empiricist historical scholarship – his first degree was in history – and an adopted allegiance to the French tradition of sociological holism as exemplified in the *Année Sociol-*

ogique school founded by Émile Durkheim. He rejected Radcliffe-Brown's view of anthropology as a natural science of society, seeing it rather as an art, akin to historiography (1950). He was generally wary of 'grand theory', regarding himself as 'first an ethnographer and secondly as a social anthropologist' (1963). He saw social anthropology as primarily concerned with the task of translation from one culture to another, an idea he owed to Malinowski. But Evans-Pritchard had no equal in his ability at rendering in sensitive and often beautiful prose, the meaning of alien modes of thought and life. This ability is outstandingly exemplified in his studies of witchcraft and other magical beliefs among the Azande people of Africa (1937), and of the religion of the Nuer, another African people (1956). Evans-Pritchard's account of the lineage and political systems of the Nuer (1940) profoundly influenced a generation of social anthropologists, but its conceptual basis has recently attracted radical criticism from several quarters (see Kuper, 1982). For general assessments of Evans-Pritchard see Bidney (1953), Hatch (1973) and Douglas (1980).

Roy Willis
University of Edinburgh

References

Bidney, D. (1953), *Theoretical Anthropology*, New York.

Douglas, M. (1980), *Evans-Pritchard*, London.

Evans-Pritchard, E. E. (1937), *Witchcraft, Oracles and Magic among the Azande*, Oxford.

Evans-Pritchard, E. E. (1940), *The Nuer*, Oxford.

Evans-Pritchard, E. E. (1950), 'Social anthropology: past and present', *Man*, 50, 198.

Evans-Pritchard, E. E. (1956), *Nuer Religion*, Oxford.

Evans-Pritchard, E. E. (1963), 'The comparative method in social anthropology' (Hobhouse Memorial Lecture), London.

Hatch, E. (1973), *Theories of Man and Culture*, New York.

Kuper, A. (1982), 'Lineage theory: a critical retrospect', *Annual Review of Anthropology*, 11.

Eysenck, Hans J. (1916–)

A voluntary expatriate from Germany in 1933, Eysenck studied at University College, London, and thus in the psychometric tradition of Galton, Spearman and Burt; he was later to extend the methodology of the study of intellectual ability to the study of human personality, and so to create one of the major schools of personality theory. The war forced him into the clinical field, and he was eventually to found the first university-based course in clinical psychology, a profession in Britain that owes much to his early initiative and scientific approach. He is quite unusual in his literary output, being the author or joint author of well over 50 books and 600 journal articles: many of the layman's modern concepts of psychology as a scientific discipline owe much to his popular writings. He has been at the centre of the longstanding debate concerning the role of genetic factors in determining individual differences in intellectual ability, with its strong overtones of political controversy, and he appears to enjoy controversy. Although reputed to be a hard-nosed scientist, and having been a leading figure in the critical onslaught against the vagaries of psychoanalytic theory, Eysenck has shown a surprising fondness for treating seriously such fringe topics as astrology and psychic research. Retiring from the chair of Psychology at the age of 67 in 1983, he is still a man of remarkable intellectual and physical vigour, and in terms of citations in learned journals, he proves to be quite the most influential of living British psychologists.

H. B. Gibson
Cambridge

Further Reading
Broadbent, D. E. (1981), 'Introduction', in R. Lynn (ed.), *Dimensions of Personality: Papers in Honour of H. J. Eysenck*, Oxford.
Eysenck, H. J. (1979), 'Autobiographical sketch', in G. Lindzey (ed.), *A History of Psychology in Autobiography*, vol. VII, San Francisco.

Gibson, H. B. (1981), *Hans Eysenck: The Man and His Work*, London.

Feyerabend, Paul K. (1924–)

Paul K. Feyerabend, a leading philosopher of science, has fundamentally challenged the logical positivist account of the scientific method and, in addition, advocated an anarchistic theory of knowledge, relying on the works of such political theorists as J. S. Mill, Marx, Lenin and Trotsky. He emphasizes the significance of political action, propaganda and political thought for the study and practice of science.

Born in Vienna, Feyerabend was induced into the Austrian army during the Nazi occupation and at the end of World War II he read history, physics and astronomy at the University of Vienna. He received his doctorate in 1951 and then went to England to study with fellow Austrian philosopher, Ludwig Wittgenstein. But Wittgenstein's untimely death resulted in Feyerabend studying with the philosopher of science, Karl Popper – whose ideas about the nature and significance of science Feyerabend has been criticizing for many years. For the past 25 years he has taught at the University of California at Berkeley, and during this time has held several teaching positions at European universities as well.

Following numerous philosophical articles on the nature of scientific inquiry, Feyerabend published in 1975 his well-known and provocative volume, *Against Method: Outline of an Anarchistic Theory of Knowledge*, which contains his vehement attack on the mainstream rationalist theory of scientific methodology. Feyerabend's thought becomes most relevant to social scientists in his conception of the traditional philosophical fields of logic, epistemology, and the philosophy of science as empirical inquiries requiring historical, sociological, psychological, anthropological and political data.

Some of Feyerabend's characteristic positions include his passionate rejection and fear of the stultifying consequences of one method of doing science which demands conformity on the part of scientists: 'Science is an essentially anarchistic enterprise: theoretical anarchism is more humanitarian and more likely to encourage progress than its law-and-order alternatives' (*Against Method*); and his corresponding deep commitment to fostering the conditions of maximum scientific creativity even to the point of claiming the creative value of violence! 'Violence . . . is *beneficial* for the individual, for it releases one's energies and makes one realize the powers at one's disposal' (*Against Method*). His admonition not to stifle scientists' creativity because of a dominant methodology is reflected in his renowned methodological credo for science of 'Anything Goes': 'All methodologies have their limitations and the only "rule" that survives is "anything goes" ' (*Against Method*).

Feyerabend argues for the democratic control of science by the lay public and replies to the critics of *Against Method* in his *Science in a Free Society* published in 1978.

Joel Kassiola
Brooklyn College of the City University of New York
See also: *Popper*.

Foucault, Michel (1926–84)

Michel Foucalt, the French philosopher, was successively a university teacher, professor at Clermont Ferrand, Paris-Vincennes, and from 1970, professor of the history of systems of thought at the Collège de France.

At first sight – and on account of the title of his chair – one might take Foucault to be engaged in a kind of history of ideas. In fact, he refuses any such definition of his work. His *L'Archéologie du savoir* (1969) (*The Archaeology of Knowledge*, 1972) is directed against the discipline called 'the history of ideas', which he takes to be something like a totalizing overview that rewrites the past in order to produce a unified object of study. In the same book he criticizes certain aspects of his own earlier work: for example, the presupposition of the existence of a 'general subject of history' contained in *Histoire de la folie à l'âge classique* (1961) (*Madness and Civilization*, 1967). In *Les Mots et les choses* (1966) (*The Order of Things*, 1970) Foucault claims that man is a modern invention and destined to disappear. Such an opinion might lead us to call him a 'structuralist', for he takes the idea of *man*, in any sense recognizable to the contemporary reader, to be a product of nineteenth-century structures (in fact, of structures of knowledge or *savoir*). But in *L'Archéologie du savoir* he had also turned against the structuralist leanings of his earlier writings.

The problem appears to have lain in the use made in those writings of the concept of an *episteme*: roughly, a structure of knowledge or – in his own terms – a 'discursive formation', which determines the manner in which the world is experienced in a given epoch. Can a study of the history of the appearance and disappearance of epistemic formations itself make use of the concept of episteme as an *explanatory* tool? If not, what does explain epistemic ruptures and eruptions? Foucault insists that the explanation must lie in 'the regime of materiality', which he then interprets as consisting in the *institutions* in which the material relations structuring discursive events are embodied.

Knowledge therefore has to be explained in terms of institutions, and of the events which take place in the latter – events of a technical, economic, social and political nature. But institutions cannot function without the exercise of *power*. Foucault therefore turns to an examination of the question of power, which, being institutional, is not and cannot be personal in origin or character. Unlike Marxists, however, he wants to study not some mechanistic process whereby power in general is explained in terms of economic ownership, but rather what he calls the 'strategies' of power. And, in order to avoid any semblance of anthropocentrism, he explains that he means by the term 'strategy' not the conscious plan or design of some human individual or group but 'the effect of a strategic position'.

The merely descriptive – and structuralist – notion of the *episteme* is now subordinated to a genuinely historical conception of the eruption of new epistemic configurations, including new sciences, a conception which – as mentioned – is avowedly materialist.

Power, he says, is located in strategies which are operative at every level: they cannot be reduced to the power of, for example, the State, or of a ruling class. Power is productive (and in particular productive of knowledge). He talks about a 'microphysics of power', power disseminated throughout the whole of society. There are of course clashes between the multi-farious and multi-levelled strategies of power. What is not clear is how the outcome of such clashes and similar processes is to be explained, given that no general mechanism of the generation of power is provided. Foucault has thus been criticized for offering, at the theoretical level, no more (nor less) than a *metaphysics* of power.

This critique does not detract from the interest of the detailed studies carried out by him (often in collaboration with pupils): for instance, his study of prisons and imprisonment (*Surveiller et punir*, 1975) (*Discipline and Punish*, 1977) and of the history of sexuality (*La Volonté de savoir*, 1976) (*The History of Sexuality*, vol. I, 1979).

Foucault's metaphysics of power – if such it is – is in any case, as we have seen, a microphysics. This point is worth underlining in the light of the exploitation made of his work by the so-called 'nouveaux philosophes' (André Glucksmann and others), who have drawn on some of its themes or vocabulary in order to produce a violently anti-Marxist metaphysics of the State – otherwise called a theory of totalitarianism – which reintroduces the idea, rejected by Foucault, of a single centre of power (see Glucksmann, 1977).

Grahame Lock
Catholic University, Nijmegen

Reference
Glucksmann, A. (1977), *Les Maitres penseurs*, Paris.

Further Reading
Dreyfus, H. and Rabinow, P. (1982), *Michel Foucault: Beyond Structuralism and Hermeneutics*, Brighton.
Foucault, M. (1977), *Language, Counter-Memory, Practice*, ed. D. Bouchard, Oxford.
Foucault, M. (1979), *Power, Truth, Strategy*, ed. M. Morris and P. Patton, Sydney.

Foucault, M. (1980), *Power/Knowledge*, ed. C. Gordon, Brighton.

Sheridan, A. (1981), *Michel Foucault: The Will to Truth*, London.

White, H. (1979), 'Michel Foucault', in J. Sturrock (ed.), *Structuralism and Since*, Oxford.

Frazer, James George (1854–1941)

Educated in Glasgow University, Frazer proceeded in 1879 to Trinity College Cambridge, where he spent the rest of his long career. He started off as a classicist, but became increasingly engaged with anthropological questions, under the influence of the orientalist W. Robertson Smith and the anthropologist E. B. Tylor.

Robertson Smith had adopted the theory that the original religion of mankind was 'totemism': members of a clan worshipped an animal from which they believed themselves to be descended. The sacrifice of an animal totem prefigured more developed religious beliefs (including Christian beliefs) about gods which were sacrificed for the sakes of their followers. Frazer published two authoritative reviews of totemism, *Totemism* (1887) and *Totemism and Exogamy* (1910), and investigated the meaning of divine sacrifice in his most famous study, *The Golden Bough*, which first appeared in 1890 and was regularly republished thereafter. Frazer compulsively added more and more documentation, bringing together classical and biblical myths, European folklore and ethnographic materials published in a number of European languages.

Frazer also drew on Comte's theory that the intellectual development of mankind was marked by a progression from magical thinking to religious thinking and, finally, to scientific thinking. Magical thought was based on an erroneous theory of causality. Objects were thought to influence one another because they were in contact (contagious magic) or because of some superficial similarity between them (sympathetic magic).

The implication of his work was that Christianity was just another primitive cult (though Frazer was circumspect about drawing such conclusions). This may explain the enormous influence of *The Golden Bough* on twentieth-century literature, but its reputation within anthropology was short-lived.

Frazer was extraordinarily prolific if never particularly original; but his greatest long-term contribution was perhaps his stimulation of ethnographers all over the world. He maintained a huge correspondence with amateur scholars in the tropics, and developed questionnaires to guide ethnographic research. He consistently argued that ethnographic studies had a far greater permanent value than any theories, and was always ready to abandon old hypotheses when confronted with awkward new information.

Adam Kuper
Brunel University, Uxbridge

Further Reading
Downie, R. A. (1979), *Frazer and the Golden Bough*, London.

Freud, Anna (1895–1982)

The youngest of Sigmund Freud's six children, Anna Freud was born in Vienna in 1905. As the only one of his children to follow her father's profession, she referred to psychoanalysis as a sibling. She was for many years her father's caretaker and confidante, and she promulgated his theories during the generation after his death. Her own work focused on child analysis and adolescence.

Beginning her career as a teacher of young children, Anna Freud presented her first paper to the Vienna Psychoanalytic Society in 1922 and joined the Society soon after. One of her first and most important works was *The Ego and the Mechanisms of Defense* (1936). In it she stressed that for psychoanalytic understanding of ego development, the defences are as important as the instincts. This insight was a major contribution not only to psychoanalytic theory, but to psychoanalytic therapy as well. She also focused on adolescence as a crucial period of ego and super-ego transformation.

Among her other notable publications are two monographs

derived from her wartime experience: *Infants Without Families* (1943) and *War and Children* (1943). These studies marked the beginning of detailed and systematic psychoanalytic observation of children and its relation to the reconstruction of childhood in the psychoanalysis of adults. *Normality and Pathology in Childhood: Assessments in Development* (1965) brought a new, developmental direction to the so-called psychoanalytic metapsychology. *Beyond the Best Interests of the Child* (1973), written with collaborators from the Yale School of Law, was an attempt to apply psychoanalytic theories to legal policy affecting children.

Anna Freud escaped with her father to London following the Nazi occupation of Austria in 1938. There, in order to advance the study and treatment of children, she established a nursery school which evolved into the Hampstead Child Therapy Course and Clinic. Anna Freud died in London in 1982.

Leo Rangell
University of California, Los Angeles
University of California, San Francisco

Further Reading

Freud, A. (1936), *The Ego and the Mechanisms of Defense*, New York.

Freud, A. (1965), *Normality and Pathology in Childhood*, New York.

See also: *Freud, S.*

Freud, Sigmund (1856–1939)

Ernest Jones, the foremost biographer of Freud, comments that Freud gave the world an incomplete theory of mind, but a new vista on man (Jones, 1953–57). The insights Freud arrived at and shared with the world changed and developed as he expanded his knowledge and understanding of himself, pursued his clinical work with patients, and broadened his interest in the world of science and letters. The perilous times in which he lived had a profound impact on his personal and professional life.

Freud was born on 6 May 1856, in Schlossergasse, Moravia, a small town in what is now Czechoslovakia (Freud, 1959 [1925]). His parents were Jewish, and though he was an agnostic he always maintained his identity as a Jew. The family moved to Vienna when Freud was four, and he lived there until 1938, when he and his family fled the Nazis to London (Hampstead). He died a year later, on 23 September 1939.

Although the family was not well off, no pressure was put on Sigmund, the oldest child, to seek a career that would be economically advantageous. Stimulated by Darwin's theories, he saw new hopes for understanding human nature. An essay by Goethe, 'On Nature', read at a popular lecture, sparked his interest in becoming a natural scientist and strengthened his desire to go to medical school. Freud's interests in social sciences, human interactions, developmental processes and ancient history were already evident during his childhood and youth; they were later to give richness to the discipline he founded: psychoanalysis.

At the university, he experienced serious disappointments. Yet the fact that his Jewishness made him an outsider seemed to strengthen his independence of mind. In Ernst Brücke's physiological laboratory, where he was allowed to work, he found role models he could respect, not only Brücke himself but his assistants, Sigmund Exner and Ernst Fleischl von Marxow. Brücke asked him to work on the histology of the nervous system, which he did before undertaking his own independent research. In 1882, when he had been at the laboratory for six years, Brücke strongly advised him, in view of his 'bad financial position', to abandon his research and theoretical career for a clinical one.

Freud entered the General Hospital in Vienna, where he pursued his neurohistological interests at the Institute of Cerebral Anatomy, published several short papers, and was encouraged by Professor Theodore Meynert to devote himself to the study of the anatomy of the brain.

In 1882 Freud's friend Josef Breuer told him about his work with a patient suffering from hysterical symptoms. After putting the patient into deep hypnosis, Breuer had asked her to tell him what was on her mind. In her awakened state she could not repeat what she had revealed under hypnosis. The major contribution of the case of Anna O. (whose real name was Bertha Pappenheim) was the discovery of a technique that was a precursor to psychoanalytic treatment – free association.

In 1885 Freud won a travelling grant and went to Paris, where he became a student at the Saltpêtrière of the eminent neurologist, Jean-Martin Charcot. Freud's interest in Breuer's work had made him eager to find out more about Charcot's studies on hysteria. Charcot demonstrated quite convincingly the genuineness of hysterical phenomena and their conformity to laws, the frequent occurrence of hysteria in men (contrary to current theories), the production of hysterical paralyses and contractures by hypnosis, and the finding that artificially induced states showed features similar to those of spontaneous attacks that were initiated traumatically. Freud determined to study neuroses in greater depth. Before returning to Vienna, he spent a few weeks in Berlin in order to gain more knowledge of childhood disorders. During the next few years he published several monographs on unilateral and bilateral cerebral palsies in children.

In 1886 he settled in Vienna as a physician, married Martha Bernays, to whom he had been engaged for several years, and became known as a specialist in nervous diseases. He reported to the Vienna Society of Medicine on his work with Charcot, an account which the medical society did not receive with favour. Some of his critics doubted that there could be hysteria in males. In response to their scepticism he found a male with a classical hysterical hemianesthesia, demonstrated it before the medical society, and was applauded – but ultimately ignored. Once again he was an outsider. He was excluded from the laboratory of cerebral anatomy, had no place to deliver his lectures, withdrew from academic life, and ceased to attend meetings of the professional societies.

Freud's therapeutic armamentarium was limited. He could use electrotherapy or hypnotism. Since it became known that the positive effects of electrotherapy were in fact the effects of suggestion, Freud turned his sole attention to hypnosis. With this shift he thus became more firmly committed to psychological rather than organic treatment. He had observed in Paris how hypnotism could produce symptoms similar to hysteria and could then remove them again. In 1889 he went to Nancy where he observed the technique developed by Liébeault and Bernheim which used suggestion, with or without hypnosis, for therapeutic purposes. As he wrote in his autobiographical study (1925), '[I] received the profoundest impression of the possibility that there could be powerful mental processes which nevertheless remained hidden from the consciousness of men.' This was one of the first statements presaging Freud's monumental discovery of the unconscious.

In the early 1890s, Freud attempted to persuade Breuer to renew his interest in the problems of hysteria and to share with the world the discoveries he had made in the case of Anna O. *Studien über Hysterie* (1895) (*Studies on Hysteria*) was the result – a collaborative effort in which Breuer and Freud presented their ideas on the origin and treatment of hysterical symptoms. Freud described the unconscious in detail and introduced two key concepts: that a symptom arises through the restraining of a conflictful affect, and that it results from the transformation of a quantum of energy which, instead of being used in other ways, was converted into the symptom. Breuer described the way in which the technique he used with Anna O. allowed for the cathartic discharge of feelings (abreaction) with symptom relief. Although subsequent clinical research has questioned the universality of the effectiveness of this technique, it was *Studies on Hysteria* that introduced psychoanalysis to the world.

Breuer ultimately left the field of psychological treatment, but Freud, undeterred by the unfavourable reception given to the *Studies* by the experts of the day, pursued his studies of patients. He discovered that what was strangulated in neurosis was not just any kind of emotional experience but those that were primarily sexual in nature. Freud then began to study the so-called neurasthenics as well as the hysterics. As a consequence of these investigations, he believed at that time that the neuroses, without exception, resulted from disturbances in sexual function.

Freud's study of Breuer's patient, Anna O., led to the discovery of the concept of 'transference', a key to clinical and applied psychoanalysis. In a patient's relationship with his analyst, Freud thought, the patient re-experiences the early emotional relations that he had with his parents. It is the analysis of this transference that becomes the most fruitful instrument of analytic treatment. As a result of his discovery of transference, Freud abandoned hypnotism and began to use other procedures that evolved into the technique used in psychoanalysis today. The patient lies on a couch with the analyst sitting behind. The patient associates freely, and the analyst listens for patterns of transference, linkages, feelings, dreams, and other products of the associative process.

Once he had abandoned the use of hypnosis, Freud came to understand that there were forces which he called resistances which kept certain patterns, linkages, and connections from awareness. An impulse barred from access to consciousness was in fact retained and pushed into the unconscious (that is, repressed), from which it was capable of re-emerging when the counterforces were weakened or the repressed impulses strengthened. Freud considered repression a mechanism of defence, comparable to the flight mechanism used to avoid external conflict. In order to keep the debarred impulse repressed in the unconscious, the mental apparatus had to deploy 'energy'. The amount of energy available for other nonconflicted activities was thereby depleted, and as a result symptoms appeared. The theory of repression became the cornerstone of the newer understanding of the neuroses, which in turn affected the task of therapy.

Freud's early 'topographic model' of the mind separated the unconscious into the preconscious and the unconscious proper. The topographic model was later to evolve into the 'structural model' of the mind, which consisted of the id, the ego, and the ego ideal or superego.

As Freud investigated his patients' lives, he was struck by the significance of events that had seemingly occurred during the first years of childhood. The impressions of that early period of life, though buried in the unconscious, still played a significant role in the individual's personality and vulnerability to later emotional disturbance. Freud's assertion that sexuality is present from the beginning of life and has a subsequent course of development was a pivotal concept of psychoanalysis and one that evoked a good deal of controversy.

At the time of this discovery, Freud believed that experiences of sexual seduction in childhood were universally the basis of neurosis. The evidence for this was derived from his clinical work. Subsequently, however, he came to realize that the seductions had not actually taken place but were fantasies. That such wishful fantasies were of even greater importance than actual external reality, however, was one of Freud's most significant discoveries.

Freud's ideas of infantile and childhood sexuality became the basis of his developmental theory of sexual progression. Initially, he believed that sexuality is connected with what he called 'component instincts', i.e., instincts which are connected with erotogenic zones of the body but which have an independent wish for pleasure. These are usually connected with the vital biological activities necessary for survival. For example, oral activities involve sucking and feeding as well as oral pleasures, anal activities involve excretion as well as anal pleasures, and genital pleasures are related to reproduction and conception. Freud called the energy of sexual instincts libido. In the course of psychosexual development, fixations of libido may occur at various points which may be returned to when later threats force a withdrawal to an earlier level. Freud called this process 'regression'. Freud also noted in *An Autobiographical Study* (1925) that, 'The point of fixation is what determines the *choice of neurosis*, that is, the form in which the subsequent illness makes its appearance.'

The first object of libidinal gratification and fulfilment is the mother. Her breasts serve as the source of oral pleasure, and she takes on the significance of the external source from which later confidence, self-esteem, and self-regulation are derived. This relationship with the mother plays a pivotal role in a developmental stage that Freud named the Oedipus complex, after the famous Greek tragic hero. Using the male child as an illustration, and reducing this developmental stage to a simple formulation that did not take into account variations, complexities and consequences, Freud noted that boys focus their sexual wishes upon their mothers and become hostile to and rivalrous with their fathers. This incestuous object choice and its feared and fantasied consequences of genital damage and retaliation give rise to a stage of latency during which the conscience (super-ego) becomes evident through feelings of morality, shame and disgust. At puberty, the earlier conflicts, including the Oedipus complex, may become reanimated. Although Freud's discoveries of the sexuality of children were made from the psychoanalyses of adults, direct observation of children as well as the analyses of children and adolescents have confirmed, extended, detailed and modified his ideas.

Freud also made a major contribution to the study of dreams – their meaning and their use in the therapeutic situation. In one of his major works, *Die Traumdeutung* (1900) (*The Interpretation of Dreams*, 1913), Freud described his researches on dreams, dream work and formation, symbolism, and his wish-fulfilment theory of the function of dreams.

In *Zur Psychopathologie des Alltagslebens* (1901) (*The Psychopathology of Everyday Life*), Freud turned his attention to slips and lapses of memory. Such symptomatic acts, so common in everyday life, he believed, have meaning, can be explained and interpreted, and indicate the presence of conflicting impulses and intentions. The study of dreams and of symptomatic acts has applicability to both pathological situations and normal healthy mental functioning.

For ten years after he and Breuer parted (1895–96 through 1906–7) Freud worked in isolation, rejected by the German-Austrian establishment. In 1900–1902, however, Bleuler and Jung, working at the Burghölzli, a large hospital near Zurich, became interested in psychoanalysis and began to extend the application of Freudian theories beyond the confines of upper-middle-class Vienna.

In 1909, Freud, Jung, and Sandor Ferenczi, a member of Freud's circle in Vienna, gave lectures at Clark University in Worcester, Massachusetts. James J. Putnam, a neurologist at

Harvard, and William James were among those present. The trip was a success, and marked the beginning of international recognition. In 1910 the International Psycho-Analytic Association was founded, an organization that still exists. Several journals, institutes, and societies were organized in Vienna, Berlin, Moscow, New York, Zurich and London.

Although many of the earlier pioneers remained loyal to Freud and to psychoanalysis, some of his followers ultimately left him to found their own movements (for example, Adler, Jung, Reich, Rank, and Stekel).

Freud's research continued at an intense pace, but gradually his students and colleagues took over increasingly from him. In 1923 he became ill with a malignancy of the jaw which was to give him pain and anguish for the rest of his life. His contributions to our understanding of art and artists, literature and writers, jokes, the psychology of religion, anthropology, myths and fairy tales, rituals, the emotional aspects of group psychology, philosophy, education, child care and rearing, and the question of educating nonphysicians to be psychoanalysts were some of the by-products of his lifelong struggle to penetrate the science of the mind.

Freud was a brilliant and a learned man, a researcher, clinician, theoretician, and writer. Psychoanalysis allowed us to understand what previously was seen as irrational human behaviour from a new perspective. His contributions to psychiatry, psychology, sociology, and biology are monumental. The science of psychoanalysis has moved on since Freud's time, correcting some of his errors and expanding into areas that he did not develop. One can only do so much in a lifetime, and Freud gave us so much that it will be many lifetimes before we have fully understood him.

George H. Pollock
Institute for Psychoanalysis, Chicago

References
Freud, S. (1953–74), *Standard Edition of the Complete Psychological Works of Sigmund Freud*, 24 vols, ed. J. Strachey, London.

Included are: Vol. XX: *An Autobiographical Study, Inhibitions, Symptoms, Anxiety, Lay Analysis and Other Works* (1925–6).
Vol. II: *Studies on Hysteria* (1893–5) (with J. Breuer).
Vols. IV and V: *The Interpretation of Dreams* (I) and (II) (1900–1).
Vol. VI: *The Psychopathology of Everyday Life* (1901).
Jones, E. (1953–7), *The Life and Work of Sigmund Freud*, 3 vols, London.

Further Reading
Schur, M. (1972), *Freud: Living and Dying*, London.
Sulloway, F. J. (1979), *Freud: Biologist of the Mind*, New York.
Wollheim, R. (1971), *Sigmund Freud*, London.

Friedman, Milton (1912–)

Since 1950, Milton Friedman has been a leader of international monetarism, methodological positivism, and traditional liberalism, as well as of the so-called 'Chicago School' which embodies these ideas. He was Nobel Laureate in 1976; his presidencies include the American Economic Association and the Mont Pelerin Society. His best-known book among the general public remains probably *Capitalism and Freedom* (1962), followed by selections from his *Essays in Positive Economics* (1953) and his *Monetary History of the United States* (1963, with Anna J. Schwartz).

Born in New Jersey of immigrant parents, Friedman was trained almost simultaneously in mathematics, economics, and statistics (AB Rutgers University, MA University of Chicago, Ph.D. Columbia University). He was initially known primarily as a mathematical statistician specializing in decision theory. His broader interests in economic theory, history, and methodology became apparent in university teaching at the Universities of Wisconsin (1949–50), Minnesota (1945–7) and Chicago (1947–77), and dominate his later work. Since his retirement from Chicago, Friedman has been affiliated with the Hoover Institute on the Stanford University campus in California.

Friedman the methodologist believes that the widely ridiculed differences of opinion and advice among economists relate primarily to questions of *what is* (positive economics) rather than of what *should be* (normative economics), and that once the 'positive' questions are satisfactorily answered the 'normative' ones will be manageable. Friedman maintains that questions in positive economics can in principle be answered at least tentatively by comparing (evaluating) the quantitative predictions, which themselves result from alternative 'models' of how the world – or the economy – works. It makes no difference to him whether the basic assumptions underlying these models are or are not themselves intuitively realistic; also, any 'general case' theory, into which wide ranges of alternative results fit equally well as 'special cases', is untestable and thus of little value.

Friedman's monetarism and his 'modernized' quantity theory of money illustrate his methodological position. He interprets the quantity theory as a theory of nominal income, and as maintaining only that the quantity of money in a country (however defined) is a more accurate determinant of both the levels and changes of that country's nominal income than is the country's 'autonomous' expenditures, in the sense of Keynesian theory. As for the division of nominal income effects between real income and the price level, and, also, as for the precise structure relating money and income, the quantity theory (in Friedman's version) has little to say. We should also note that Friedman has favoured exchange-rate flexibility, whereas most 'international monetarists' prefer a fixed-rate system.

In their *Monetary History of the United States* and related works, Friedman and Schwartz apply their monetary insights to the period since the American Civil War, tracing changes in both price levels and business activity to monetary uncertainties – fluctuations of monetary growth above and below any smooth relationship with the long-term growth rate of the real economy. It contains two disconcerting results: (1) The inauguration of the Federal Reserve System in 1914 seems to have made things worse rather than better than they were previously – Friedman favours 'rules', including the pre-1914 gold standard, over 'authorities', like the Federal Reserve Board, as regulators of the money supply. (2) The main explanation for the depth and the persistence of the Great Depression of the 1930s is a series of errors in Federal Reserve policy, whose fears of 'going off gold' permitted the American money supply to fall by approximately one-third over the 3-year period following the stock-market collapse of October 1929, without preventing America's departure from the gold standard.

Friedman's overall liberal faith in the market as an economic regulator is a matter of 'second best' and does not regard market determinations as utopian. This liberalism arises primarily from Friedman's understanding and interpretation of the record of intervention, extending even to attempts like the American Anti-Trust Laws at enforcement of closer approaches to 'pure and perfect competition' upon an imperfectly competitive market-place. Friedman's negative judgement embraces both the errors of well-intentioned voting majorities and of well-intentioned intellectual meritocrats, along with the errors of tyrants, dictators, and despots. A secondary Friedman argument for the market is the shelter its anonymity offers to social, religious, racial, and ideological minorities doomed to failure so long as success requires employment of licensure by the majority or by the Establishment. At the same time, Friedman's liberal individualism does not go so far as the 'libertarianism' of some other American writers for whom the State is illegitimate and taxation, in particular, is robbery. Friedman's major concession to the contemporary (twentieth-century) concept or distortion of liberalism has been his advocacy of a minimum income below which individuals and families should not be required to fall, but which should replace the myriad of social services programmes embodied in the contemporary 'Welfare State'.

Martin Bronfenbrenner
Duke University

Further Reading
Breit, W. and Ransom, R. (1982), *The Academic Scribblers*, rev. edn, Chicago.

Thygessen, N. (1975), 'The scientific contributions of Milton Friedman', *Scandinavian Journal of Economics*.

Tobin, J. (1972), 'Friedman's theoretical framework', *Journal of Political Economy*, 80.

Goffman, Erving (1922–82)

A Canadian-born social scientist, Goffman graduated from the University of Toronto, and received his MA (1949) and Ph.D. (1953) from the University of Chicago. He taught at the Universities of Edinburgh, Berkeley and Pennsylvania, and carried out field research in the Shetland Islands, and in a public mental hospital in Washington DC. Among his many books are: *The Presentation of Self in Everyday Life* (1959), *Asylums* (1961), *Encounters: Essays on the Social Situation of Mental Patients and Other Inmates* (1961), *Stigma: Notes on the Management of Spoiled Identity* (1963), *Frame Analysis* (1974), and *Gender Advertisements* (1979).

Goffman took as his focus the microanalysis of everyday behaviour, in a variety of contexts. He analysed social situations in terms of the linkage between sociocultural frames of meaning and the ability of the actor to manage and interpret his environment. His topics were aspects of social behaviour such as games, public gatherings, stigmatizing behaviour, the interaction of 'staff' and 'inmates', and so on. In interpreting these phenomena, Goffman used theoretical constructs such as 'ritual', 'the management of impression', 'social encounters', 'role distance', and others, designed to formulate the principles whereby social situations and relationships were constituted. He was often linked to the tradition of social interactionism, but especially in his later work he appeared to be taking a different path. He emphasized that human interaction is structured by the position of actors in a wider social setting, governed by a symbolic code which defines its boundaries, rules of conduct and universe of meaning. Like Simmel, Goffman was more interested in the structure of social situations than in their content.

In Goffman's world, the actor is assumed to be aware of his role, and to interpret it. The individual is allowed to manœuvre within the web of interactional contingencies which constitute the frame of action. The actor responds to shifting involvements and breaches in communication. Failure to sustain an acceptable performance in social encounters is liable to lead to embarrassment, self-reproach and sanctions. Here, perhaps, Goffman's perspective is grounded in a structural model rather than in a social-psychological approach, but (perhaps because he was working in a complex society) his analyses exhibit a flexibility and subtlety which mute any tendency to functionalist analysis.

Methodologically, Goffman is open to criticism. His work is rife with cultural preconceptions, and he depends on unsystematic observations. This limits the force of his work, and diminishes its value as a model for further research and thought.

Haim Hazan
Tel-Aviv University

Further Reading

Gonos, G. (1977), 'Situation versus frame: the "interactionist" and the "structuralist" analysis of everyday life', *American Sociological Review*, 42.

Perry, N. (1974), 'The two cultures and the total institution', *British Journal of Sociology*, 24.

Psathas, G. and Waksler, C. (1973), 'Essential features of face to face interaction', in G. Psathas (ed.), *Phenomenological Sociology: Issues and Implications*, London.

Gouldner, Alvin Ward (1920–80)

Alvin Gouldner, born in New York in 1920, was both a Marxist and a sociologist, yet neither. Gouldner's *The Coming Crisis in Western Sociology* (1971) is the classic interpretation of the social basis for the failure of post-Second World War sociological functionalism in the West and of Marxism in the East. This book was broadly influential, especially among those who turned to sociology in response to their disappointment with the political radicalism of the 1960s.

Coming Crisis was also a major work in his life's project – the critical interpretation of the history of social theory. *Enter Plato* (1966) was the first in this series. It turned social scientists' attention to Greek thought. (Classicists were annoyed that an outsider would dare to enter their scholarly domain.) After *Coming Crisis*, *The Dialectic of Ideology and Technology* (1976) and *The Future of Intellectuals and the Rise of the New Class* (1979) examined the fate of critical thinking and political action in late industrial society. The latter made the controversial claim that the new class, comprising intellectuals, managers, and the technical intelligentsia, was the best hope for revolution in light of the failure of the industrial proletariat. He thus challenged the central political and theoretical premise of Marxism. But in *The Two Marxisms* (1980) he carefully distinguished scientific and critical Marxisms and clearly identified himself with the latter, more humanistic, course. *Against Fragmentation: The Origins of Marxism and the Sociology of Intellectuals* (posthumous, 1985) is an extension of his historical theory of intellectuals to Marxism – thus completing a twenty-year project that began with Greeks and ended with twentieth-century Marxism.

Of his fourteen books, *Patterns of Industrial Bureaucracy* (1954) stands with *Coming Crisis* as a sociological classic. The former is a *locus classicus* of American industrial sociology, just as the latter became the manifesto of post-1960s social scientists seeking a third way between their academic disciplines and the political visions of Marxism. *Theory and Society*, the international journal which he founded in 1974 and edited until his death, was the institutionalization of this third-way strategy.

Charles Lemert
Wesleyan University, Connecticut

Further Reading
Theory and Society II (1982) (issue devoted to the comprehensive assessment of Gouldner's life and work).

Gramsci, Antonio (1891–1937)

Antonio Gramsci, a native of Sardinia, was one of the outstanding Marxist thinkers of this century. After leaving Turin University, he became a leading activist and journalist in the Italian Socialist Party (PSI). During Italy's *biennio rosso* of 1919–20, a period of great unrest, he championed the cause of factory councils, and he developed his theory of councils in *L'Ordine Nuovo*, a weekly review which he co-edited. The network of councils was seen as both the main agency of revolutionary change and the embryonic structure of the future society. After the rise of Fascism, however, Gramsci abandoned this theory – denounced as 'syndicalist' by his more orthodox comrades – and turned his attention to the co-ordinative and educational role of the party. In 1921, he, along with fellow left-wing dissidents, split off from the PSI to form the *Partito comunista d'Italia*, an organization which he led from 1924 to 1926, the year he was imprisoned by Mussolini's regime.

While in prison Gramsci composed his *Prison Notebooks*, a massive, disordered, and unfinished work which is nevertheless a classic of our time. The *Notebooks*, elaborating ideas which had often been implicit in his earlier newspaper articles, put forward a humanist conception of Marxism, focusing on human subjectivity – on beliefs, values, aspirations and theories. Influenced by Croce's brand of idealist philosophy, and with scant regard for orthodoxy, Gramsci challenged crucial theoretical elements of classical Marxism: the reductive physicalism which denied reality to anything but matter; the passive, or contemplative, conception of knowledge; the attempt to extend the methods of the natural sciences to the study of man; the belief that history obeys universal causal laws similar to those of the physical sciences; the dismissal of cultural and political activities as pale reflections of economic practices; the assumption that capitalism is a conflict-ridden system precariously held together by coercion; and the optimistic conviction that the downfall of capitalism is guaranteed by its inherent contradictions. In Gramsci's view, conventional Marxism had disastrously imposed a metaphysical, or transcendent, design on history, independent of human will and action – though the 'hidden God' was no longer Hegel's 'Spirit' but an equally abstract and impersonal 'Nature'.

Gramsci is best remembered for his doctrine of 'hegemony', or moral/spiritual supremacy, according to which the ascendancy of a class or group rests, essentially, on its ability to translate its own world-view into a pervasive dominant ethos, guiding the patterns of daily life. Because of bourgeois hegemony, Marxists should, in his opinion, adopt a non-Bolshevik strategy, whereby the revolutionary party effects a mental transformation of the masses *before* seizing power. The emphasis shifts from political to cultural revolution, to the long-term task of scraping away 'the muck of ages'. This patient, 'gradualist' approach was, as Gramsci realized, incompatible with the Leninist conception of the party as a monolithic, quasi-military structure, aloof from the everyday concerns of the people. His version of Marxism, with its stress on persuasion, culture and mass participation, has given inspiration to the 'Eurocommunists', in their efforts to distance themselves from Moscow. Gramsci himself, however, remained a committed revolutionary, though he wanted a 'majority' not a 'minority' revolution.

Joseph V. Femia
University of Liverpool

Reference
Gramsci, A. (1975), *Quaderni del Carcere*, 4 vols, ed. V. Gerratana, Turin (trans. Q. Hoare and G. Nowell Smith, *Selections from the Prison Notebooks*, London 1971).

Further Reading
Adamson, W. L. (1980), *Hegemony and Revolution: Antonio Gramsci's Political and Cultural Theory*, Berkeley and Los Angeles.
Femia, J. V. (1981), *Gramsci's Political Thought: Hegemony, Consciousness, and the Revolutionary Process*, Oxford.

Habermas, Jürgen (1929–)

Jürgen Habermas has been the most prolific and influential representative of the 'second generation' of the Frankfurt School. He has both continued the theoretical tradition of his teachers Adorno and Horkheimer and his friend Marcuse, and has also significantly departed from 'classical' critical theory and made many important new contributions to contemporary philosophy and social theory. In particular, he has opened critical theory to a dialogue with other philosophies and social theories such as the hermeneutics of Gadamer, systems theory and structural functionalism, empirical social sciences, analytic and linguistic philosophy, and theories of cognitive and moral development. In recent years, he has been synthesizing these influences into a theory of 'communicative action', which presents the foundation and framework of a social theory that builds on the tradition of Marx, Weber and classical critical theory, but which also criticizes his predecessors and breaks new theoretical ground.

Habermas was born on 18 June 1929 in Dusseldorf, and grew up in Gummersbach, Germany. His father was head of the Bureau of Industry and Trade, and his grandfather was a minister and director of the local seminary. He experienced the rise and defeat of Fascism, and was politicized by the Nuremberg trials and documentary films of the concentration camps shown after the war. Habermas began his university studies in Göttingen in 1949 and finished a dissertation of *Das Absolute und die Geschichte* in 1954. In the 1950s, Habermas studied – and was strongly influenced by – Lukács's *History and Class Consciousness* and Adorno and Horkheimer's *Dialectic of Enlightenment* which he first read in 1955. He studied the young Marx and the young Hegelians with Karl Löwith, one of Germany's great scholars and teachers.

Habermas resolved to work with Adorno and Horkheimer because he believed that they were establishing a dialectical and critical theory of society from within a creative and innovative Marxist tradition. He thus went to Frankfurt and continued his studies in the Institute for Social Research. In this context, he wrote his first major book *Strukturwandel der Öffentlichkeit* (1962).

Combining historical and empirical research with the theoretical framework of critical theory, Habermas traced the historical rise and decline of what he called the 'bourgeois public sphere' and its replacement by the mass media, technocratic administration, and societal depoliticization. This influential work continues to animate discussion concerning problems of representative democracy in contemporary capitalist societies and the need for more participatory, democratic and egalitarian spheres of sociopolitical discussion and debate.

In the 1960s, Habermas taught at the Universities of Heidelberg (from 1961–4) and Frankfurt (from 1964–71). At this time he also became more interested in politics and published *Student und Politik* with others in 1961 which called for university reforms, and *Protestbewegung und Hochschulreform* in 1969 which continued his concern with university reform and also criticized what he saw as the excesses of the German student movement in the 1960s. Habermas was also engaged in intense theoretical work during this period. His *Theorie und Praxis* appeared in 1963 (*Theory and Practice*, Boston, 1973), which contained theoretical papers on major classical and contemporary social and political theorists, as well as anticipations of his own theoretical position; *Zur Logik der Sozialwissenschaften* in 1967 contained a detailed and critical summary of contemporary debates in the logic of the social sciences; *Erkenntnis und Interesse* in 1968 (*Knowledge and Human Interests*, Boston, 1971) traced the development of epistemology and critical social theory from Kant to the present; and several collections of essays: *Technik und Wissenschaft als Ideologie* (1968); *Arbeit-Erkenntnis-Fortschritt* (1970); and *Philosophische-politische Profile* (1971).

During the 1970s Habermas intensified his studies of the social sciences and began restructuring critical theory as communication theory. Key stages of this enterprise are contained in a collection of studies written with Niklas Luhmann: *Theorie der Gesellschaft oder Sozialtechnologie* (1971); *Legitimationsprobleme im Spätkapitalismus* (1973); *Zur Rekonstruktion des Historischen Materialismus* (1976); and essays collected in several other books. In these works, Habermas sharpened his critique of classical Marxism and his critical theory predecessors. He attempted to develop his own reconstruction of historical materialism, a critical theory of society, and a philosophical theory rooted in analyses of communicative action. During much of this period since 1971, Habermas was director of the Max Planck Institute in Starnberg where he involved himself in various research projects and was in close touch with developments in the social sciences. After a series of disputes with students and colleagues, he resigned in 1982 and returned to Frankfurt where he is now Professor of Philosophy and Sociology.

In 1981, Habermas published his two-volume magnum opus, *Theorie des kommunikativen Handelns*. This impressive work of historical scholarship and theoretical construction appraises the legacies of Marx, Durkheim, Weber, Lukács and 'Western Marxism', including critical theory, and criticizes their tendencies towards theoretical reductionism and their failure to develop an adequate theory of communicative action and rationality. Habermas also contributes his own analysis of the importance of communicative action and rationality for contemporary social theory. The book points both to his continuity with the first generation of the Frankfurt school and his significant departures. *Theorie des kommunikativen Handelns* also manifests Habermas's continued interest in the relationship between theory and practice with his discussion of new social movements. The concluding section is a testament to his interest in systematic social theory with a practical intent in his summation of the status of critical theory today. The work as a whole thus sums up Habermas's last decade of theoretical work and points to some issues and topics that will probably constitute future projects. Habermas's legacy thus remains open to new theoretical and political developments and is an important part of contemporary discussions within social theory and science.

Douglas Kellner
University of Texas, Austin

Further Reading
Horster, D. and von Reijen, W. (1979), 'Interview with Jürgen Habermas', *New German Critique*, 18.
McCarthy, T. (1978), *The Critical Theory of Jürgen Habermas*, London.
See also: *Marcuse*.

Hayek, Friedrich A. (1899–)

Recipient of the Nobel Prize in Economic Science (together with Gunnar Myrdal) in 1974, Friedrich August von Hayek was born in Vienna on 8 May 1899. He earned two doctorates at the University of Vienna – Dr. jur. (1921) and Dr. rer. pol. (1923) – and became Privatdozent in Political Economy in 1929. He was director of the Austrian Institute for Economic Research from 1927 to 1931. In 1931 he accepted an appointment at the University of London as Tooke Professor of Economic Science and Statistics. He was awarded a D.Sc. degree by that institution in 1944. He remained at London until 1950, when he accepted a position at the University of Chicago. He returned to Europe in 1962 as Professor of Economic Policy at the University of Freiburg, and upon retirement from that institution in 1967 he accepted a position as honorary professor at the University of Salzburg, from which he received an honorary doctor's degree in 1974.

Hayek was instrumental in the founding of the Mont Pelerin Society in April 1947, a society whose aims were to contribute to the preservation and improvement of the free society. He served as president of the Society for twelve years.

Hayek's broad scope of inquiry is reflected in his contributions to economic science. These include: the theory of economic fluctuations; the pure theory of capital; the theory of economic planning under socialism and competitive capitalism; and the methodology of economics.

In addition to many articles, his theory of economic fluctuations was presented in two books: *Monetary Theory and the Trade Cycle* (1926 and 1933) and *Prices and Production* (1931). Beginning with Wicksell's theory of the 'cumulative process', Hayek expanded and modified Wicksell's theory and then proceeded to develop his own theory of economic fluctuations which included such elements as how changes in the quantity of money affect relative prices, rather than general price levels, as well as allocation of resources, especially between producer and consumer goods; the related disturbances in investment period and voluntary saving, as well as 'forced saving'; bank credit and its effects on 'forced saving' and capital deepening; a model of the price mechanism and its operation in the context of fluctuations.

In 1941, Hayek published the *Pure Theory of Capital*, a treatise on capital theory. Among the topics treated and which represented a contribution to the theory of capital were: the concept of 'intertemporal equilibrium'; physical productivity of investment; the phenomenon of natural growth; 'period of investment', the idea of the 'force of interest'; and finally, 'durable goods'.

In spite of his contributions to economic theory, Hayek was never accorded the recognition of his contemporary J. M. Keynes, whose *General Theory* (1936) was accepted as the standard paradigm of economic fluctuations in economics. Also, the Austrian theory of capital had fallen out of fashion by the time his *Pure Theory of Capital* appeared, and his work in this area was largely ignored. The later period of his career was devoted to political and social philosophy and methodology, the most popular of his books being *The Road to Serfdom* (1944) and *The Counter-Revolution in Science* (1952).

Vincent J. Tarascio
University of North Carolina

References

Hayek, F. A. (1928), *Geldtheorie und Konjunkturtheorie*, Vienna. (English edn, *Monetary Theory and the Trade Cycle*, London, 1933.)

Hayek, F. A. (1931), *Price and Production*, London.

Hayek, F. A. (1941), *The Pure Theory of Capital*, London.

Hayek, F. A. (1944), *The Road to Serfdom*, London.

Hayek, F. A. (1952), *The Counter-Revolution in Science*, Glencoe, Ill.

Further Reading
Machlup, F. (1974), 'Friedrich von Hayek's contribution to economics', *Scandinavian Journal of Economics*, 76.
Machlup, F. (ed.) (1976), *Essays on Hayek*, New York.

Hegel, Georg Wilhelm F. (1770–1831)

Probably no other philosophy dominates the modern European consciousness to the same extent as Hegel's. Yet few great thinkers have been so consistently misunderstood and their teaching so distorted by friend and foe alike, even today, in spite of the work of specialist Hegel scholars, who in the last decade or two have swarmed as never before. The old stereotypes still persist: the allegedly 'tender-minded' reality-behind-appearance Idealist; the arch-rationalist; the professional historian's *bête noire* with his *a priori* philosophy of history; the apologist of Prussian authoritarianism and the conservatism of the Restoration, the apostle of *Machtpolitik* and totalitarianism, if rarely in their cruder shapes, yet often nowadays in more subtle and sophisticated kinds of criticism. Scholars are reluctant, even timid, to start at the other end of the spectrum: to accept Hegel without reserve as the thoroughly down-to-earth realist that he always was, interested especially in what we would call sociological phenomena (and Hegel's *Volksgeist*, for instance, is to be seen in this light and not that of Romantic nationalism); or to see him as the lifelong enthusiast for the ideals of the French Revolution, in many ways closer to Benthamite radicalism than Burkian conservatism, who tried to use philosophy to expound the logic of the claim of modern man to self-realization and freedom and therefore the rationale of the modern democratic state as such, a thinker who is not outside the liberal democratic tradition, but sociologically realistic within it.

It is a strange paradox that Marx did accept much of this, precisely because in his critique of Hegel's political philosophy he was attacking the idea of the state as such, in its most plausible form, and wanted to show that it was self-contradictory, because it was an illusion of the alienated false consciousness of bourgeois society or, rather, non-society, which could not possibly become a reality in the modern world. Marx admired the detail and clarity of Hegel's account of modern society and its sociological realism – only it was 'upside down', like a photographic negative. And for modern Marxists it is an unshakeable dogma that Marx 'demystified' Hegel, removed the centre of gravity from *Geist* to man, and so on. In fact they have created a new myth: not the state, but what in Hegel is one of its 'moments', namely, 'civil society', is all-in-all, and the state is powerless to intervene and correct the self-destructive evils of this sphere of rampant economic liberalism that he analysed so acutely, especially the production of an alienated 'pöbel' or proletariat. Hegel is said to be describing something on its way out. Although this sort of interpretation involves too much looking down the wrong end of the telescope, it does come closer to the real Hegel than traditional liberal distortions, for example, that Hegel 'equated' state and society, in so far as Hegel's view of modern industrial and commercial civilization was not only profoundly critical but closely related to a dialectic designed to develop fully the inherent self-contradictions in all partial truths, and which applies not only to thinking but to the reality that is thought.

An interpretation which spotlights the theme of alienation generally and the need for community need not be Marxist, and in England and America especially this has recently been fashionable. The influence of the *Zeitgeist* seems fairly obvious in this concentration on community rather than state in Hegel, a concentration which is inclined to lean heavily on certain aspects of his immature thought, especially his enthusiasm for the 'beautiful wholeness' of the life-style of the ancient Greeks. The mature Hegel is then interpreted in this light.

All these interpretations suffer from failure to understand the meaning and significance of the religious dimension of Hegel's philosophy, his claim that philosophy is the fully rational truth of Christianity, and how this is reflected in the Hegelian 'concept' or 'notion', the concrete universal that is the tool of Reason, as opposed to the scientific 'Understanding' which knows its objects by separating and dividing. This means accepting the reality and necessity of continuing division and conflict for true harmony and unity in the human spirit and society, and rejecting all belief in a 'beyond' as a pathological symptom of alienation. A true unity is a unity of differences, unlike the primitive undifferentiated wholeness of the Greek *polis*, and a 'rational' state, as understood by philosophy, will be the reverse of totalitarian: it must in fact be pluralistic, since the universal needs the particular as much as the particular needs the universal. It is the 'prodigious strength' of the modern state that it is able to contain its negation: the world of self-seeking particularity that destroyed the primitive unity of the Greek *polis*. This is the fully developed freedom (fully developed in every relevant objective sense, ethical, legal, political and social), of the modern state that makes sense of history, and whose development the philosopher can trace in history. Beyond history and the state is the timeless 'absolute freedom' of art, religion and philosophy; the state and its freedom is not an end in itself. Hegel was in fact 'describing' something on its way in: the *Geist* of modern man, his claim to freedom and the institutions necessary to make that claim real. In many ways he anticipated Max Weber in his account of the modern rational state as an essentially public impersonal institution that belongs to no one but which everyone recognizes as his own in so far as it is seen to uphold his own particular interests, and which generates a perpetual tension between freedom and control, liberty and order.

In the *Grundlinien der Philosophie des Rechts*, 1821 (*Philosophy of Right*, 1942) Hegel spells this out in meticulous detail far surpassing anything to be found in most philosophers who call themselves empirical, and in this he was unnecessarily and dangerously extending his lines into matters that were contingent and time-bound. But it is a superficial view that writes off this sort of thing as 'out-of-date': it is more rewarding to seek the rationale that underlies such obvious anachronisms. And this is in accordance with the Hegelian dialectic, which is not a strict and logically brittle deduction of 'thesis, antithesis and synthesis', but a way of thinking concretely and multidimensionally about human experience and of exhibiting such thought, which is one reason why Hegel is 'difficult'. The only test is trueness to life. But anyone who approaches the *Philosophy of Right* in the correct spirit, a book which it should be remembered is not a 'book', but a compendium for a course of lectures, will be repeatedly struck by his soundness and common sense and be able to appreciate the force of his criticism of all abstract thinking about freedom and the state in purely legal or purely ethical or, for that matter, purely sociological modes. But a proper understanding of Hegel requires a sound knowledge of the historical background (which most critics do not have), so that one can make the necessary adjustments in order to arrive at its relevance. The beginner, however, should start with the lectures on the philosophy of history, which Hegel himself designed for beginners, though this too has its dangers. There is simply no short cut to this philosophy, which is a circle, whose end is its beginning. Hegelian dialectic was able to bring home the bacon of sociological realism, as Marx in his own way realized, and political liberalism would have been a lot sounder and healthier if its exponents had realized it too, and not been so busy hunting 'totalitarian' and 'conservative' hares, in country for which they did not possess an adequate map.

Duncan Forbes
University of Cambridge

Further Reading
Avineri, S. (1972), *Hegel's Theory of the Modern State*, Cambridge.
Fleischmann, E. J. (1964), *La Philosophie politique de Hegel*, Paris.
Hegel, G. H. (1975), *Reason in History*, Cambridge.
Knox, T. M. (1967), *Hegel's Philosophy of Right*, London.
Marcuse, H. (1941), *Reason and Revolution*, New York.
Plant, R. (1973), *Hegel*, London.
Pöggeler, O. (ed.) (1977), *Hegel: Einführung in seine Philosophie*, Munich.

Reyburn, H. A. (1921), *Hegel's Ethical Theory*, Oxford.

Rosenzweig, F. (1920), *Hegel und der Staat*, Munich.

Verene, D. P. (ed.) (1980), *Hegel's Social and Political Thought*, New York.

Weil, E. (1950), *Hegel et l'état*, Paris.

Hobbes, Thomas (1588–1679)

Thomas Hobbes is one of the most important figures in the development of modern science and modern politics. As a contemporary of Bacon, Galileo and Descartes, he contributed to the radical critique of medieval Scholasticism and classical philosophy that marked the beginning of the modern age. But he alone sought to develop a comprehensive philosophy – one that treated natural science, political science and theory of scientific method in a unified system. He published this system in three volumes, under the titles *Body*, (1655) *Man* (1957), and *Citizen* (1642). In the course of his long career, Hobbes also published treatises on mathematics, on free will and determinism, on the English common law system, and on the English Civil War. Although his work covered the whole of philosophy, Hobbes made his greatest contribution to modern thought in the field of political philosophy. On three separate occasions, he presented his theory of man and the state; the most famous of his political treatises, the *Leviathan* (1651), is generally recognized as the greatest work of political philosophy in the English language.

In all branches of knowledge, Hobbes's thought is characterized by a pervasive sense that the ancient and medieval philosophers had failed to discover true knowledge, and that a new alternative was urgently needed. It is this sense that defines Hobbes as a modern thinker and gives his work its originality, verve and self-conscious radicalism. In natural science (metaphysics and physics), he rejected the Scholastic and Aristotelian ideas of 'abstract essences' and immaterial causes as nothing more than vain and empty speech. The nature of reality is 'matter in motion', which implied that all phenomena of nature and human nature could be explained in terms of mechanical causation. In the theory of science, Hobbes dismissed the disputative method of Scholasticism and classical dialectics as forms of rhetoric that merely appealed to the authority of common opinion and produced endless verbal controversies. The correct method of reasoning combined the resolutive-compositive method of Galileo and the deductive method of Euclidean geometry. By combining these, Hobbes believed that every branch of knowledge, including the study of politics, could be turned into an exact deductive science.

In political science proper, Hobbes was no less radical in his rejection of the tradition. He opposed the republicanism of classical antiquity, the ecclesiastical politics of medieval Europe, and the doctrine of mixed-monarchy prevalent in seventeenth-century England. All these doctrines, Hobbes claimed, were seditious in intent or effect, because they were derived from 'higher' laws that allowed men to appeal to a standard above the will of the sovereign. Hobbes blamed such appeals, exploited by ambitious priests and political demagogues, for the political instability of his times, culminating in the English Civil War. The solution he proposed was political absolutism – the unification of sovereignty in an all-powerful state that derived its authority not from higher laws but from *de facto* power and the consent of the people.

With these three teachings – mechanistic materialism, exact deductive science, and political absolutism – Hobbes sought to establish science and politics on a new foundation that would produce certain knowledge and lasting civil peace.

From the first, Hobbes's philosophical system generated controversy. In the seventeenth century, Hobbes was treated as a dangerous subversive by all who believed in, or had an interest in, the traditional order. Christian clergymen condemned his materialist view of the world as atheistic and his mechanistic view of man as soulless; legal scholars attacked his doctrine of absolutism for placing the sovereign above the civil laws; even kings, whose power Hobbes sought to augment, were wary of accepting the teaching that political authority rested on force and consent rather than on divine right (Mintz, 1962). In the eighteenth and nineteenth centuries his defence of absolute and arbitrary power ran counter to the general demand for constitutional government. Hobbes has been treated more favourably in this century than ever before. Although some scholars have seen certain parallels between Hobbes's Leviathan state and twentieth-century tyrannies (Collingwood, 1942), most clearly recognize that Hobbes's 'enlightened despot', whose primary goal is to secure civil peace, is vastly different from the brutal and fanatical heads of totalitarian states (Strauss, 1959).

Such studies can be divided into several groups, each reflecting the perspective of a contemporary school of philosophy as it probes the origins of modernity. (1) Guided by the concerns of contemporary analytical philosophy, one group argues for the primacy of method and formal logic in Hobbes's system and views his politics as a set of formal rules which serve as utilitarian guidelines for the state (McNeilly, 1968; Watkins, 1965). (2) Another group has examined Hobbes's theory of 'political obligation' from a Kantian point of view. According to this interpretation, Hobbes's argument for obedience goes beyond calculations of utility by appealing to a sense of moral duty in keeping the social contract, and by requiring citizens to have just intentions (Taylor, 1938; Warrender, 1957). (3) Developed by Marxist scholars, a third interpretation uses Hobbes to understand the ideological origins of bourgeois society and to provide a critical perspective on bourgeois liberalism by exposing its Hobbesian roots (Macpherson, 1962; Coleman, 1977). (4) The fourth interpretation reflects the concerns of the natural law school. According to the foremost scholar of this school, Hobbes is the decisive figure in transforming the natural law tradition from classical natural right to modern natural 'rights'; Hobbes accomplished this revolution by asserting that the right of self-preservation, grounded in the fear of violent death, is the only justifiable moral claim (Strauss, 1936).

Robert P. Kraynak
Colgate University

References
Coleman, F. M. (1977), *Hobbes and America: Exploring the Constitutional Foundations*, Toronto.
Collingwood, R. G. (1942), *The New Leviathan*, Oxford.
Macpherson, C. B. (1962), *The Political Theory of Possessive Individualism*, Oxford.
McNeilly, F. S. (1968), *The Anatomy of Leviathan*, London.
Mintz, S. I. (1962), *The Hunting of Leviathan*, Cambridge.
Strauss, L. (1936), *The Political Philosophy of Hobbes*, Chicago.
Strauss, L. (1959), 'On the basis of Hobbes's political philosophy', in *What Is Political Philosophy?*, New York.
Taylor, A. E. (1938), 'The ethical doctrine of Hobbes', *Philosophy*, 13.
Warrender, H. (1957), *The Political Philosophy of Hobbes: His Theory of Obligation*, Oxford.
Watkins, J. W. N. (1965), *Hobbes's System of Ideas: A Study in the Political Significance of Philosophical Theories*, London.

Hull, Clark L. (1884–1952)

An American neobehavioural psychologist whose influence within psychology was most profound during the 1940s and 1950s, Clark L. Hull was himself influenced by Darwin's theory of evolution, Pavlov's concept of delayed or trace-conditioned reflexes, and Thorndike's law of effect. Hull firmly believed that psychology is a true natural science concerned with the 'determination of the quantitative laws of behaviour and their deductive systematization', and set out during his years at Yale University (1929–52) to develop a comprehensive general theory of behaviour constructed of variables linked systematically to experimentally derived data. An extensive study of rote learning led to the publication in 1940 of a monograph entitled *Mathematico-Deductive Theory of Rote Learning*. This work served as a prelude to a more general behaviour system first detailed in *Principles of Behavior* (1943) and later, with modifications, in *A Behavior System*, published posthumously in 1952. The system was based on the assumption that most response sequences leading to the reduction of bodily tension associated with need reduction are learned or reinforced. Hull proposed that the tendency for an organism to make a particular response when a stimulus is presented is a multiplicative function of habit strength (reflecting the number of previous reinforcements) and drive (based on bodily needs), minus certain inhibitory tendencies (associated with previous conditioning trials). These, along with other factors such as stimulus intensity and momentary behavioural oscillation, were seen as variables relating to response acquisition in the context of reinforced trials. Through careful experimentation, much of it with laboratory rats in mazes, Hull sought to quantify the functional relationships among these variables. While he failed to construct a comprehensive behaviour system, his theory led to important studies in the areas of motivation and conflict, frustration and aggression, manifest anxiety, social learning theory, and biofeedback. Early in his career Hull also made contributions in the areas of concept formation, hypnosis and aptitude testing. In the late 1930s and early 1940s, he conducted seminars to explore the congruencies between psychoanalytic and behavioural theories. These seminars did much to bring Freudian ideas to the attention of experimental psychologists.

Albert R. Gilgen
University of Northern Iowa

Further Reading
Hilgard, E. R. and Bower, G. H. (1975), *Theories of Learning*, New York.

Hume, David (1711–76)

Though it is now a cliché that Hume's philosophy is a 'Newtonian' science of man, and that all through this century students of it have noticed such things as the role played by sympathy as a mechanism of communication and factor in the development of self-consciousness and attacked the view of its allegedly atomistic, unhistorical individualism, it seems fair to say that Hume has not occupied a particularly important place in the history of social science, except perhaps negatively. His friends Ferguson and A. Smith have attracted more attention as founding fathers of a truly sociological method and outlook, and there are some good reasons for this: Hume's social theory, compared with theirs, was in many ways 'backward'. Its negative side has attracted those who value it as a useful political hygiene. There has been too much use of hasty generalizations and abridgements of a philosophy which is controversial and difficult to interpret. His social and political thought is no less complex and many-sided, as anyone knows who has tried to make sense of it as a whole. Those determined to place him in the tradition of conservative politics ignore his 'republicanism'; those who collect evidence of his 'civic humanism', or the 'politics of nostalgia' of the country gentlemen, neglect what is forward-looking and 'sociologically' positive in him.

Hume's contribution to 'politics', which he defined as the science of 'men united in society and dependent on each other', can be divided roughly into three main sections or phases: (1) a theory of justice and government as such, as part of a naturalistic ethics; (2) essays covering a wide range of topics in economics and politics; and (3) a *History of England*. All can be seen as parts of a programme not only of political 'moderation' but also of modernization, an attempt to give the Revolution and Hanoverian regime a proper, that is, 'philosophical' or scientific and empirical, foundation, and to understand the nature of modern European political civilization.

The natural law that Hume accepted as the ground of political science was, in its contemporary modes, open to the attacks of sceptics, moral relativists and Hobbists, but what Hume provided in his account of 'Justice' – the three 'natural laws' concerning property without which settled society is impossible and which government is instituted to uphold – was wholly secular and too avant-garde for his contemporaries. It was regarded, as was Hume's philosophy generally, as sceptical in a wholly destructive sense, a socially dangerous virus, not a healthy vaccine producing 'moderation', and the view that it destroyed the rational foundations of natural law became canonical in the text-book histories of jurisprudence and political thought. Even when Hume was praised for the socio-

logical realism of his account of the origin of justice and government, allegedly doing away with the 'state of nature' and the
social contract, this was usually misunderstood, and Hume's
real contribution to social science was overlooked: an empirical,
secular and 'one-dimensional' idea of society as the exclusive
locus of justice and all moral obligation and social ties and
rules. Hume had no use for the idea of a God-governed 'society'
of men *qua* rational agents as such; his philosophy could not
accommodate it.

Hume's 'philosophical' approach to politics had little more
success in the other parts of his programme. Contemporaries in
England did not appreciate his ability, both as a cosmopolitan
Scotsman and a 'Newtonian' scientist, to take a detached view
of the British government and political scene or its history, and
to compare them, not altogether favourably, with the 'civilized'
absolute monarchies of Europe. And the *History* became notori-
ously the 'Tory' apologia for the Stuarts: its broader theme, the
development of 'regular' government in Europe, was invisible
through the key-hole of English party politics.

A broader-based, more thorough and intensive study of
Hume's 'politics' is a comparatively recent development.

Duncan Forbes
Clare College, University of Cambridge

Further Reading
Forbes, D. (1975), *Hume's Philosophical Politics*, Cambridge.
Miller, D. (1981), *Philosophy and Ideology in Hume's Political
Thought*, Oxford.
Stewart, J. B. (1963), *The Moral and Political Thought of David
Hume*, New York.

Illich, Ivan (1926–)

Ivan Illich is the 'leading contemporary exponent of the
romantic anarchist tradition' (Thomas, 1983). He was born in
Vienna in 1926 and grew up in Europe, obtaining degrees in
natural sciences, history, philosophy and theology. In 1950 he
went to New York where he worked for five years as a parish

priest in an Irish and Puerto Rican neighbourhood. Between 1956 and 1960 he was vice-rector of the Catholic University of Puerto Rico. In 1962 he founded the Centre for Intercultural Documentation in Cuernavaca, Mexico, where he is now based, dividing his time between his writing and teaching medieval history in West German universities. His chief works are *Celebration of Awareness* (1971); *Deschooling Society* (1971); *Tools for Conviviality* (1973); *Energy and Equity* (1974); *Medical Nemesis* (1976); *Toward a History of Need* (1978); *Shadow Work* (1981); and *Gender* (1983).

His work can be understood as a sustained historical polemic against the logic of modern economic development, especially in the Third World. Instead of seeing economic growth as the progressive mastery of need and scarcity, he argues that it is a process in which previously self-subsistent peasant peoples are dispossessed of their own 'vernacular' skills and made to depend on doctors for their health, teachers for their schooling, automobiles for their transport, television for their entertainment, and wage labour for their subsistence. Development is enslavement to need, not liberation from scarcity. His latest work, *Gender*, extends this analysis to women, arguing that economic development has freed them from the segregated domain of 'gender' only to enslave them to the violence and inequality of modern 'sex'.

Illich underestimates the extent to which the new needs created by the modern division of labour actually do correspond to what people desire, but he has made an extremely effective critique of the assumption that economic progress means greater freedom. His writing has had a major influence on post-1968 critiques of Western consumer affluence and, more importantly, on Third World development strategies, which seek to protect the 'vernacular' skills and self-subsisting capacities of indigenous populations from the false needs engendered by capitalist economic development.

Michael Ignatieff
King's College, Cambridge

Reference

Thomas, K. (1983), 'Review of *Gender* by Ivan Illich', *New York Review of Books*, 12 May.

Jakobson, Roman Osipovič (1896–1982)

Roman Jakobson was born in Moscow in 1896, the son of a chemical engineer and prominent industrialist. He was educated at the renowned Lazarev Institute of Oriental Languages from which he graduated *cum laude* in 1914, and at Moscow University. His academic training predisposed him to treat language as a *functional system* rather than advocating the historical-comparative approach characteristic of the traditional neogrammarian doctrine. Moreover, following the Russian scholarly tradition, he was prepared to link the study of language with that of literature and folklore.

No less important than his formal training was the artistic milieu in which the young Jakobson grew up. As early as 1913–16 he associated with the most avant-garde painters and poets, including K. Malevich and V. Majakowskij. With other students he formed the Moscow Linguistic Circle, which had an impact on the famous Russian Formalist School – and paid especial attention to the analysis of poetry as the most marked, semioticized form of discourse.

Jakobson lived and taught in Czechoslovakia from 1920 to 1939, a period which, as Morris Halle (1979) has said, 'saw the full development of his scientific genius'. In 1939, fleeing the Nazi occupation, he went to Scandinavia, and then in 1941 to the United States. He held chairs in Slavic and General Linguistics at Columbia and Harvard Universities and at MIT.

The main areas that had always captivated Jakobson's mind were: (1) the general theory of language (including poetics); (2) neurolinguistics, and (3) Slavic studies. Each of these areas he either totally reshaped or enriched with fundamental contributions.

(1) Jakobson's principal contribution to the science of language – and a turning point in the development of both modern linguistics and the science of man – is his theory of phonology. He developed his new approach in close collabor-

ation with N.S. Trubetzkoy, and forced a revision of the concept of the phoneme, which until then was assumed to be the smallest component of language. He showed that the phoneme could be further resolved into a set of specific properties – *distinctive features*. These properties, defined in articulatory/motor/acoustic terms, are *relative* in character and form *binary oppositions* which make up the phonemic *system* of language. A phoneme as a global unit does not stand in any clear relation to another phoneme, but sets of distinctive features (such as strident vs. non-strident, voiced vs. voiceless, and so on) are the necessary and sufficient components for the specification of the phonemes of a given language. This reduction provides 'the minimum number of the simplest operations that would suffice to encode and decode the whole message' ('Phonology and phonetics', with M. Halle, *Selected Writings*, vol. I). His phonological theory contains another important principle, the principle of *markedness*. The marked member of an opposition is the member that carries more information than its partner. In this way he established the *hierarchical* nature of phonemic oppositions and of phonemic system as a whole. Another concept elaborated in this framework concerns the relation of the *invariant* to *variation*, an idea Jakobson adapted from topology in mathematics. Thus the distinctive features retain their invariant properties amidst the continuous stream of contextual variations.

These principles, which were first developed and refined in the field of phonology, were subsequently applied by Jakobson to all other levels of language, in particular to morphology, resulting in studies of the Russian case system, of the structure of the Russian verb, and of the nominal and pronominal inflections (*Russian and Slavic Grammar: Studies 1931–1981*).

Jakobson revised the doctrine of F. de Saussure and reassessed the Saussurean opposition between synchrony, that is language as a static system, and diachrony – its dynamic, developmental aspect. Jakobson regarded this opposition as false because it excluded the role of the time factor in the present moment of the language state. While Saussure considered the linguistic sign to reflect an arbitrary connection between sound and meaning, Jakobson insisted upon the close and intricate ties between the two parts of the sign. These and other aspects of Jakobsonian theory were guided by semiotic considerations. He worked also to develop semiotics as a discipline of its own, and he contributed pivotal studies to the classification and typology of semiotic systems, with special attention to language ('Language in relation to other communication systems', *Selected Writings*, vol.II). His main inspiration in semiotics came from the works of Charles Sanders Peirce, whom Jakobson considered the greatest American philosopher.

Jakobson worked on poetics all his life and found new insights into its development in the mathematical theory of information. Within this framework he built a model of language in operation in which he showed the integration of poetry and the poetic function into the speech event, and the specific role of language in poetry. He also pointed out the particular role that grammatical categories play in poetry.

(2) Jakobson's most significant contribution to neurolinguistics is reflected in the title of his study 'Two aspects of language and two types of aphasic disturbances' (*Selected Writings*, vol. II). Basing himself on the pioneering work of the Polish linguist Mikołaj Kruszewski, Jakobson showed that our entire linguistic activity gravitates around the axis of selection and the axis of combination. The two axes in question are connected respectively with the metaphoric and metonymic poles, since a process of selection underlies the metaphoric operation, while combinatorial procedures are related to the metonymic operation. The structure and function of the brain are thus reflected in the two types of discourse, poetry and prose, the metaphoric tendency being typical of the former and the metonymic of the latter.

(3) In his research in Slavic studies, Jakobson followed the same integrated approach he displayed in every area of his scientific endeavour. He held that Slavic unity is defined most importantly by the common language patrimony. This patrimony in turn determines the stock of poetic (literary) devices common to all Slavic peoples. These factors permit the reconstruction and thus the explanation of changes in national

literary borrowings, convergences and coincidences. His main efforts were focused on reconstructing the archaic forms of Slavic oral and written tradition.

Jakobson's methodology, rooted in linguistics, influenced such disciplines as social anthropology, psychology, psychiatry and biology. Internationally recognized, he received honorary degrees from twenty-six universities. Several *Festschriften* all over the world were devoted to him.

Krystyna Pomorska
Massachusetts Institute of Technology

Reference
Halle, M. (1979), 'Roman Jakobson', in D. L. Sills (ed.), *International Encyclopedia of the Social Sciences, Biographical Supplement*, 18, New York.

Further Reading
I. Works of Roman Jakobson
(1962), *Selected Writings*, 7 vols; vol I: *Phonological Studies* (1962); (2nd, expanded edn, 1971); vol. II: *Word and Language* (1972); vol. III: *Poetry of Grammar and Grammar of Poetry* (1981); vol. IV: *Slavic Epic Studies* (1966); vol. V: *On Verse, Its Masters and Explorers* (1979); vol. VI: *Early Slavic Paths and Crossroads* (1985); vol. VII: *Contributions to Comparative Mythology. Recent Studies in Linguistics and Philology. Retrospections. Bibliography* (forthcoming); The Hague-Paris-Berlin-New York.
(ed.) (1975), *N. S. Trubetzkoy's Letters and Notes*, The Hague.
(1978), *Six Lectures on Sound and Meaning*, Cambridge, Mass.
(1979) [With L. R. Waugh], *The Sound Shape of Language*, Bloomington.
(1980), *Brain and Language: Cerebral Hemispheres and Linguistic Structure in Mutual Light*, Columbus, Ohio.
(1980), *The Framework of Language*, Ann Arbor.
(1982) [With K. Pomorska], *Dialogues*, Cambridge, Mass.
(1983), *Russian and Slavic Grammar: Studies 1931–1981*, Berlin.

II Works on Roman Jakobson

Armstrong, D. and van Schooneveld, C. H. (1977), *Roman Jakobson: Echoes of His Scholarship*, Lisse, Holland.
Holenstein, E. (1976), *Roman Jakobson's Approach to Language*, Bloomington.
Holenstein, E. (1983), *A Tribute to Roman Jakobson*, Berlin.
Waugh, L. R. (1976), *Roman Jakobson's Science of Language*, Lisse, Holland.

See also: *Peirce; Saussure.*

James, William (1842–1910)

William James, eminent psychologist and philosopher, was born in New York City. He, his novelist brother, Henry, and his sister were the main recipients of an unusually unsystematic education supervised by their father which consisted largely of European travels and private tutors. After an interval in which he studied painting, James enrolled in the Lawrence Scientific School at Harvard in 1861. In 1864 he entered Harvard Medical School and received the MD in 1869. His life was marked by periods of acute depression and psychosomatic illnesses which occasioned solitary trips to Europe for rest and treatment. These periods, however, produced two benefits. they gave James firsthand experience of abnormal psychological states concerning which he was later to be a pioneer investigator; and they provided opportunities for extensive reading of science and literature in French, German and English. His marriage in 1878 appears to have been an important factor in improving his health and focusing his concentration on teaching and writing. His academic life was centred at Harvard where he became an instructor in psychology in 1875 and taught anatomy and physiology. Subsequently he offered courses in philosophy until his retirement in 1907.

James's work in psychology and philosophy was interfused and is not completely separable. His greatest effort and achievement was *The Principles of Psychology* (1890) which, some ten years in writing, made him world-famous and is now regarded a classic in both fields of study. James stated his intention to establish psychology as a natural science. By this he meant that metaphysical questions would be avoided and, wherever possible, explanations in psychology should be based on experimental physiology and biology rather than on introspective procedures which had dominated philosophic psychology since Locke and Hume. In contrast to a widely prevailing conception of mind as composed of ideas, like atoms, ordered and compounded by association, James proposed that mentality is a 'stream of consciousness' including in it feelings and interests. For James, the mental is to be construed in evolutionary and teleological forms: mental activity is evidenced where there are selections of means to achieve future ends. Darwinian theory had an important influence on James's psychological and philosophical views. Ideas and theories are interpreted as instruments enabling us to adapt successfully to and partly transform reality according to our interests and purposes of action.

In an address of 1898, 'Philosophical Conceptions and Practical Results', James inaugurated the theory of pragmatism which soon became the major movement in American philosophy. He also drew attention to the neglected work of Charles S. Peirce whom he credited with having originated pragmatism. The main thesis is that the value and significance of concepts, their meaning and truth, is determined not by their origins but by their future practical consequences. An application of this view is found in 'The Will to Believe' (1896) and in James's Gifford Lectures (1901–2); 'The Varieties of Religious Experience'; it is argued explicitly in *Pragmatism* (1907) and *The Meaning of Truth* (1909). In his later writings and lectures, James refined and defended his metaphysical doctrines of the pluralistic character of reality, indeterminism, and 'radical empiricism' according to which the world is conceived as a growing continuous structure of experience.

H. S. Thayer
The City College of The City
University of New York

Further Reading
James, W. (1975–), *The Works of William James*, ed. F.
    Burkhardt and F. Bowers, Cambridge, Mass.
Perry, R. B. (1935), *The Thought and Character of William James*,
    2 vols, Boston.

Jung, Carl Gustav (1875–1961)

Carl Gustav Jung was a Swiss psychiatrist whose theories form
the basis of Analytical or Jungian psychology. Concepts that
Jung introduced to psychology include: the stages of life with
age-related tasks, psychological types with differing attitudes
(extraversion-introversion) and functions, the collective unconscious, archetypes, individuation or transformation as an aim of
analysis, feminine and masculine principles, and synchronicity
(meaningful coincidence).

Jung's depth psychology considers spirituality important. It
is considered especially suitable for people in the second half of
life, who may be well adapted but plagued by a sense of the
meaninglessness of life. His psychology is also of particular
value in working with psychosis, since his insights into symbolic
material help make delusions and hallucinations, as well as
dreams intelligible

Jung was a prolific writer; his *Collected Works* (1953–79)
contains eighteen volumes. His theories have also had a major
impact on literature, history and anthropology.

Training centres in Jungian analysis exist in Europe and the
United States. Certified analysts are members of local or
regional Societies of Jungian Analysts and the International
Association for Analytical Psychology.

Jung's life and his theories are intertwined, as he emphasized
in his autobiography, *Memories, Dreams, Reflections*, (1961): 'My
life is a story of self-realization of the unconscious. Everything
in the unconscious seeks outward manifestation, and the personality too desires to evolve out of its unconscious conditions and
to experience itself as a whole.'

Jung was born in 1875 in Kesswil, Switzerland. A sensitive
child who played alone in his early years, he mulled over questions raised by his dreams and by observations of himself and

others. As a student, he was powerfully drawn to science, especially zoology, paleontology, and geology. His other fascinations were comparative religion and the humanities, especially Graeco-Roman, Egyptian and prehistoric archaeology. These interests represented his inner dichotomy: 'What appealed to me in science were the concrete facts and their historical background, and in comparative religion the spiritual problems, into which philosophy also entered. In science I missed the factor of meaning; and in religion, that of empiricism.' Later in his psychology he would attempt to bridge the distance between these two poles.

Jung's medical studies were at the Universities of Basel (1895–1900) and Zurich (MD, 1902). At that time psychiatry was held in contempt, mental disease was considered hopeless, and both psychiatrists and patients were isolated in asylums. Jung had no interest in psychiatry, until he read the introduction to Krafft-Ebing's textbook. It had a galvanizing effect: 'My excitement was intense, for it had become clear to me, in a flash of illumination, that for me the only possible goal was psychiatry. Here alone the two currents of my interest could flow together and in a united stream dig their own bed. Here was the empirical field common to biological and spiritual facts, which I had everywhere sought and nowhere found. Here at last was the place where the collision of nature and spirit became a reality.' Jung became an assistant at the Burghölzli Mental Hospital in Zurich in 1902, which alienated him from his medical colleagues.

At Burghölzli, Jung concerned himself with the question: 'What actually takes place inside the mentally ill?' He developed the word association test, which provided insight into emotion-laden complexes, discovered that a patient's secret story is a key in treatment, and found that delusions are not 'senseless'. He became a lecturer in psychiatry at the University of Zurich, senior physician at the Psychiatric Clinic, and acquired a large private practice.

In 1903, Jung discovered the convergence of Freud's *The Interpretation of Dreams* with his own ideas. Jung had frequently encountered repressions in his experiments in word association.

In 1907, he published *Über die Psychologie der Dementia Praecox* (*The Psychology of Dementia Praecox*, 1953) which led to a meeting with Freud. Jung considered Freud the first man of real importance he had encountered; Freud believed he had found in Jung his spiritual son and successor.

An idealized father-son relationship betwen Freud and Jung ended over theoretical differences. Jung could not agree with Freud that all neuroses are caused by sexual repression or sexual traumata. Freud considered Jung's interest in religion, philosophy and parapsychology as 'occultism'. The final personal and theoretical divergence concerned mother-son incest; Jung considered incest symbolically, in opposition to Freud's literal, sexual interpretation.

After the break with Freud in 1914, Jung was professionally alone. Then followed a four-year period of uncertainty that Jung called his 'confrontation with the unconscious'. In his private practice, he resolved not to bring any theoretical premises to bear upon his patient's dreams, instead asking them, 'What occurs to you in connection with that?' This method, which arose from theoretical disorientation, became the basis of the 'amplification' approach to dreams in analytical psychology.

This period was characterized by intense inner confusion and discovery for Jung. As he groped to understand himself, he became emotionally engaged in building a small villa out of stones and sticks at the lakeshore. Going about this project with the intensity of a participant in a rite released a stream of memories, fantasies and emotion. (This experience would later influence the development of sandplay therapy.)

Jung had vivid and frightening dreams, fantasies and visions, and feared that he was menaced by a psychosis. Despite his fear of losing command of himself, and motivated in part by 'the conviction that I could not expect of my patients something I did not dare to do myself', Jung committed himself to the 'dangerous enterprise' of plummeting down to the 'underground'. He kept a record of his fantasies and dreams, and painted and conversed with the figures populating his inner world. (This technique would lead to 'active imagination' as a therapy tool.) Jung's effort to understand and assimilate the meaning of his inner reality proved to be a germinal period for ideas that he would develop and write about for the rest of his life.

In 1918, the phase of Jung's intense journey inward ended, and a period of writing followed. The first major work, *Psychologische Typen*, was published in 1921 (*Psychological Types, Collected Works* vol.6). In it, he introduced his concepts of introversion and extraversion as fundamental differences in attitude, and the four functions by which experience is assessed and perceived: thinking, feeling, intuition and sensation. Through this work, he came to understand why he, Freud and Adler could have such divergent theories about human nature.

He continued to write prolifically until his death in Zurich in 1961. Everything he wrote about began as an inquiry into a subject that was personally relevant. He sought empirical data, read widely and travelled considerably. Jung remains of continuing interest to students of religion, literary criticism and humanities. There has been some controversy about Jung's supposed racial theories of the collective unconscious and his alleged sympathies with ideologies of racial superiority.

Jean Shinoda Bolen
Training Analyst, C. G. Jung Institute, San Francisco

References
Jung, C. G. (1961), *Memories, Dreams, Reflections*, recorded and edited by A. Jaffe, New York.
Jung, C. G. (1953–79), *Collected Works of C. G. Jung*, 20 vols, eds, H. Read, M. Fordham and I. Adler, Princeton, N.J.

Further Reading
Jacobi, J. (1969), *The Psychology of C. G. Jung*, London.
Storr, A. (1973), *C. G. Jung*, London.

Keynes, John Maynard (1883–1946)

The son of John Neville Keynes, a Cambridge economist, philosopher and administrator, and Florence Ada (Brown),

Cambridge's first woman town councillor and later its mayor, Maynard Keynes made contributions that extended well beyond academic economics. After an education at Eton and King's College, Cambridge (BA in Mathematics 1905), his first career was that of a Civil Servant in the India Office (1906–8). Although he soon returned to Cambridge to lecture in economics (1908–20) and be a Fellow of King's (1909–46), he never lost his connection with the world of affairs. He served as a member of the Royal Commission on Indian Finance and Currency (1913–14), was a wartime Treasury official eventually in charge of Britain's external financial relations (1915–19), a member of the Macmillan Committee on Finance and Industry (1929–31), a member of the Economic Advisory Council (1930–9), an adviser to the Chancellor of the Exchequer (1940–6) and a director of the Bank of England (1941–6). After 1919, he also had an active career in the world of finance as a company director, insurance company chairman and bursar of King's College, Cambridge. Moreover, under the influence of his Bloomsbury friends, Vanessa Bell and Duncan Grant, as well as Lydia Lopokova of the Diaghilev Ballet whom he married in 1925, he played an active and important role in the cultural life of his time as a patron of the arts, founder of the Arts Theatre, Cambridge (which he gave to the City and University in 1938), trustee of the National Gallery, chairman of the Council for the Encouragement of Music and the Arts, and initiator and first chairman of the Arts Council of Great Britain.

Keynes's reputation as an academic economist arises from work that he started after his fortieth year and published after he was 47. Prior to that, he was much better known as a publicist and commentator on economic affairs, a career he began in 1919 after his resignation as the senior Treasury official at the Paris Peace Conference with his bestselling and influential indictment of the negotiation and terms of the Peace Treaty in *The Economic Consequences of the Peace* (1919). He continued in this popular vein with *A Revision of the Treaty* (1922), *A Tract on Monetary Reform* (1923), *The Economic Consequences of Mr Churchill* (1925), *The End of Laissez-Faire* (1926) and prolific journalism, notably for the liberal *Nation and Athenaeum* (1923–31) and the more socialist *New Statesman and Nation*, for both of which he was chairman of the board. This does not mean that he was unknown as an academic: he was editor of the Royal Economic Society's *The Economic Journal* (1911–45) and the author of *A Treatise on Probability* (1921), a philosophical examination of the principles of reasoning and rational action in conditions of incomplete and uncertain knowledge, the earliest ideas of which date from 1904 when Keynes was strongly influenced by G. E. Moore. Nevertheless, it would be fair to echo Sir Austin Robinson's comment (1947): 'If Maynard Keynes had died in 1925 it would have been difficult for those who knew intimately the power and originality of his mind to have convinced those who had not known him of the full measure of Keynes' ability.'

The bases for Keynes's academic reputation as an economist were his *Treatise on Money* (1930) and *The General Theory of Employment, Interest and Money* (1936). Both were stages in the development in theoretical terms of the principles which should underlie attempts by governments to achieve economic stability. In the *Treatise*, as in the more popular *Tract*, the main concern was with monetary and price stability and the role that monetary policy alone could play in achieving them. As was common in contemporary monetary economics, Keynes dichotomized the economy into its monetary and real sectors and, on the assumption that money was neutral in the long run, looked for the principles of monetary practice which would ensure price stability, in the *Treatise* case a monetary policy which made the long-term market rate of interest equivalent to the 'natural rate' at which savings equalled investment. This initial approach to the problem was found to be inadequate by Keynes's critics, who included R. G. Hawtrey, F. A. Hayek and D. H. Robertson, as well as a group of younger economists in Cambridge (R. F. Kahn, James Meade, Joan and Austin Robinson, and Piero Sraffa). When convinced of the inadequacies of the *Treatise*, Keynes began reformulating his ideas. The major breakthrough came in 1933 when, contrary to traditional theory, Keynes hit on the crucial role of changes in output and employment in equilibration savings and investment, thus providing the basis for a more general theory than his own or his predecessors' previous work. The new theory seemed to offer the possibility of equilibrium at less than full employment, something missing in previous work. From his 1933 breakthrough, which hinged on the consumption-income relationship implicit in the multiplier, after considerable further work, everything fell into place.

During the last ten years of his life, although his activities were inhibited by a severe heart condition after 1937, Keynes devoted less time to defending and somewhat refining his theoretical views than to seeing them implemented. Even before the outbreak of war in 1939, he had started to influence Treasury thinking in Britain, while his students and his writings were becoming influential in such places as Washington and Ottawa. However, the problems of war finance and post-war planning appear to have been crucial in the spread of his ideas into day-to-day policy making, for as he demonstrated in *How to Pay for the War* (1940) the new ideas when married to another contemporary development – national income and expenditure accounting – provided a powerful new way of thinking about the economy and its management. The resulting 'new economics' put less emphasis than Keynes would have done on the roles of monetary policy and the control of public investment in the achievement of full employment, yet, along with a political determination to avoid the wastes of the inter-war years, it led to widespread official commitments to post-war policies of high or full employment. By then, however, Keynes was less involved in such matters: the last years of his life saw him devoting much more of his efforts to shaping other aspects of the post-war world, most notably the international monetary order of the International Monetary Fund and the World Bank, and to securing Britain's post-war international economic position. Gaining these, or at least a semblance of them, finally exhausted him.

Donald Moggridge
University of Toronto

Reference
Robinson, E. A. G. (1947), 'John Maynard Keynes,
 1883–1946', *Economic Journal*, 57.

Further Reading
Harrod, R. F. (1951), *The Life of John Maynard Keynes*, London.
Keynes, J. M. (1971–), *The Collected Writings of John Maynard
 Keynes*, ed. E. Johnson and D. Moggridge, 30 vols, London
 and New York. (Those approaching Keynes's ideas for the
 first time are advised to look at volume 9, *Essays in
 Persuasion*.)
Moggridge, D. E. (1980), *Keynes*, 2nd edn, London.

Klein, Melanie (1882–1960)

Born to an intellectual Jewish Viennese family, Melanie Klein
had intended to study medicine until an early engagement and
marriage intervened. Then, in her thirties, when she was a
housewife and mother of three, she discovered Freud's writing.
Entering analysis with Ferenczi, she began an analytic career.
Ferenczi encouraged her interest in analysing children, virtually
an unknown procedure. In 1921, she accepted Abraham's invi-
tation to continue her work in Berlin, and began publishing her
observations on child development. After Abraham's death in
1925, she took up permanent residence in London, where she
became doyenne of a distinct psychoanalytic school and the
centre of a still active, and sometimes passionate, theoretical
controversy.

Klein began her psychoanalytic career by developing a technical innovation – play therapy – which permitted the analysis
of very young children. Klein came to believe that two broad
formations successively organize the child's inner world: 'the
paranoid-schizoid position' and the 'the depressive position'.
While she ascribes them initially to the first and second half-
year of life (an inference which has occasioned considerable
criticism), Klein views these 'positions' as constellations of
anxieties, defences, and object relations which are reactivated
continually throughout development.

The paranoid-schizoid position is established before the achievement of object constancy. During this period, the real external mother contributes a number of quite separate figures to the child's inner world, via introjection of aspects of her in different situations. Thus there come to be 'good objects', introjected during gratifying experiences with the real mother, and eventually these images develop temporal continuity and merge. Moments of deprivation and pain are experienced by the infant as wilful persecution by his care-givers, so introjection during these states establishes sadistic, 'bad objects' in the inner world. The child's anxieties in this stage are that the persecutory objects will succeed in annihilating either the self or the good objects.

In normal development, this fantasy structure is gradually modified so that the various separate internal images of the real mother coalesce into a single object, with aspects both gratifying and frustrating, good and bad. But when the 'bad mother' begins to coalesce with the beloved mother in the child's internal psychic reality, the child comes to feel that his own (fantasized) attacks against the persecutor also damage the adored, essential good object. Guilt and mourning now develop. A new inner constellation, 'the depressive position', gradually emerges.

In addition to defensive regression ('splitting' of the internal object), the pain of the depressive position can also be temporarily assuaged through denial of the effects of one's own aggression (the 'manic defences'). But resolution of the depressive position depends on a different response: acceptance of responsibility, with attempts to repair the damaged objects. The cement for internal integration is the child's growing confidence in the reparative powers of his love.

While Klein's play therapy technique became universally accepted, her conclusions generated intense controversy and led to a schism within the psychoanalytic community. Most of the controversy concerns not the descriptive theory summarized above, but subsidiary issues – such as the timing of psychic phases in development, and the relative influence of constitutional versus environmental factors. Currently, as psychoanalysis struggles to conceptualize more primitive mental states, Klein's formulations are increasingly being integrated into the main body of analytic thought.

Alan S. Pollack
McLean Hospital, Belmont, Massachusetts
Harvard University

Further Reading
Klein, M. (1975), *Love, Guilt, and Reparation and Other Works 1921–1945*, New York.
Segal, H. (1964), *Introduction to the Work of Melanie Klein*, New York.

Kropotkin, Peter (1842–1921)

After Bakunin's death in 1876, Kropotkin became the leading anarchist theorist in Europe. Born in Moscow into an ancient princely family, and educated at the élite Corps of Pages in St Petersburg, he served from 1862 to 1867 as an army officer in Siberia, where his geographical and geological explorations and research won him immediate acclaim. In 1871, his social conscience having been awakened, he abandoned a scientific career of great promise to devote himself to revolutionary activity. Kropotkin was imprisoned in 1874 and escaped two years later to the West, where he became greatly respected in radical circles. He spent three years in prison in France on spurious charges of sedition, and on his release in 1886 settled in England, where he remained until the Revolution of 1917 allowed him to return to Russia.

Kropotkin attempted (as Bakunin had never done) to construct a coherent 'scientific' theory of society. He argued that mutual aid, not Darwinian competition, was the fundamental law of evolution in nature and society, and that the centralized state with its large-scale production, specialization of function and coercive powers, was a temporary aberration which social revolution would sweep away. In several books (notably *The Conquest of Bread* (1892), *Fields, Factories and Workshops* (1899), and *Mutual Aid* (1902)), and numerous articles,

Kropotkin outlined his ideal: a society of small communities based on voluntary co-operation, in which integration of industry and agriculture, replacing the division of labour, would give full scope to the individual's mental and manual capacities.

Kropotkin's faith in man's inherent virtue, founded on an idealization of primitive communities, seems naively optimistic in our century; but his belief in the dehumanizing effects of centralized mass production now seems prescient, and he anticipated some modern solutions to these problems in arguing for 'integral' education and small-scale economic units: hence a recent revival of interest in his works, after half a century of neglect.

But Kropotkin deserves to be remembered most as a moralist: for his inflexible opposition to the principle that the end justifies the means, his belief (exemplified by his life) that the revolutionary's personal conduct should reflect his humanist ideals, and his prophetic warnings of the dangers of despotism inherent in revolutions made for, but not by, the majority.

Aileen Kelly
King's College, Cambridge

Further Reading
Miller, M. (1976), *Kropotkin*, Chicago.
Miller, M. (ed.) (1970), *P. A. Kropotkin, Selected Writings on Anarchism and Revolution*, Cambridge, Mass.
Woodcock, G. and Avakumović, I. (1950), *The Anarchist Prince*, London.

Kuhn, Thomas Samuel (1922–)

Thomas Kuhn, born in Cincinnati, Ohio in 1922, was trained as a theoretical physicist, but it was his experience teaching a course in the theory and practice of science for non-scientists that first undermined his preconceptions about science and the reasons for its special success. Under the influence of J. B. Conant at Harvard (where Kuhn took his degree), Kuhn began to explore the divergence between the idealized accounts of science produced by philosophers and the reality unearthed by research into its historical development. His subsequent work can be seen as a consistent attempt to bring the former into line with the latter. It is therefore clear why, with these preoccupations, Kuhn is one of the few historians of science to produce a general model of science.

His most influential book is *The Structure of Scientific Revolutions* (1970), first published in 1962, in which science is portrayed as an activity bound by precedent and tradition. Scientific contributions are modelled on past achievements. These exemplary achievements Kuhn calls 'paradigms'. Paradigms are not simply theories but pieces of work which embody all the elements of scientific practice within some specialized area of inquiry. They exhibit the important parameters to be measured, define required standards of accuracy, show how observations are to be interpreted, and the kind of experimental methods to be used. An example is John Dalton's *New System of Chemical Philosophy*, published in 1808, which showed how to understand chemical reactions in terms of atom to atom linkages, and how to make inferences about atoms by measuring the relative weights of combining substances. Paradigms leave many problems unsolved, and hence allow the growth of research traditions in which their concepts are refined to account for new results and applications. Kuhn calls this process of articulation and exploitation 'normal science', because it is what most scientists do most of the time. Normal science is a creative form of puzzle solving, whose difficulties are seen as tests of the ingenuity of the scientist rather than tests of the truth of the paradigm. Kuhn then argues that it is this very commitment of scientists to their paradigm that eventually brings about its overthrow. As it is pressed into service in ever more detail, the expectation of success sensitizes scientists to failures. If experimental results continue to resist explanation in terms of the accepted paradigm, a crisis of confidence may ensue. A new approach based on a new paradigmatic achievement may gain favour if it appears to resolve the difficulty and opens up new lines of puzzle-solving activity. This constitutes a revolution, but the rejected paradigm will not have been decisively proven false, because no one knows what greater persistence with it might have revealed. The cycle of paradigm, normal science and revolution then repeats itself.

Kuhn's picture has two important consequences:

(1) Scientific knowledge cannot be simply 'read off' from nature: it is always mediated by historically specific and culturally shared paradigms. This challenges our intuitions about scientific truth and progress.

(2) Neither continuity nor change in science can be understood by means of abstract rules. The coherence of normal science derives from the family resemblances between work modelled on a paradigm, and the change of paradigm requires an intuitive judgement that cannot be fully justified by abstract and independent principles. Not surprisingly Kuhn has been charged with 'irrationalism', though he is really only challenging certain philosophical preconceptions about rationality. His position has affinities with Wittgenstein's, because we can say that each paradigm gives rise to a particular 'language-game'. In conjunction with Kuhn's stress on tradition, commitment and precedent, this explains why his work has proved an important stimulus and resource for studies in the sociology of science.

In 1961, Kuhn took up a professorship in the history of science at the University of California, Berkeley, and in 1964 he moved to Princeton University.

David Bloor
University of Edinburgh

Reference
Kuhn, T. S. (1977), *The Structure of Scientific Revolutions*, 2nd edn, Chicago.

Further Reading
Barnes, B. (1982), *T. S. Kuhn and Social Science*, London.
Fleck, L. (1979), *Genesis and Development of a Scientific Fact*, Chicago. (First published in German in 1935.) (A pioneering book in the sociology of knowledge which

anticipated many of the themes in Kuhn's work and to which Kuhn was himself indebted.)

Kuhn, T. S. (1957), *The Copernican Revolution*, Cambridge, Mass.

Kuhn, T. S. (1977), *The Essential Tension: Selected Studies in Scientific Tradition and Change*, Chicago.

Kuhn, T. S. (1978), *Black Body Theory and the Quantum Discontinuity, 1894–1912*, Oxford.

Lacan, Jacques (1901–83)

Jacques Lacan has been called the 'French Freud'. He was probably the most controversial European psychoanalyst of the post-Second World War era. Lacan was a scathing critic of the 'American' developments in psychoanalysis which moved away from Freud's unconscious to what was called 'ego psychology'. In America, psychoanalytic therapy focused on forming an alliance with the healthy ego, interpreting pathological defences, and promoting the growth of conflict-free adaptation. Lacan entirely rejected this approach. There was, in his view, no conflict-free sphere: the 'ego' was hostile to the unconscious and the essential analytic process. Analysis was an inquiry, not a cure. Lacan, in his characteristic play-on-words style, described American empirical research intended to make psychoanalyis an experimental science as 'ex-peri-mental' (that is, ex-mental and peri-mental). To Lacan, such research with animals left out the mental, because the mental has to do with language, meaning and signification.

Lacan regarded Freud's early and introspective works such as *the Interpretation of Dreams* (1913) as the essence of psychoanalysis. Lacan theorized that the unconscious is structured as a natural language; psychoanalysis, as a theory and as a therapy, was the discovery of this other language by recapturing associative chains of signification. An example of Lacan's theoretical emphasis on linguistics is his reintepretation of the Oedipal complex. In greatly oversimplified terms, he believed it encompassed the child's movement from the order of images to the order of polysemic symbols. Lacan describes the infant's mental life as beginning in a mirror phase, like Narcissus by the stream seeing reflected images. When language and symbols are acquired, these images are mediated, their signification changes, and the infant becomes a divided subject. The unconscious is 'The Other' and the other language. The hydraulic and mechanistic theories of Freud are replaced in Lacan by a linguistic theory, for example, repression as metaphor formation.

Lacan's writing is arcane, convoluted, technical, poetic and difficult. Existentialist, neo-Hegelian and linguistic theories all influenced Lacan as much as did Freud. Lacan's later work became even more difficult as he emphasized the centrality of topology and mathematics to his theories.

Lacan became a central figure in French intellectual and radical thought, and was of particular interest to literary and social criticism in the West. Whatever Lacan's place may be in the history of modern thought, he was rejected by organized psychoanalysts because of his clinical methods. Most notable was his practice of dismissing patients after 5- or 10-minute sessions because, he said, they had nothing interesting to say or they were getting into a routine which silenced the unconscious. Lacan, in turn, attacked the psychoanalytic establishment which sought to 'authorize' those who would be analysts. Lacan claimed that analysis was a calling and the analyst must authorize himself.

Alan A. Stone
Harvard University

Further Reading

Bär, E. S. (1974), 'Understanding Lacan', in *Psychoanalysis of Contemporary Science*, vol. 3, New York.

Lacan, J. (1966), *Ecrits*, Paris. (English translation, *Ecrits*, London, 1977.)

Schneiderman, S. (1983), *Jacques Lacan: The Death of an Intellectual Hero*, Cambridge, Mass.

Laing, Ronald David (1927–)

The philosopher Kant wrote, 'The only general characteristic of Insanity is the loss of a sense of ideas that are common to all and its replacement with a sense for ideas peculiar to ourselves.' The question remains, however, how does one decide which *peculiar ideas* are delusions? R. D. Laing, born in Glasgow in 1927, began his career as a psychiatrist by attempting to make the *peculiar ideas* of schizophrenic patients (which he assumed were delusions) comprehensible. But in his subsequent work as a psychiatrist-philosopher he concluded that normality, 'the ideas that are common to all', is madness and, therefore, a psychiatry founded on such ideas was unable to declare any beliefs delusions.

Laing, his critics would say, went further than this epistemological relativism; he romanticized insanity and particularly schizophrenia. Madness became a breakthrough, a way of being in the world that rejects the 'pseudo-social' reality, the most awesome psychedelic trip.

Laing's early writings are both psychoanalytic and existential in character, as he attempted to portray the subjective experience of the schizophrenic. There are brilliant descriptions of the divided self unable to be a 'whole person with the other'. Perhaps most powerful are his descriptions of the family interactions out of which comes 'schizophrenic disorder'. It is the family that seems mad in Laing's description, and the patient's delusions and 'bizarre communication' are explained as a symbolic and visionary commentary on that family's madness (Laing and Esterson, 1964). His subsequent writings are less detailed, more prophetic in tone. The schizophrenic experience becomes a divination of the madness of society, not to be cured by drugs or to be interfered with by psychiatrists but perhaps to be learned from. As one of Laing's critics noted, 'Schizophrenia became a State of Grace.' Laing's writings were seized upon by the radical critics of psychiatry and by other radicals seeking liberation during the late 1960s and the 1970s. Laing's influence in psychiatry was short-lived. He turned to mysticism and poetry as his own liberation. In *The Politics of Experience* (1967) he wrote, 'True sanity entails in one way or another the dissolution of the normal ego, that false self competently adjusted to our alienated social reality: the emergence of the "inner" archetypal mediators of divine power, and through this death a rebirth, and the eventual re-establishment of a new king of ego-functioning, the ego now being the servant of the divine, no longer its betrayer.'

Alan A. Stone
Harvard University

References
Laing, R. D. (1967), *The Politics of Experience*, London.
Laing, R. D. and Esterson, A. A. (1964), *Sanity, Madness and the Family*, London.

Further Reading
Laing, R. D. (1959), *The Divided Self*, London.

Leontief, Wassily (1906–)

Input-output analysis is unquestionably the crowning achievement of Wassily Leontief for which he was awarded the 1973 Nobel Memorial Prize in Economic Sciences. With its roots in Quesnay's *Tableau Économique* and in Walrasian general equilibrium (though Leontief is highly critical of general equilibrium theories since they offer little insight into operational propositions about the measureable properties of specific economic systems), input-output provides a comprehensive breakdown of macroeconomic aggregates, as it is a useful tool for studying the quantitative interdependence among interrelated economic activities, and is a valuable device for national economic planning. Leontief, a prophet enjoying greater honour outside his own country, is a strong advocate of the use of input-output for democratic economic planning.

Originally elaborated to analyse and measure the flows among the different producing and consuming sectors of a national economy, input-output has been sucessfully used in studying more compact economic systems, such as regions or very large enterprises. It was later extended to the analysis of international economic relations and, in its most ambitious form, to the structure of the world economy. Whatever needs to be said about Leontief's pioneering effort (and its subsequent refinements), it was a major *tour de force* in posing the problems of mutual compatibility and accommodation between theoretical formulation and observational capability (development of the empirical data base), and the difficulties in analysing and describing in concrete numerical magnitudes the specific operational features of the modern economy characterized by supercomplexity of the intersectoral links.

Born in 1906 in St Petersburg, the son of an economics professor, Leontief studied at the Universities of Leningrad and Berlin. He began his research career at the Institute for World Economics (University of Kiel), moving in 1931 to the US National Bureau of Economic Research. From 1932 he taught at Harvard University from which he resigned in 1975 to become Professor of Economics and Director of the Institute of Economics Analysis, New York University.

Though many Harvard students first learned mathematical economics at Leontief's knees, he is very critical of abstract economic theorizing. He warns that in interpreting the models, all too often we forget their restrictive assumptions, and he underlines that the usefulness of the exercise really depends on the empirical validity of these assumptions. Throughout his research he has taken this warning to heart; there runs an overwhelming current of empirical relevance.

George R. Feiwel
University of Tennessee

Further Reading

Dorfman, R. (1973), 'Wassily Leontief's contribution to economics', *Scandinavian Journal of Economics*, 75.

Leontief, W. (1951), *The Structure of the American Economy, 1919–1939*, New York.

Leontief, W. (1977), *Essays in Economics*, 2 vols, New York.

Leontief, W. *et al.* (1977), *The Future of the World Economy*, New York.

Miernyk, W. H. (1979), 'Leontief, Wassily', in D. L. Sills (ed.), *International Encyclopedia of the Social Sciences*, Vol. 18, New York.

Le Play, Frédéric (1806–82)

The French social scientist Frédéric Le Play was a nineteenth-century pioneer of the direct observation of social reality. Before becoming a professional sociologist, he was a mining engineer, and as professor of metallurgy at the École des Mines he travelled frequently to European metal works and mines, developing a keen eye for the connection between technical innovation and social change. His official reports covered management and manufacturing methods as well as conditions of work and life of the industrial workers. In 1844, Le Play was commissioned to investigate mines and works in the Ural Mountains which employed about 45,000 serfs, and was even persuaded to take over the management of the enterprise.

After an initial enthusiasm for the 1848 Revolution and the Republic, he became disillusioned, and moved to the right on political issues. From then on he gave priority to social studies. He was appointed to the Conseil d'État by Emperor Napoleon II, partly as a result of his work as head of the organization of the 1855 World Exhibition in Paris. In the same year he published his first book on social studies, *Les Ouvriers Européens* (Paris, 1855).

The social data collected on his early travels formed a basis for his later numerous case studies. 'Study the facts,' he urged, advocating a thoroughgoing inductivism; laws as well as suggestions for social reform will emerge from empirical study. For the six volumes on European workers, he and his collaborators wrote 'monographs' consisting largely of the budgets of working-class family expenditures, collected through interviews whose use he pioneered.

Le Play argued that the family was the basic social unit. The patriarchal family was the most stable; the two-generation family with its individualism was the most unstable. It was by the material well-being and the stability of the family that the condition of society could be measured. Technological and industrial innovations did not automatically require social innovations. Customs and traditional values, stable families and the commands of the Decalogue had to set bounds to social change. Constantly referring to the 'original sin', he strongly opposed Rousseau and his optimistic views about human nature.

Among his other works are: *La réforme social en France*, Paris, 1864; *L'Organisation du travail*, Tours, 1870; *L'Organisation de la famille*, Paris, 1871; and *La Méthode de la science sociale*, Tours, 1879.

Sacha Bem
University of Leiden

Further Reading

Brooke, M. Z. (1970), *Le Play: Engineer and Social Scientist*, London.

Le Play, F. (1982), *Frédéric Le Play on Family, Work and Social Change*, ed. C. B. Silver, Chicago.

Lévi-Strauss, Claude (1908–)

Claude Lévi-Strauss was born in Brussels, of French parents. After attending the Lycée Janson de Sailly in Paris he studied at the Faculty of Law in Paris, where he obtained his license, and at the Sorbonne, where he received his teacher's qualification in philosophy (*agrégation*) in 1931. After teaching for two years at the lycées of Mont-de-Marsan and Laon, he was appointed to the French university mission in Brazil, serving as professor at the University of Sao Paulo from 1935 to 1938. Between 1935 and 1939 he organized and directed several ethnographic expeditions in the Mato Grosso and the Amazon. Returning to France on the eve of the war, he was mobilized. After the armistice, in June 1940, he succeeded in reaching the United States, where he taught at the New School for Social Research in New York. Volunteering for the Free French forces, he was attached to the French scientific mission in the United States, and founded with H. Focillon, J. Maritain, J. Perrin and others the École Libre des Hautes Études in New York of which he became secretary-general. In 1945 he was appointed cultural counsellor of the French Embassy to the United States, but resigned in 1948 in order to devote himself to his scientific work.

Lévi-Strauss's doctoral thesis, submitted at the Sorbonne, was made up of his first two studies, *La Vie familiale et sociale des Indiens Nambikwara* (1948) and *Les Structures élémentaires de la parenté* (1949) (*The Elementary Structures of Kinship*, 1969). In 1949 he became deputy director of the Musée de l'Homme, and later director of studies at the École Pratique des Hautes Études, chair of the comparative religion of non-literate peoples, in succession to Maurice Leenhardt. In 1959 he was appointed to the Collège de France, establishing a chair in social anthropology. He taught there until his retirement in 1982.

The name of Claude Lévi-Strauss has become linked indissolubly with what later came to be called structural anthropology. Reading his first articles, such as 'Structural analysis in linguistics and in anthropology' (1963 [1945]), one is struck by the clarity with which from the first he formulated the basic principles of structuralism. As the title of the essay suggests, he found his inspiration in the linguistics of Saussure and above all in the phonological method developed by Trubetzkoy and by Jakobson (with whom he was associated in New York during the war). He drew from them rules of procedure: concentrate not on conscious phenomena but on their unconscious infrastructure; do not attribute an independent value to the elements of a system but rather a positional meaning, that is to say, the value of the elements is dependent upon the relations which combine and oppose them, and these relations must be the foundation of the analysis; recognize at the same time that these relations also have a merely positional significance within a system of correlations whose structure must be extracted.

Lévi-Strauss applied this method first to the study of kinship systems, demonstrating their formal analogy with phonetic systems. His article of 1945 paid especial attention to the problem of the avunculate, sketching some of the central themes of his *Elementary Structures*, which he was then elaborating. These included the central role of marriage exchange, which implies a prohibition on incest (of which exchange is, in a sense, the other, positive, side of the coin). Marriage exchange is the condition of kinship: 'Kinship is allowed to establish and perpetuate itself only through specific forms of marriage.' He also stressed the social character of kinship, which has to do not with 'what it retains from nature', but rather with 'the essential way in which it diverges from nature' (1963). Finally, Lévi-Strauss proposed the definition of kinship systems, and of social systems more generally, as systems of symbols.

Another influence which is also apparent, and which Lévi-Strauss has always acknowledged, is the work of Marcel Mauss. His sympathy for the thought of Mauss is apparent when he compares the method of analysis in Mauss's *Essai sur le don* with the approach of structural linguistics, or when, in the same essay, he charges anthropology with the task of studying 'the unconscious mental structures which one may discern by investigating the institutions, or better still the language', and which render intelligible the variety and apparent disorder of appearances (Lévi-Strauss, 1983 [1950]).

This was the goal which had been set by the author of *The Elementary Structures of Kinship*:

> The diversity of the historical and geographical modalities of the rules of kinship and marriage have appeared to us to exhaust all possible methods for ensuring the integration of biological families within the social group. We have thus established that superficially complicated and arbitrary rules may be reduced to a small number. There are only three possible elementary kinship structures; these three structures are constructed by means of two forms of exchange; and these two forms of exchange themselves depend upon a single differential characteristic, namely the harmonic or disharmonic character of the regime considered. Ultimately, the whole imposing apparatus of prescriptions and prohibitions could be reconstructed *a priori* from one question, and one alone: in the society concerned, what is the relationship between the rule of residence and the rule of descent? (1969 [1949], p. 493)

Furthermore, these kinship structures rest upon universal

mental structures: the force of the rule as a rule, the notion of reciprocity, and the symbolic character of the gift.

Lévi-Strauss returned to deal with one unanswered question fifteen years later, in *The Raw and the Cooked*. Are these kinship structures really primary, or do they rather represent 'the reflections in men's minds of certain social demands that had been objectified in institutions'? Are they the effect of what one might term an external logic? His *Mythologiques*, of which this was the first volume, put this functionalist hypothesis out of court, demonstrating that in mythology, which, in contrast to kinship, 'has no obvious practical function . . . is not directly linked with a different kind of reality', processes of the same order were to be found. Whether systems were actually 'lived', in the course of social life, or like the myths, simply conceived in an apparently spontaneous and arbitrary manner, they led back to the same sources, which one might legitimately describe as 'mental'. This answer had in fact been given earlier, in 1962, in *Le Totémisme aujourd'hui* (*Totemism*, 1962) and *La Pensée sauvage* (*The Savage Mind*, 1966), the latter book asserting, in opposition to Lévy-Bruhl's notion of a 'prelogical mentality', that 'savage' forms of thinking are to be found in us all, providing a shared basis which is domesticated by our various cultures.

The issue was whether the structuralist method applied only to kinship structures, and moreover only to those Lévi-Strauss termed 'elementary', which are not universal, even among those societies which traditionally are called traditional. The re-examination of totemism demonstrated how successfully this method could be applied to the symbolic systems with the aid of which people structure their representations of the world. The analysis of myths demonstrated, further, that the method worked not only for closed systems, like kinship systems, but applied also to open systems, or at least to systems whose closure could not be immediately established and whose interpretation could be developed only in the manner of a 'nebula' in the absence of 'the general appearance of a stable and well-defined structure' (*The Raw and the Cooked*).

In his last lectures at the Collège de France, between 1976 and 1982, Lévi-Strauss took up problems of kinship once more, but moved on from the systems based on unilineal descent and preferential alliance, concerning which he had developed his theory of elementary structures in 1949. He now investigated societies whose fundamental grouping brought together 'either cognates and agnates, or else cognates and maternal kin', and which he termed the 'house', borrowing a term which was used in medieval Europe. These studies are described in his latest book, *Paroles données*, published in 1984. Here he demonstrates that structuralism is by no means disqualified from the study of 'a type of institution which transcends the traditional categories of ethnological theory, combining descent and residence, exogamy and endogamy, filiation and alliance, patriliny and matriliny' and can analyse the complex matrimonial strategies which simultaneously or in succession employ principles 'which elsewhere are mutually exclusive'. What is the best alliance? Should one seek a spouse in the vicinity, or far away? These are the questions which dominate the myths. But they are not posed by savages alone. At a conference held in 1983 (whose proceedings were published in *Annales*, November-December, 1983) Lévi-Strauss cited materials from Blanche de Castille, Saint-Simon and the peasant populations of Japan, Africa, Polynesia and Madagascar to show that 'between societies which are called "complex" and those which are wrongly termed "primitive" or "archaic", the distance is less great than one might think'.

It is therefore mistaken to criticize anthropologists, certainly if they are structuralists, for ignoring history and considering the societies they study as though they were static, despite the fact that, like our own, they exist in time, even if they may not situate themselves in time in the same fashion. This criticism rests upon a misunderstanding which Lévi-Strauss, however, tried to forestall very early. It is significant that it was in 1949 – the year in which his *Elementary Structures* appeared – that he published an essay with a title – 'History and Ethnology' – which he was to use again for his conference paper in 1983. In his article of 1949 he emphasized that the difference between the two disciplines was a consequence of their very complementarity, 'history organizing its data with reference to conscious characterizations, ethnology with reference to the unconscious conditions of social life'. In 1983, taking into account what has come to be called the 'nouvelle histoire', this complementarity is restated, but at another level. In fact 'it was through their contact with ethnology that the historians recognized the importance of those obscure and partly submerged facets of life in society. In return, as a consequence of the renewal of its field of study and its methods, history, under the name of historical anthropology, has become a source of considerable assistance to ethnologists'. Thus anthropology and history can serve each other, at least if the historian does not concern himself only with the succession of kings and queens, with wars, with treaties and with the conscious motives of actors, but studies customs, beliefs, and all that which is covered by the vague term 'mentalité', in a given society at a given time; especially if the anthropologist recognizes that the past of so-called complex societies increases 'the number of social experiments which are available for the better knowledge of man'.

It is true that in his inaugural lecture at the Collège de France in 1960 Lévi-Strauss opposed 'cold' societies – those which chose to ignore their historical aspect, and which anthropologists had traditionally preferred to study   and 'hot' societies – those which, on the contrary, valued their historicity and which were of especial interest to historians. Nevertheless, this opposition did not put in question the historicity of one or other type of society, but rather their attitude to their respective pasts. Every society presents a double aspect: structural and historical. But while one aspect might be especially favoured, this does not lead to the disappearance of the other. And in truth, the 'cold' societies do not deny the past: they wish to repeat it. For their part, 'hot' societies cannot totally deny their 'coldness': the history that they value is theirs only by virtue of a certain continuity which guarantees their identity. This explains the paradox that the very peoples who are most concerned with their history see themselves through stereotypes. And recognizing, or desiring, a history does not prevent them from thinking of others, and especially their neighbours, in a static mode. One might instance the set fashion in which, for example, the French and the English represent each other. Thus structuralism does not put history in question, but rather an idea of history which is so common: the idea that history can concern itself only with flux, and that change is never-ending. Yet although nature does not, apparently, make jumps, history does not seem to be able to avoid them. Certainly one might interest oneself in the moments of transition. One might equally interest oneself in the intervening periods, and is history not in essence constituted by such periods? The times within which different states of society succeed each other are not less discontinuous than the space within which societies contemporary in time but equally different, often ignorant of each other, share a border. It matters little whether the distancing – which appears to the ethnologist to be the condition of his research, since it is the other as such which is the object of his research – is temporal or spatial.

Obviously it is not necessary to accept the notion of a possible fusion between anthropology, as conceived by Lévi-Strauss, and history. The historian strives to surmount discontinuity, his goal being to establish genealogical connections between one social state and another. The anthropologist, on the contrary, tries to profit from discontinuity, by discovering among distinct societies (without concerning himself as to whether or not they figure in the same genealogical tree) homologies which attest to the reality of a shared foundation for humanity. Lévi-Strauss has always striven to recognize this 'original logic' beneath a diversity of expressions which have often been judged to be absurd, explicable only by positing the priority of affect over intellect, but which are 'a direct expression of the structure of the mind . . . and not an inert product of the action of the environment on an amorphous consciousness' (*Totemism*, 1962).

If one might talk of a Kantian aspect to structuralism (and Lévi-Strauss has never denied it), one should note that its course inverts that of Kant in two ways. First, instead of positing a transcendental subject, it tries to detach, from the variety of concrete systems of representations, collective modes of thought. Secondly, from among these systems it selects those which diverge most from ours. Kantianism without a transcendental subject thus, although the ambition of discovering in this way 'a fundamental and communal matrix of constraints', or in other words invariants, would seem nevertheless at the least to evoke its shade.

Such an enterprise appears to dispose of subjectivity, or at least to put it within parentheses, and this has indeed been one of the reproaches directed at structuralism: that it does not deal with man as a subject. There is a misapprehension here. As Lévi-Strauss, indeed, remarked in his 'Introduction à l'oeuvre de Marcel Mauss' (1983):

> Every society different from ours is an object; every group in our society, apart from our own, is an object; indeed, each usage, even of our own group, which we do not share, is an object. Yet this unlimited series of objects, which together constitute the object of the ethnographer, whatever its historical or geographical features, is still, in the end, defined in relation to himself. However objective in analysis, he must in the end achieve a subjective reintegration of them.

And again, in the same text: 'In the last analysis, the ethnological problem is a problem of communication.' That is to say, communication between subjects, between 'the Melanesian of whatever island', as Mauss put it, 'and the person who observes him, listens to him . . . and interprets him'. A similar point was made in *La Pensée sauvage*, published twelve years later, which ended with a consideration of the convergence between the laws of 'savage thought' and modern theories of information, that is, of the transmission and reception of messages. Thus the subject is not neglected or denied, but (while avoiding a solipsism which would obviously be the negation of anthropology) one might say that there is always a plurality of subjects, without which indeed the problem of communication would not present itself, and it is their relations which are significant. This remains a constant principle of Lévi-Strauss's structuralism: it is the relations which matter, not the terms.

That is also the principle which has guided this brief review. It has been concerned less with the analysis of texts, each considered in itself, than with their relations – from a point of view as much synchronic as diachronic – the aim being to abstract the invariant features of a body of work which is at once complete yet always open.

Jean Pouillon
Laboratory of Social Anthropology, Collège de France, Paris

References

Lévi-Strauss, C. (1963), 'Structural analysis in linguistics and anthropology', *Structural Anthropology*, New York. (Originally published in French as 'L'analyse structurale en linguistique et en anthropologie', *Word*, l, 1945.)

Lévi-Strauss, C. (1969), *The Elementary Structures of Kinship*, London. (Original French edn, *Les Structures élémentaires de la parenté*, Paris, 1949.)

Lévi-Strauss, C. (1983), *Introduction to Marcel Mauss*, London, 1983. (Originally published in French as 'Introduction à l'oeuvre de Marcel Mauss', in Marcel Mauss, *Sociologie et anthropologie*, Paris, 1950.)

Lévi-Strauss, C. (1984), *Paroles données*, Paris.

Further Reading

Hayes, E. N. and Hayes, T. (eds) (1970), *Claude Lévi-Strauss: The Anthropologist as Hero*, Cambridge, Mass.

Lévi-Strauss, C. (1961), *A World on the Wane*, New York. (Original French edn, *Tristes Tropiques*, Paris, 1955.)

Lévi-Strauss, C. (1963), 'History and ethnology', *Structural Anthropology*, New York. (Originally published in French as 'Histoire et ethnologie', *Révue de Métaphysique et de Morale*, 1949.)

Lévi-Strauss, C. (1963), *Structural Anthropology*, New York. (Original French edn, *Anthropologie structurale*, Paris, 1958.)

Lévi-Strauss, C. (1970), *The Raw and the Cooked*, London. (Original French edn, *Le Cru et le cuit* ([vol. l of *Mythologiques*]), Paris, 1964.)

Lévi-Strauss, C. (1972), *From Honey to Ashes*, London. (Original French edn, *Du Miel aux cendres* ([vol. 2 of *Mythologiques*]), Paris, 1966.)

Lévi-Strauss, C. (1978), *The Origin of Table Manners*, London. (Original French edn, *L'Origine des manières de table* ([vol. 3 of *Mythologiques*]), Paris, 1968.)

Lévi-Strauss, C. (1981), *The Naked Man*, London. (Original French edn, *L'Homme nu* ([vol. 4 of *Mythologiques*]), Paris, 1971.)

Lévi-Strauss, C. (1977) 'The scope of anthropology', *Structural Anthropology*, II. (Inaugural lecture, Collège de France, 1960; published in *Anthropologie structurale*, II, Paris, 1973.)

Lévi-Strauss, C. (1983), *Le Regard éloigné*, Paris.

Steiner, G. (1966), 'A conversation with Claude Lévi-Strauss', *Encounter*, 26.

See also: *Mauss*.

Lévy-Bruhl, Lucien (1857–1939)

Lucien Lévy-Bruhl, anthropologist and philosopher, belonged to the Republican generation of French academics, which, strongly influenced by positivist philosophy and imbued with the ideals of lay (anti-clerical) democracy, took command of the new Sorbonne around the turn of the century. He was educated at the École Normale Superieure and following a rapid university career was appointed to a chair in the history of modern philosophy at the Sorbonne in 1904.

The nomination represented a turning point in his intellectual development: from then on most of his work was dedicated to problems of cultural relativity and, specifically, to the theory of 'primitive mentality'. His first major statement in this area, which was formulated in *La Morale et la science des mœurs* (1903) (*Ethics and Moral Science*, 1905), referred to the variability of morals in space and time, and suggested that a rational art of human conduct (ethics) should follow the observed laws of morality and be only applicable to local social circumstances.

His later books, starting with *Les Fonctions mentales dans les sociétés inférieures* (1910) (*How Natives Think*, 1926) and ending with *L'Expérience mystique et les symboles chez les primitifs* (1938), are based largely upon ethnological evidence from secondary sources. The main focus of this work is the study of mental functions in modern and archaic societies. Lévy-Bruhl postulated a basic difference in mental functions in the two forms of society. Primitive mentality, as expressed in collective representations, ignored the rules of logic, particularly the law of contradiction – hence its definition as 'prelogical'. The principle of contradiction was replaced by a notion of mystical participation. Affective elements supplemented logical generalizations, and no clear-cut distinction was made between ordinary and mystical experience. Lévy-Bruhl's theory altered over time. In his later years he argued that the two types of mentality coexisted, rather than postulating two separate socio-mental structures. Indeed, in his posthumous *Les Carnets de Lucien Lévy-Bruhl* (1949) (*The Notebooks on Primitive Mentality*, 1975), he largely repudiated his original notion of the fundamental differences between modern and archaic mentalities.

Lévy-Bruhl significantly influenced structuralist cultural anthropology and Jungian psychoanalysis. Though he was consistently criticized by Durkheim and Mauss, his teaching provided a powerful impetus to the renewal of anthropological studies in France. He was co-founder, together with Marcel Mauss and Paul Rivet, of the Ethnological Institute of Paris University in 1925.

Victor Karady
Centre National de la Recherche Scientifique, Paris

Further Reading

Cazeneuve, J. (1963), *Lucien Lévy-Bruhl, sa vie, son oeuvre, avec un exposé de sa philosophie*, Paris. (English translation, *Lucien Lévy-Bruhl*, Oxford, 1972.)

Locke, John (1632–1704)

John Locke was born in 1632 at Wrington in Somerset. He entered Christ Church College, Oxford in 1652 where he received his MA in 1658. In that same year he was elected student of Christ Church; in 1660 he became lecturer in Greek; lecturer in Rhetoric in 1662, and censor of Moral Philosophy in 1664. From 1667 to 1681 Locke was physician and secretary to Anthony Ashley Cooper, Lord Ashley (later, First Earl of

Shaftesbury). He was elected fellow of the Royal Society in 1668, and was secretary to the Lords Proprietors of Carolina from 1668 to 1675. In 1684, he was deprived of his appointment to Christ Church by royal decree. He lived in Holland from 1683 to 1689; was Commissioner on the Board of Trade from 1696 to 1700, and died at Otes (Oates) in the parish of High Laver, Essex in 1704.

Locke's *Essay Concerning Human Understanding* (1690) made a major contribution to psychology and to philosophical psychology. That work offered the outlines of a genetic epistemology, and a theory of learning. Locke's interest in children is reflected not only in his pedagogical work, *Some Thoughts Concerning Education* (1693), but in many passages of the *Essay* where he traced the development of awareness in children. The oft-quoted metaphor used by Locke to characterize the mind as a blank tablet should not blind us to the fact that the Lockean mind comes equipped with faculties, that the child has specific 'tempers' or character traits which the educator must learn to work with, and that human nature for Locke has basic self-preserving tendencies to avoid pain and seek pleasure. These tendencies were even called by Locke 'innate practical principles'. The innate claim his psychology rejected was for truths (moral and intellectual) and specific ideational contents.

Much of the *Essay* is occupied with discussing how we acquire certain ideas, with showing how a combination of physical and physiological processes stimulate and work with a large number of mental operations (for example, joining, separating, considering, abstracting, generalizing) to produce the ideas of particular sense qualities and many complex notions, such as power, existence, unity. One such complex notion is the idea of self or person.

The account of the idea of self – or rather, *my* idea of *my* self, for Locke's account of this notion is a first-person account – emerges out of a discussion of the question, 'Does the soul always think?' That question had been answered in the affirmative by Descartes. For Locke, not only was it empirically false that the soul always thinks; that question suggested wrongly that something in me (my soul), not me, thinks. *I* am the agent of my actions and the possessor of my thoughts. Moreover, all thinking is reflexive; when I think, I am aware that I am thinking, no matter what form that thinking takes (sensing, willing, believing, doubting or remembering). It is the awareness of my act of thinking which also functions in awareness of self. Consciousness appropriates both thoughts and actions. The self or person for Locke consists in that set of thoughts and actions which I appropriate and for which I take responsibility through my consciousness.

Appropriation is a fundamental activity for Locke. I appropriate my thoughts and actions to form my concept of self. The *Essay* details the appropriation by each of us of ideas and knowledge. Education is also an appropriation of information, but more importantly of habits of good conduct. Education is a socializing process. It takes place usually within the family, with a tutor (for Locke writes about the education of a gentleman's son). But the account of the socialization process extends to Locke's political writings, *Two Treatises on Government* (1690), where he discusses the family, duties parents have to their children and to each other (a marriage contract is part of his account of the family), and the rights and duties of citizens in a political society. The appropriation of land, possessions and eventually money by the activities of the person constitutes an early stage in Locke's account of the movement from the state of nature to a civil (political) society.

The political society, as the pre-political state of nature, is grounded in law and order; order is respect and responsibility to each other and ultimately to God whose law of nature prescribes these duties. Locke's law of nature is a Christianized version of that tradition. The individual laws which he cites on occasion prescribe and proscribe the actions sanctioned or denied by the liberal religion of his day. These laws differed little in content from those innate moral truths Locke attacked; it was not the truths he rejects, only the claim that they were innate. Locke's society is fairly slanted in favour of the individual: preservation of the person, privacy of property, tacit assent, the right of dissent. At the same time, the pressures towards conformity and the force of majority opinion are also strong. The structure of his civil society, with its checks and balances, its separation of powers, its grounding on the law of nature, is designed to achieve a balance between the rights and needs of the individual and the need for security and order. His views on toleration (which were expressed in a series of tracts), while directed mainly against religious intoleration, match well with his insistence that government does not have the right to prescribe rites, rituals, dress and other practices in religion. Locke's toleration did not, however, extend to unbelief, to atheism.

The methodology for acquiring knowledge recommended by Locke and illustrated in his *Essay* stressed careful observation. Both in the physical sciences and in learning about ourselves and others, it was the 'plain, historical method' (that is, experience and observation) which holds the promise of accurate knowledge, or sound probability. Knowledge was not limited to demonstrative, deductive processes. Truth claims were always open to revision through further reports and observations. These concepts of knowledge and this experiential method were extended by Locke to what was later termed (for example, by Hume) 'the science of man' or 'of human nature'. His detailed attention to his own thought processes enabled him to map the wide variety of mental operations and to begin the development of a cognitive psychology. His interest in children, throughout his life, led to observations and descriptions of their behaviour. He had many friends who had children, and lived for several years on different occasions with families who had several young children. The *Essay* uses some of these observations as the basis for a brief genetic learning theory, and his *Some Thoughts* contains many remarks and recommendations for raising children based upon his firsthand experience with children in their natural environment.

Locke's social theory grew out of his reading and (more importantly) out of these habits of observing people in daily life. In his travels in France and Holland, he often recorded details of activities and practices, religious, academic and ordinary. Where direct observation was not possible, he used the new travel literature for reports on other societies, other customs and habits. He had his own biases and preferences, to be sure, but with his dedication to reason and rationality, he seldom allowed emotions to affect his observations or his conclusions. He was an articulate representative of the Royal Society's attitudes in the sciences, including what we know as the social sciences.

John W. Yolton
Rutgers College

Locke's Writings:
Epistola de Tolerantia, Gouda, 1689.
Essay Concerning Human Understanding, London, 1690.
Further Considerations Concerning Raising the Value of Money, London, 1695.
Letter Concerning Toleration, London, 1689.
A Letter to Edward Lord Bishop of Worcester, London, 1697.
The Reasonableness of Christianity, as Delivered in the Scriptures, London, 1695.
A Second Letter Concerning Toleration, London, 1690.
Short Observations on a Printed Paper, Intituled 'For Encouraging the Coining Silver Money in England, and After, for Keeping it Here', London, 1695.
Some Considerations of the Consequences of the Lowering of Interest and Raising the Value of Money, London, 1692.
Some Thoughts Concerning Education, London, 1693.
A Third Letter for Toleration, London, 1692.
Two Treatises of Government, London, 1690.
Works, London, 1714, 3 vols.

Further Reading
Aaron, R. I. (1971), *John Locke*, 3rd edn, Oxford.
Colman, J. (1983), *John Locke's Moral Philosophy*, Edinburgh.
Cranston, M. (1957), *John Locke, A Biography*, New York.
Dunn, J. (1969), *The Political Thought of John Locke*, Cambridge.
Tully, J. (1980), *A Discourse on Property. John Locke and his Adversaries*, Cambridge.
Yolton, J. W. (1956), *John Locke and the Way of Ideas*, Oxford.

Yolton, J. W. (1970), *Locke and the Compass of Human Understanding*, Cambridge.

Lukács, George Szegedy von (1885–1971)

Born the son of a wealthy Jewish banker, the Hungarian Georg (Gyorgy) Lukács became internationally famous as a literary critic and as an interpreter of Marx. He was additionally a man of action who played a major role in the revolution of 1919, was a member of the Hungarian, Austrian and German Communist Parties between the wars, and was Minister of Culture in the abortive uprising of 1956.

After moving in Budapest literary circles after the turn of the century, Lukács was increasingly influenced by the Heidelberg neo-Kantians and studied first in Berlin under Simmel, and then in Heidelberg, where he met Lask and Weber. His first major work of literary criticism, *Die Seele und die Formen* (1911) (*Soul and Form*, 1971) aimed at a 'philosophy of art in order to pinpoint the ultimate questions of life' and maintained that the critic's role was to relate particular artistic forms to various mental states, or ways of understanding the world. However, tiring of the ahistorical nature of neo-Kantian argument and increasingly influenced by the work of Hegel, Lukács sought in his next major work, *Die Theorie des Romans* (1916) (*The Theory of the Novel*, 1971) to historicize aesthetic categories and already employed that concept which was to become crucial to his later work, the concept of *totality*. It has to be said of this early work, of his subsequent criticism of modernism while living in exile in Russia from 1933 to 1944, and of his account of irrationalism in German intellectual history (*Die Zerstörung der Vernunft*, 1954) (*The Destruction of Reason*, 1954) that it is often crude and omits those events, thinkers or literary works which fail to match Lukács's crassly manipulated schemata. (It is an odd theory of the novel indeed which cannot embrace Stendhal or Dostoevsky.) However, the later *Wider den misverstandenen Realismus* (1958) (*Meaning of Contemporary Realism*, 1963) and especially *Die Eigenart des Aesthetischen* (*The Peculiarity of Aesthetics*, 1963) have to a large extent made good the deficit, proved much more open-minded towards modernism and writers such as Kafka, and have sought to prove that there is such a thing as a *Marxist* aesthetics which does not – *pace* Mehring – require borrowings from other intellectual traditions.

It is none the less in his interpretation of Marx that Lukács has probably been most influential. Lukács had always loathed the autocratic politics of pre-1914 Hungary, had been influenced by the anarchic-syndicalist ideas of Erwin Szabó and had never been attracted to the 'positivism' of the Western democracies. The crude materialism of 'orthodox' Second-International Marxism, represented above all by Kautsky, appalled his neo-Kantian and Hegelian inheritance. The solution to this dilemma Lukács found in Lenin, in the Russian Revolution, and in an interpretation of Marx which was all the more remarkable for the fact that the so-called *Paris Manuscripts* of 1844 had not yet been discovered. Rediscovering the concepts of alienation and praxis in the writings of the mature Marx, Lukács argued that scientistic interpretations of Marxism failed to recognize the transitory nature of the capitalist mode of production, reduced man to a cog in an economic machine and thus reduced the world-historical actor, the proletariat, to a fatal impotence, as was only too clear from the history of Social Democracy. What the proletariat required was not a pseudo-scientific theory of economic evolution but an awareness of the *historical* nature of capitalist society, a *total* view. But this could only come through the self-liberation of the proletariat. Thus Lukács initially identified the workers' council as *the* form of proletarian revolution, in which the worker would reappropriate his own fate and become the subject, no longer merely the object, of history. These views, expressed in a series of essays published in 1923 as *Geschicht und Klassenbewusstsein* (*History and Class Consciousness*, 1971), however, stand in a certain tension to Lukács's increasingly Leninist identification of the Communist Party with working-class consciousness and his difficulty, which remained with him to the end of his days, in accepting that there could be a distinction between the interests of the party and those of the working class. Although Lukács subsequently disowned *History and Class Consciousness*, it is perhaps to its image of working-class self-liberation that Lukács owes his fame, at least among the Western intelligentsia.

Dick Geary
University of Lancaster

Further Reading
Lichtheim, G. (1970), *Lukács*, London.
Meszaros, I. (1972), *Lukács' Concept of Dialectics*, London.
Parkinson, G. H. R. (ed.) (1970), *Georg Lukács: The Man, His Work and His Ideas*, London.

Luria, Alexander Romanovich (1902–1977)

Alexander Romanovich Luria, the Russian pioneer of neuropsychology, was born in Kazan in Soviet Central Asia, and died in Moscow. After graduating in social sciences from the University of Kazan in 1921, he entered the Kazan medical school. However, he had already become interested in psychology, and in 1923 he took up a position at the Institute of Psychology at Moscow State University. His earliest work used measures of word association and motor reaction to study the effects of stress and anxiety upon the expression of affective states. His account of this research sought to integrate an objective, behaviouristic approach with psychoanalytic notions about personality dynamics (Luria, 1932; 1979).

In 1924 Luria was joined by Lev Vygotsky, who was formulating his ideas on the role of language and other culturally transmitted devices in the mediation of higher mental functions. From then until Vygotsky's death in 1934 they carried out research together with Alexei Leontiev on the nature of conscious mental processes, on the social aspects of intellectual development and on the effects of brain damage upon cognitive function. Following the Marxist-Leninist thesis that consciousness is the product of sociohistorical processes, they stressed that human cognition evolved at both the individual and the societal level within a historical context. Moreover, this development should be reflected in the cerebral organization of cognition function and in the patterns of dysfunction associated with neurological damage (Luria, 1979).

In 1931 and 1932 Luria led two expeditions to Uzbekistan and Kirghizia to examine the intellectual abilities of peasant communities under the impact of collectivization. Their findings were generally consistent with Levy-Bruhl's notion that socio-cultural differences in cognitive behaviour reflected different stages of intellectual development. Brief reports of these expeditions appeared in Western journals. However, in the USSR it was felt undesirable that such research should be published when the central government was trying to get these communities to participate in the national economy, and fuller accounts did not appear until the 1970s (Luria, 1976b; 1979).

The same ideological perspective led to an interest in the relative importance of biological and environmental determinants of behaviour. Luria and others at the Medico-Genetic Institute in Moscow investigated this in many studies comparing twins who received different methods of instruction. But these studies, too, were felt to be politically controversial, and Luria's own findings once again remained largely unpublished.

Vygotsky, Luria, and many of their colleagues were also attacked during the early 1930s because of their association with the mental testing movement and their promotion of Western psychological traditions in contrast to the work of Pavlov and the 'reflexologists'. Although they set up an alternative centre for teaching and research in Kharkhov, in 1936 Luria decided to return full time to his medical training, which he had been doing on a part-time basis since the late 1920s. He graduated from the First Moscow Medical School in 1937, and then specialized in neurology. Following on his earlier work with Vygotsky, he focused on studying psychological consequences of neurological damage and disease, the discipline now known as clinical neuropsychology, and especially upon the typology of acquired speech disorders.

After the outbreak of the Second World War, in 1941, Luria became head of a rehabilitation hospital in the southern Urals for patients with brain injuries. His extensive experience before and during the War resulted in two major books on traumatic aphasia (Luria, 1970) and on recovery from neurological damage (Luria, 1963a). In these books, and in all his subsequent work, he emphasized the detailed symptomatology of individual patients. In 1945 he was appointed professor of psychology at Moscow State University, and continued his work at the Bourdenko Institute of Neurosurgery, on the impairment of higher mental functions following local brain lesions. He explored the nature of both normal and abnormal cognitive function and the representation of such function in the human brain (Luria, 1966b).

Soviet academic life experienced a considerable upheaval in the late 1940s and early 1950s. Although Luria had followed Pavlov and Bekhterev in emphasizing neural plasticity and the possibility of functional reorganization within the damaged brain, his own work once again came under criticism for paying insufficient regard to Pavlovian principles, and in 1950 he was dismissed from his post at the Institute of Neurosurgery. But since he had been elected to the Russian Academy of Pedagogical Sciences in 1947, he was able to take up a position at the Academy's Institute of Defectology. During the 1950s he studied mentally handicapped children. He hypothesized that they were retarded because in their case speech had failed to assume its normal regulative functions (Luria, 1963b; 1979). He was also able to publish a study done in the 1930s of a pair of identical twins with retarded speech and behaviour (Luria & Yudovich, 1959); this has since become very influential among teachers and educationalists in Western Europe.

In the late 1950s Luria was allowed to return to the Institute of Neurosurgery to continue his work in clinical neuropsychology. During the last twenty years of his life, in a series of books Luria developed a comprehensive theory on the systematic organization of higher cognitive functions (Luria, 1966a, 1966b, 1973, 1976c, 1981). This built upon Vygotsky's ideas concerning the role of language in the development of cerebral control over behaviour (reflected in his interest in the neurophysiology of the frontal lobes), and upon Pavlov's notion of cerebral reflexes as the basic elements of behaviour. The theory also had close affinities to the information-processing accounts of human cognition prevalent in the West during the same period. His basic assertion was that the brain should be regarded as 'a *complex functional system*, embracing different levels and different components each making its own contribution to the final structure of mental activity' (Luria, 1973). While there were undoubted differences in functional organization among different parts of the brain, there was nevertheless considerable 'equipotentiality' within relatively large anatomical regions. In his work, he emphasized careful qualitative description rather than detailed quantitative assessment. This was very much in the tradition of classical neurological examination.

Two studies published in the 1960s based on case material extending back more than 25 years attempt to revive the traditions of 'romantic science' in opposition to the reductionism of 'classical' science. *The Mind of a Mnemonist* (Luria, 1968) described an individual with a remarkable ability to remember specific experiences and episodes, but who nevertheless was not able to abstract meaning from those experiences; and *The Man with a Shattered World* (Luria, 1972) described the rehabilitation of a case of severe brain damage from the Second World War by means of extracts from the patient's own diary.

Towards the end of his life, Luria returned to the analysis of the particular disorders of language function resulting from local brain damage. Influenced directly by Roman Jakobson's ideas on the structure of language, he attempted to provide a comprehensive neuropsychological analysis of the comprehension and production of both spoken and written language and a rigorous classification of aphasic disorders (Luria, 1976a). While taking note of recent developments in semiotics, linguistics, and psycholinguistics, he considered that he was taking 'the first steps towards a general scheme of a new branch of science – that of Neurolinguistics, using observations on disturbances of language and speech in patients with local brain lesions as a method for a better understanding of some components of language itself'.

John T. E. Richardson
Brunel University, Uxbridge

References

Luria, A. R., (1932 [1930]), *The Nature of Human Conflicts; or Emotion, Conflict, and Will: An Objective Study of Disorganization and Control of Human Behavior* (ed. and trans., W. H. Gantt), New York.

Luria, A. R. (1936), 'The development of mental functions in twins', *Character and Personality*, 5.

Luria, A. R. (1963a [1948]), *Restoration of Function after Brain Injury* (B. Haigh, trans.; O. L. Zangwill, Ed.), Oxford.

Luria, A. R. (ed.) (1963b), *The Mentally Retarded Child: Essays Based on a Study of the Peculiarities of the Higher Nervous Functioning of Child-Oligophrenics* (W. P. Robinson, trans.; B. Kirman, ed.), Oxford.

Luria, A. R. (1966a [1962]), *Higher Cortical Functions in Man* (B. Haigh, trans.), New York.

Luria, A. R. (1966b [1963]), *Human Brain and Psychological Processes* (B. Haigh, trans.), New York.

Luria, A. R. (1968 [1965]), *The Mind of a Mnemonist: A Little Book about a vast Memory* (L. Solotaroff, trans.), New York.

Luria, A. R. (1969), 'The neuropsychological study of brain lesions and restoration of damaged brain function', in M. Cole & I. Maltzman (eds.) *A Handbook of Contemporary Soviet Psychology* (pp. 277–301), New York.

Luria, A. R. (1970 [1947]), *Traumatic Aphasia* (D. Bowden, trans.), The Hague.

Luria, A. R. (1972 [1971]), *The Man with a Shattered World: The History of a Brain Wound* (L. Solotaroff, trans.), New York.

Luria, A. R. (1973), *The Working Brain* (B. Haigh, trans.), Harmondsworth.

Luria, A. R. (1976a [1975]), *Basic Problems of Neurolinguistics* (B. Haigh, trans.), The Hague.

Luria, A. R. (1976b [1974]), *Cognitive Development: Its Cultural and Social Foundations* (M. Lopez-Morillas & L. Solotaroff, trans.; M. Cole, ed.), Cambridge, Mass.

Luria, A. R. (1976c [1974; 1976]), *The Neuropsychology of Memory*, New York.

Luria, A. R. (1979), *The Making of Mind: A Personal Account of Soviet Psychology* (M. Cole & S. Cole, eds.), Cambridge, Mass.

Luria, A. R. (1981 [1978]), *Language and Cognition* (J. V. Wertsch, ed.), New York.

Luria, A. R. and Yudovich, F. I. (1959 [1956]), *Speech and the Development of Mental Processes in the Child* (O. Kovasc and J. Simon, trans. J. Simon, ed.), London.

Machiavelli, Niccolo (1469–1526)

Machiavelli was a Florentine patriot, civil servant and political theorist. Entering the service of the Council of Ten which ruled republican Florence in 1498, he was sent abroad on diplomatic missions which provided much of the experience later to be distilled as advice on political and military skill. In 1512 the republic crumbled and the Medici family, who had long dominated Florentine politics, returned to power. Accidentally and unjustly implicated in a plot against them, Machiavelli was arrested and tortured. On his release he was exiled from the city, and retired to a small farm in Sant' Andrea, seven miles south of the city. The remainder of a disappointed life was devoted to writings, some of them intended to persuade the new rulers to restore him to the centre of affairs which he so dearly loved.

The Prince (1513), written soon after his downfall, was a short work of advice to princes, focused in its last chapter on the local problem of liberating Italy from foreign domination. Some writers (Spinoza and Rousseau most notably) have taken the work as a satire on monarchy, but it seems evidently a piece of self-advertisement in the service of ingratiation. Settling in to a life of exile, Machiavelli farmed, and wrote the *Discourses on the First Ten Books of Titus Livius* ([1532] 1950), a sequence of reflections on political skill, largely as exemplified in the Roman republic. His republican sympathies are evident in this work, but the frank discussion of ruthless and immoral options, for which he is notorious, is no less to be found here than in *The Prince*. By 1520 he had written on *The Art of War* and commenced *The History of Florence*. His comedy *Mandragola* is one of the classics of Italian literature. In 1525, the Medici regime was overthrown and a republic restored, but the new regime failed to employ him. He died in 1526.

Machiavelli criticized previous writers on politics for dealing with ideal and imaginary states, and claimed himself to deal with the 'effective truth' (*verita effettuale*) of politics. Situated firmly within the tradition of civic humanism, he was deeply preoccupied with the constitution of cities and the glory of heroes. His contribution to the unblinking realism of the period was to recognize that the heroes of statesmanship had not invariably followed the moral advice current in a Christian community, and indeed that some of the maxims conventionally pressed upon princes might well lead directly to their ruin. A prince must therefore know, he argued, how not to be good, and to use this knowledge according to necessity. Beyond that, however, he thought that those rulers who are in the process of consolidating their power must know how to dominate the imaginations of men. One who did was Cesare Borgia, a prince with whom Machiavelli dealt while serving the Florentine republic. Borgia had used one of his lieutenants, Ramirro da Orca, to pacify, with all necessary brutality, the newly conquered Romagna; he then had da Orca killed, and his body cut in two, and left in the piazza at Cesena, to satisfy the grievances and no doubt dominate the imaginations of the people. The ferocity of this spectacle, he wrote in chapter VII of *The Prince*, 'caused the people both satisfaction and amazement'. It is often said that Machiavelli believed in one kind of morality for private life, another for statesmen. Yet for all his cynicism, there is nothing actually relativist to be detected in his straightforward recognition of good and evil. Rulers are not accorded a different morality; they are merely construed as the guardians of morality itself and accorded a licence to violate moral norms when necessary. Transposed out of the idiom of advice to princes and into a characterization of the emerging modern state (of which Machiavelli was an acute observer) this became the idea of reason of state.

Machiavelli was very far from encouraging any sort of enormity. Statesmen are the creators of civilization, and their ambitions are without glory unless they serve the public good. Machiavelli talked with some diffidence of the proper use of cruelty in politics. The test of necessary cruelty is that it is economical, and this combination of utility with an ethic of honour was highly distinctive of his attitude. 'When the act accuses him, the outcome should excuse him,' wrote Machiavelli, in a passage often translated as 'the end justifies the means'. But Machiavelli is concerned not with moral justification but with the proper judgement to be made by subjects, and historians. From this technical point of view, religion is important because it binds men to commitments and intensifies their virtue. Machiavelli is deeply anticlerical in a Latin style, and often directly hostile to Christianity because its ethic of humility weakens governments and discourages a serious military ferocity. His admiration goes to the heroic actor in this world rather than to the pious devotee of the next.

The Machiavelli of the *Discourses* is less well known but more enduring. Here we find a conflict theory of society, with men struggling to hold states together against the tendencies of dissolution. Machiavelli bequeathed to later thinkers the classical idea that any enduring constitution must balance monarchic, aristocratic and democratic elements. To create and sustain such a state, in which mere private and familial preoccupations are transcended in the public realm of citizenship, is the supreme human achievement, but contains its own ultimate doom. For states create peace, and peace allows prosperity, and when men grow accustomed to peace and prosperity, they lose their civic virtue and indulge private passions: liberty, to use Machiavelli's terms, gives way to corruption. This tradition of thought, with its emphasis on citizenly participation, never ceased to be cultivated even in the absolute monarchies of early modern Europe, and became dominant from the time of the French Revolution onwards. It composes much of what the modern world calls 'democracy'.

The Machiavelli of popular imagination, however, has always been the exponent of the pleasures of manipulation, the supreme pornographer of power. Many revolutionary adventurers have found in him conscious formulae to cover what they were inclined to do by instinct. And in this role, Machiavelli has been remembered by social psychologists constructing a questionnaire to measure the manipulative tendencies of personality.

Those who score high are called 'high machs', while less manipulative people are called 'low machs'.

Kenneth Minogue
London School of Economics and Political Science

Further Reading
Chabrol, F. (1958), *Machiavelli and the Renaissance*, London.
Hale, J. R. (1961), *Machiavelli and Renaissance Italy*, London.
Skinner, Q. (1981), *Machiavelli*, London.
Pocock, J. (1975), *The Machiavellian Moment*, Oxford.

Malinowski, Bronislaw Kaspar (1884–1942)

Malinowski was born in Cracow in Poland, the son of a distinguished linguist and folklorist. His parents apparently belonged to the landed gentry. After reading exact sciences at the Jagellonian University (receiving his doctorate in 1908), he moved to the University of Leipzig, where he spent two crucial years, studying psychology with Wundt and economic history with Bücher. In 1910 he left Leipzig for the London School of Economics, where he worked under Westermarck. He was in Australia when war broke out in 1914, and as an Austrian subject was considered an enemy alien. However, he was permitted to do fieldwork in New Guinea, and even granted an official subsidy to do so. After preliminary work among the Mailu he went on to the Trobriand Islands. He spent two years there, from 1915–16 and from 1917–18, and invented modern anthropological fieldwork methods. He began lecturing at the London School of Economics in 1920, and was appointed Reader in 1924. He remained at the LSE until 1938 when he went to the United States, teaching at Yale. He died in New Haven in 1942 at the age of fifty-eight. Although he never did further intensive fieldwork after his Trobriand studies, he spent a few months in Africa, as a consultant and visiting students in the field, and he carried out collaborative research on Mexican markets (See Drucker-Brown (ed.), 1982).

Malinowski is regarded as one of the founders of scientific anthropology. He transformed the 'field' into a laboratory, in which the entire social life of the community provided a sort of experiment from which data were collected. The 'field' was no longer just a place where one met individuals and questioned them about their strange lives and ideas. Previously the classic resource of the anthropological armchair scholar was the questionnaire, circulated among missionaries, traders, planters and travellers. Malinowski revolutionized the relationship between theory and ethnography; henceforth only the man in the field himself could perhaps aspire to be a theorist (Kuper, 1983). Another facet of the same breakthrough is that it now became interesting and valid to study a living 'primitive' people *per se*, instead of as a mere token of ages past, or as the repository of survivals of interest to a prehistorian. The day-to-day life of exotic communities came to the fore as a scientific object, which in turn demanded from the anthropologist both proficiency in the vernacular and a full involvement in the lives of the tribesmen. Malinowski's special talent for 'participant observation' helped demonstrate the value of a method which had been proposed but never previously applied. His diary, published after his death, reflects the hardships he had to suffer, and so perhaps suggests why the advent of participant observation was so long delayed.

The results yielded by participant observation were impressive. No tribal community had ever been described as thoroughly as Malinowski described the Trobrianders. In part, however, his success was due also to his literary talent. His model was his great Anglo-Polish predecessor, Joseph Conrad, and he strove for something of the insight of a sensitive novelist into the minds of the Trobrianders. His discovery that Melanesian gardens were works of art, and that labour and magic spent on subsistence agriculture cannot be separated from aesthetic considerations (*Coral Gardens and Their Magic*, 1935), reflect the same spirit.

Argonauts of the Western Pacific (1922) was his most characteristic achievement. Besides providing an enduring lesson (and object-lesson) in an ethnographic methodology, the monograph offers a now classic description of a Melanesian exchange and trading system, the *kula*, which was to serve as the starting-point for most future debates on economic anthropology. At the same time it demonstrates Malinowski's literary skills and exemplifies his functionalism in action. One might even argue that in this case functionalism and literary form are virtually one and the same thing (Panoff, 1972).

At the LSE, Malinowski occupied a position somewhere between the ethnologist Seligman and the sociologists Westermarck and Hobhouse. He held joint seminars with them, but his charismatic personality impelled him to go his own way, attack the establishment, and recruit his own students for 'functionalism'. Though he wrote and lectured much on functionalism, he never succeeded in formulating a comprehensive theory (see *A Scientific Theory of Culture*, 1944). Instead he oscillated between crude biological platitudes (basic needs must be met) and absurdities (in a society everything necessarily operates). In fact Malinowski's theory was fortunately to remain immanent in his ethnography. Its main theme here was that cultures are integrated wholes which should not be dismembered for comparative purposes, any single aspect or institution being a riddle forever unless it is illuminated by its cultural context. His analysis of the complex *kula* exchange system was the crucial vindication of this rule, and it has even been argued that Malinowski's functionalism was generated by the peculiarities of this Melanesian institution (see Jarvie, 1964). *Argonauts* had a seminal influence on Mauss (*Essai sur le don*, 1925), and it inspired many anthropologists, but it failed to establish a functionalist school of anthropology.

Given his views on culture and social change, Malinowski was inevitably opposed to both historical and diffusionist approaches, at least at the theoretical level. His insistence that cultures were working wholes laid him open to the charge that he neglected the disruptive impact of colonial rule and the collapse of tribal societies, and even that he was an accomplice of colonialism. While his missionary zeal for functionalism led him to advise a few colonial officials, his work eventually had a very different impact, as is evident today. It shook European certainties about the pre-eminence of Western civilization, and (as citizens of now-independent New Guinea have repeatedly told contemporary anthropologists) it helped Melanesians regain a sense of dignity and identity, after the humiliations inflicted by their oppressors.

Michel Panoff
Centre National de la Recherche Scientifique, Paris

References
Drucker-Brown, S. (ed.) (1982), *Malinowski in Mexico*, London.
Jarvie, I. C. (1964), *The Revolution in Anthropology*, London.
Kuper, A. (1983), *Anthropology and Anthropologists: The Modern British School*, London.
Malinowski, B. (1922), *Argonauts of the Western Pacific*, London.
Malinowski, B. (1935), *Coral Gardens and their Magic*, London.
Malinowski, B. (1944), *A Scientific Theory of Culture*, Chapel Hill, North Carolina.
Malinowski, B. (1967), *A Diary in the Strict Sense of the Term*, London.
Mauss, M. (1954 [1925]), *The Gift*, London.
Panoff, M. (1972), *Bronislaw Malinowski*, Paris.

Further Reading
Firth, R. (ed.) (1957), *Man and Culture; An Evaluation of the Work of Bronislaw Malinowski*, London.
Uberoi, S. (1962), *Politics of the Kula Ring*, London.
Weiner, A. (1976), *Women of Value, Men of Renown: New Perspectives on Trobriand Exchange*, Austin, Texas.
Young, M. (ed.) (1979), *The Ethnography of Malinowski*, London.

Malthus, Thomas Robert (1766–1834)

Thomas Robert Malthus, one of the leading figures of the English classical school of political economy, was born near Guildford, Surrey. He entered Jesus College, Cambridge in 1784, graduated in mathematics in 1788 and was a fellow of his college from 1793 until his marriage in 1804. From 1805 until his death he served as professor of history and political economy at Haileybury College, then recently founded by the East India Company for the education of its cadets. The tranquillity of his life and the gentleness of his personality contrasted sharply with the harshness of his doctrines and the fierce controversies which they evoked.

Malthus's most famous contribution to classical political economy was the theory stated in 1798 in his *Essay on the Principle of Population*: 'Population, when unchecked, increases in a geometrical ratio. Subsistence increases only in an arithmetical ratio . . . . By that law of our nature which makes food necessary to the life of man, the effects of these two unequal powers must be kept equal. This implies a strong and constantly operating check on population from the difficulty of subsistence.'

In the first edition of his *Essay*, Malthus identified the checks to population as either preventive (keeping new population from growing up) or positive (cutting down existing population); hence followed the bleak conclusion 'that the superior power of population cannot be checked without producing misery or vice'. In the second, much enlarged, edition (1803) he extended the category of preventive checks to include 'moral restraint', thus admitting the possibility of population being contained without either misery or vice as necessary consequences. Even when thus modified, Malthus's doctrine still seemed to impose narrow limits on the possibilities of economic growth and social improvement. Idealists and reformers consequently railed against the implications of the theory, but his fellow economists accepted both its premises and its logic, and for most of the nineteenth century it remained one of the accepted 'principles of political economy'.

Malthus was also one of the first economists to state (in 1815) the theory of rent as a surplus, generally associated with the name of his friend and contemporary, David Ricardo. Both were followers of Adam Smith but Malthus's development of Smith's system differed significantly from Ricardo's, notably in his use of demand and supply analysis in the theory of value as against Ricardo's emphasis on labour-quantities, and his explanation of the 'historical fall' of profits in terms of competition of capitals rather than by the 'necessity of resort to inferior soils' which Ricardo stressed.

Since the time of Keynes the difference between Malthus and Ricardo which has attracted most attention relates to 'the possibility of a general glut'. In a lengthy debate Ricardo argued the validity of Say's Law, that 'supply creates its own demand', while Malthus asserted the possibility of over-saving (and investment) creating an excess supply of commodities. Ricardo's superior logic won acceptance for Say's Law for over a century, but modern economists now see Malthus's *Principles of Political Economy* as containing many insights which anticipate twentieth-century theories of investment and employment.

R. D. Collison Black
Queen's University of Belfast

References
Malthus, T. R. (1798), *An Essay on the Principle of Population*, London. (Second edn, 1803.)
Malthus, T. R. (1820), *The Principles of Political Economy, considered with a View to their Practical Application*, London. (Second edn, 1836.)

Further Reading
James, P. (1979), *Population Malthus, His Life and Times*, London.
Petersen, W. (1979), *Malthus*, London.

Mannheim, Karl (1893–1947)

Karl Mannheim, one of the founders of the sociology of knowledge (*Wissensoziologie*), was born in Budapest in 1893, and held academic posts at the universities of Heidelberg and Frankfurt and The London School of Economics and Political Science. He died in London in 1947. His biography, which is one of intellectual and forced geographical migration, falls into three phases: Hungarian (to 1920), German (1920–33) and British (1933–47). Among the important intellectual influences on

Mannheim are Georg Lukács, Georg Simmel, Edmund Husserl, Karl Marx, Alfred and Max Weber, Max Scheler and Wilhelm Dilthey. Through these and other writers, German historicism, Marxism, phenomenology, sociology and, later, Anglo-Saxon pragmatism became decisive influences on his work.

The writings of Mannheim's Hungarian phase – primarily on literary and philosophical themes – demonstrate a first attempt to go beyond the German idealist view of history and society. The German phase was Mannheim's most productive; he gradually turned from philosophy to sociology (although he never completely abandoned philosophical questions), inquiring into the possible social roots of culture and knowledge. Many of his essays on the sociology of knowledge have become classics. Mannheim's.most influential work, *Ideologie und Utopie*, Bonn, 1929 (English translation, *Utopia*, London, 1936), was also written during this period. These writings became the focus of a vigorous intellectual dispute in Germany towards the end of the Weimar Republic, in part because of what many critics regarded as the 'relativistic' implications of Mannheim's sociology. Mannheim, however, claimed that his ideas prepared the ground for a new comprehensive perspective capable of transcending the fragmented and partial social and political views held up till then. He maintained that the 'socially unattached' intelligentsia had an instrumental role in developing such a synthesis.

Mannheim's British phase was in some ways foreshadowed by the more practical orientation already evident in his work prior to his emigration from Germany. Applied sociology should be concerned with the comprehensive analysis of the structure of modern society, especially through democratic social planning, in which education should occupy a central role.

The original themes of the sociology of knowledge were formulated in Germany during a period of major social crisis, and may be seen, as Mannheim himself saw them, as the product of one of the greatest social, political and economic dissolutions and transformations, accompanied by the highest form of reflexivity, self-consciousness and self-criticism. The renewed interest in the problems posed by the sociology of knowledge reflects a similar crisis in our own period and may therefore be said to owe more to the course of events than to analytical progress.

Volker Meja
Memorial University
St John's, Newfoundland

Nico Stehr
University of Alberta, Edmonton

Further Reading
A.
Other Works by Mannheim in translation include:
Man and Society in an Age of Reconstruction, London, 1941.
Essays on Sociology and Social Psychology, London, 1953.
Essays on the Sociology of Culture, London, 1956.
Systematic Sociology: An Introduction to the Study of Society, London.
B.
Kettler, D., Meja, V. and Stehr, N. (1984), *Karl Mannheim*, London.
Loader, C. (1985), *Culture, Politics and Planning: The Intellectual Development of Karl Mannheim*, London.
Simonds, A. P. (1978), *Karl Mannheim's Sociology of Knowledge*, Oxford.
Wolff, K. H. (ed.) (1971), *From Karl Mannheim*, London.

Marcuse, Herbert (1898–1979)

A German-American philosopher and social theorist, Herbert Marcuse was associated with the Frankfurt School. He developed his own version of 'critical Marxism' which attempted to update the Marxian theory in response to changing historical conditions from the 1920s through to the 1970s. Marcuse gained notoriety as 'father of the New Left' in the 1960s when he was perceived as both an influence on and defender of the so-called 'New Left' in the United States and Europe.

Marcuse's first published article in 1928 in Weimar Germany attempted a synthesis of phenomenology, existentialism and Marxism which decades later would be carried out again by various existential and phenomenological Marxists. He also published in 1932 the first major review of Marx's *Economic and Philosophical Manuscripts of 1844* and anticipated the tendency to revise interpretations of Marxism from the standpoint of the works of the early Marx. His study of *Hegel's Ontology and Theory of Historicity* (1932) contributed to the Hegel renaissance taking place in Europe.

In 1934 Marcuse fled from Nazism and emigrated to the United States where he lived for the rest of his life. His first major work in English, *Reason and Revolution* (1941), traced the genesis of the ideas of Hegel, Marx and modern social theory. It demonstrated the similarities between Hegel and Marx, and introduced many English-speaking readers to Hegel, Marx and dialectical thinking. Marcuse worked for the US government from 1941–50 and claimed that his involvement was motivated by a desire to struggle against fascism. He later returned to intellectual work and in 1955 published *Eros and Civilization* which attempted an audacious synthesis of Marx and Freud and sketched the outlines of a non-repressive society.

Marcuse next published a critical study of the Soviet Union in 1958 (*Soviet Marxism*) and a wide-ranging critique of both advanced capitalist and communist societies in *One-Dimensional Man* (1964). This book theorized the decline of revolutionary potential in capitalist societies and the development of new forms of social control. It was severely criticized by orthodox Marxists and theorists of various political and theoretical commitments. Despite its pessimism, the book influenced many in the New Left as it articulated their growing dissatisfaction with both capitalist societies and Soviet communist societies. *One-Dimensional Man* was followed by a series of books and articles which articulated New Left politics and critiques of capitalist societies in 'Repressive Tolerance' (1965), *An Essay on Liberation* (1969), and *Counterrevolution and Revolt* (1972). Marcuse also dedicated much of his work to aesthetics, and his final book, *The Aesthetic Dimension* (1979), briefly summarizes his defence of the emancipatory potential of aesthetic form in so-called 'high culture'. His work in philosophy and social theory generated fierce controversy and polemics, and most critical studies of his work are highly tendentious and frequently sectarian. Although much of the controversy involved his critiques of contemporary capitalist societies and defence of radical social change, in retrospect, Marcuse left behind a complex and many-sided body of work comparable to the legacies of Ernst Bloch, Georg Lukács, T. W. Adorno and Walter Benjamin.

Douglas Kellner
University of Texas, Austin

Further Reading
Kellner, D. (1984), *Herbert Marcuse and the Crisis of Marxism*, Berkeley and Los Angeles.
See also: *Habermas*.

Marshall, Alfred (1842–1924)

The English economist Alfred Marshall was one of the dominant figures in his subject during the late nineteenth and early twentieth centuries. His 1890 masterwork, the *Principles of Economics*, introduced many of the tools and concepts economists use in price theory even today. The book also presented an influential synthesis of received theories of value and distribution.

Marshall was born on 26 July 1842 at Bermondsey, a London suburb, his father William being at the time a clerk at the Bank of England. Alfred was educated at Merchant Taylors' School, revealing there his aptitude for mathematics. Somewhat against his father's wishes, he entered St John's College, Cambridge, to embark on the mathematics tripos, graduating in 1865 as Second Wrangler. He was then elected to a Fellowship at St John's. Soon abandoning mathematics for ethics and psychology, his growing interest in social questions led him to economics, which by 1870 he had chosen as his life's work. He took a prominent part in the teaching for the moral sciences tripos until leaving Cambridge in 1877 on marriage to his one-time student, Mary Paley.

Although Marshall published little, these early years were the formative ones for his economic views. He mastered the classical tradition of A. Smith, D. Ricardo and J. S. Mill and was encouraged towards a mathematical approach by early acquaintance with the works of A. A. Cournot and J. H. von Thünen. Priority for the marginal 'revolution' of the early 1870s clearly goes to W. S. Jevons, L. Walras and C. Menger, but Marshall had been working on similar lines before 1870. However, his attitude towards these new developments remained somewhat grudging, and he was always reluctant to publish merely theoretical exercises. More general influences significant in this early period were those of H. Sidgwick (perhaps more personal than intellectual), H. Spencer and G. W. F. Hegel. The last two, in tune with the spirit of the age, led Marshall towards an organic or biological view of society. He found the early socialist writers emotionally appealing, but unrealistic in their views as to evolutionary possibilities for human nature. Somewhat later, he saw merit in the programme of the German Historical School of economics, but deplored its anti-theoretical stance. It was from these and other varied sources, including energetic factual enquiry, that he distilled and long pondered his subtle, complex and eclectic approach to economic questions.

Marshall returned to Cambridge in 1885, from exile in Bristol and Oxford, as professor of political economy and the acknowledged leader of British economists. He had already commenced work on his *Principles*. His first two significant publications had appeared in 1879. One was a selection of theoretical chapters from a never-completed book on foreign trade, printed by Sidgwick for private circulation under the title *The Pure Theory of Foreign Trade: The Pure Theory of Domestic Values*. These superb chapters did much to establish Marshall's reputation among British economists. The other was an ostensible primer, the *Economics of Industry*, co-authored by his wife, which foreshadowed many of the ideas of the *Principles*. It was this work that first brought Marshall's views to the attention of foreign economists.

Marshall resided in Cambridge for the rest of his life, resigning his chair in 1908 to devote all his energies to writing. The years were externally uneventful and dominated by the internal struggle to give vent and adequate expression to his vast store of knowledge. The first volume of what was intended as a two-volume work on *Principles of Economics* appeared in 1890 and cemented his international reputation. Although this first volume went through eight editions, little progress was made with the second volume, which had been intended to cover money, business fluctuations, international trade, labour and industrial organization. Among the famous concepts introduced in the *Principles*, as it soon came to be known, were consumer surplus, long and short-period analysis, the representative firm, and external economies. The elucidation and criticism of these and related concepts were to occupy English-speaking economists for many years.

In 1903, under the influence of the tariff agitation, Marshall embarked on a tract for the times on national industries and international trade. This too grew vastly in his hands and, when it eventually appeared in 1919, *Industry and Trade* realized his earlier intentions only incompletely. The book's tone, historical and descriptive rather than theoretical, has made it better known among economic historians than among economists. The years that remained were devoted to a last-ditch effort to salvage some of his unpublished earlier work. Some important early contributions to the theories of money and international trade at last saw the light in *Money, Credit and Commerce* in 1923, but the book remains an unsatisfactory pastiche. Marshall died on 13 July 1924 at the age of eighty-one having failed to do much that he had wished, yet still having achieved greatness.

During his years as professor, Marshall was instrumental in establishing the specialized study of his subject at Cambridge, which eventually became a leading centre for economic study and research. As teacher and adviser he inspired his students with his own high and unselfish ambitions for his subject. Among the several students who were to attain professional prominence and influence, A. C. Pigou and J. M. Keynes should especially be mentioned. Nationally, Marshall was a public figure and played an important role in government inquiries and in the professionalization of economics in Britain. Internationally, he was cosmopolitan in outlook and kept close contact with economists and economic events abroad.

Marshall was anxious to influence events and deeply concerned for the future of Britain, and especially of its poorer and less privileged citizens. Yet he preferred to remain above the fray of current controversy, whether scientific or concerned with policy, trusting that 'constructive' work and patient study would provide the surer if slower route towards the desired goals. His desire for historical continuity and the avoidance of controversy led him frequently to underplay the novelty of his ideas and to exaggerate their closeness to those of his classical forebears.

John K. Whitaker
University of Virginia

Further Reading
Guillebaud, C. W. (ed.) (1965), *Marshall's Principles of Economics, Variorum Edition*, London.
Pigou, A. C. (ed.) (1925), *Memorials of Alfred Marshall*, London.
Whitaker, J. K. (ed.) (1975), *The Early Economic Writings of Alfred Marshall, 1867–1890*, London.

Marx, Karl Heinrich (1818–83)

Marx was a German social scientist and revolutionary, whose analysis of capitalist society laid the theoretical basis for the political movement bearing his name. Marx's main contribution lies in his emphasis on the role of the economic factor – the changing way in which people have reproduced their means of subsistence – in shaping the course of history. This perspective has had a considerable influence on the whole range of social sciences.

Karl Heinrich Marx was born in the town of Trier in the

Moselle district of the Prussian Rhineland on 5 May 1818. He came from a long line of rabbis on both his father's and his mother's sides. His father, a respected lawyer in Trier, had accepted baptism as a Protestant in order to be able to pursue his career. The atmosphere of Marx's home was permeated by the Enlightenment, and he assimilated a certain amount of romantic and early socialist ideas from Baron von Westphalen – to whose daughter, Jenny, he became engaged in 1835 and later married. In the same year he left the local gymnasium, or high school, and enrolled at the University of Bonn. He transferred the following year to the University of Berlin, where he soon embraced the dominant philosophy of Hegelianism. Intending to become a university teacher, Marx obtained his doctorate in 1841 with a thesis on post-Aristotelian Greek philosophy.

From 1837 Marx had been deeply involved in the Young Hegelian movement. This group espoused a radical critique of Christianity and, by implication, a liberal opposition to the Prussian autocracy. Finding a university career closed to him by the Prussian government, Marx moved into journalism. In October 1842 he became editor, in Cologne, of the influential *Rheinische Zeitung*, a liberal newspaper backed by Rhenish industrialists. Marx's incisive articles, particularly on economic questions, induced the government to close the paper, and he decided to emigrate to France.

Paris was then the centre of socialist thought and on his arrival at the end of 1843, Marx rapidly made contact with organized groups of emigré German workers and with various sects of French socialists. He also edited the shortlived *Deutschfranzösische Jahrbücher*, which was intended to form a bridge between nascent French socialism and the ideas of the German radical Hegelians. It was also in Paris that Marx first formed his lifelong partnership with Friedrich Engels. During the first few months of his stay in Paris, Marx rapidly became a convinced communist and set down his views in a series of manuscripts known as the *Ökonomisch-philosophische Manuskripte* (*Economic and Philosophic Manuscripts of 1844*). Here he outlined a humanist conception of communism, influenced by the philosophy of Ludwig Feuerbach and based on a contrast between the alienated nature of labour under capitalism and a communist society in which human beings freely developed their nature in co-operative production. For the first time there appeared together, if not yet united, what Engels described as the three constituent elements in Marx's thought – German idealist philosophy, French socialism, and English economics. It is above all these Manuscripts which (in the West at least) reorientated many people's interpretation of Marx – to the extent of their even being considered as his major work. They were not published until the early 1930s and did not attract public attention until after the Second World War; certain facets of the Manuscripts were soon assimilated to the existentialism and humanism then so much in vogue, and presented an altogether more attractive basis for non-Stalinist socialism than textbooks on dialectical materialism.

Seen in their proper perspective, these Manuscripts were in fact no more than a starting-point for Marx – an initial, exuberant outpouring of ideas to be taken up and developed in subsequent economic writings, particularly in the *Grundrisse* (1857–8) and in *Das Kapital* (1867). In those later works the themes of the '1844 Manuscripts' would certainly be pursued more systematically, in greater detail, and against a much more solid economic and historical background; but the central inspiration or vision was to remain unaltered: man's alienation in capitalist society, and the possibility of his emancipation – of his controlling his own destiny through communism.

Because of his political journalism, Marx was expelled from Paris at the end of 1844. He moved (with Engels) to Brussels, where he stayed for the next three years. He visited England, then the most advanced industrial country in the world, where Engels's family had cotton-spinning interests in Manchester. While in Brussels, Marx devoted himself to an intensive study of history. This he set out in a manuscript known as *The German Ideology* (also published posthumously); its basic thesis was that 'the nature of individuals depends on the material conditions determining their production'. Marx traced the history of the various modes of production and predicted the collapse of the present one – capitalism – and its replacement by communism.

At the same time that he was engaged in this theoretical work, Marx became involved in political activity and in writing polemics, as in *Misère de la Philosophie* (1847) (*The Poverty of Philosophy*), against what he considered to be the unduly idealistic socialism of Pierre Joseph Proudhon. He joined the Communist League, an organization of German emigré workers with its centre in London, for which he and Engels became the major theoreticians. At a conference of the league in London at the end of 1847, Marx and Engels were commissioned to write a *Manifest der kommunistischen Partei* (1848) (*Manifesto of the Communist Party*), a declaration that was to become the most succinct expression of their views. Scarcely was the *Manifesto* published when the 1848 wave of revolutions broke in Europe.

Early in 1848, Marx moved back to Paris, where the revolution had first erupted. He then went on to Germany where he founded, again in Cologne, the *Neue Rheinische Zeitung*. This widely influential newspaper supported a radical democratic line against the Prussian autocracy. Marx devoted his main energies to its editorship, since the Communist League had been virtually disbanded. With the ebbing of the revolutionary tide, however, Marx's paper was suppressed. He sought refuge in London in May 1849, beginning the 'long, sleepless night of exile' that was to last for the rest of his life.

On settling in London, Marx grew optimistic about the imminence of a fresh revolutionary outbreak in Europe, and he rejoined the rejuvenated Communist League. He wrote two lengthy pamphlets on the 1848 revolution in France and its aftermath, entitled *Die Klassenkämpfe in Frankreich 1848 bis 1850* (1850) (*The Class Struggles in France*) and *Der achzehnte Brumaire des Louis Bonaparte* (1852) (*The Eighteenth Brumaire of Louis Bonaparte*). But he soon became convinced that 'a new revolution is possible only in consequence of a new crisis', and devoted himself to the study of political economy to determine the causes and conditions of this crisis.

During the first half of the 1850s the Marx family lived in three-room lodgings in the Soho quarter of London and experienced considerable poverty. The Marxes already had four children on their arrival in London, and two more were soon born. Of these, only three survived the Soho period. Marx's major source of income at this time (and later) was Engels, who was drawing a steadily increasing income from his father's cotton business in Manchester. This was supplemented by weekly articles he wrote as foreign correspondent for the *New York Daily Tribune*. Legacies in the late 1850s and early 1860s eased Marx's financial position somewhat, but it was not until 1869 that he had a sufficient and assured income settled on him by Engels.

Not surprisingly, Marx's major work on political economy made slow progress. By 1857–8 he had produced a mammoth 800-page manuscript – a rough draft of a work that he intended should deal with capital, landed property, wage-labour, the state, foreign trade, and the world market. This manuscript, known as *Grundrisse* (or 'Outlines'), was not published until 1941. In the early 1860s he broke off his work to compose three large volumes, entitled *Theorien über den Mehrwert* (1861–3) (*Theories of Surplus Value*), that discussed his predecessors in political economy, particularly Adam Smith and David Ricardo.

It was not until 1867 that Marx was able to publish the first results of his work in Volume One of *Das Kapital*, devoted to a study of the capitalist process of production. Here he elaborated his version of the labour theory of value, and his conception of surplus value and exploitation that would ultimately lead to a falling rate of profit and the collapse of capitalism. Volumes Two and Three were largely finished in the 1860s, but Marx worked on the manuscripts for the rest of his life. They were published posthumously by Engels. In his major work, Marx's declared aim was to analyse 'the birth, life and death of a given social organism and its replacement by another, superior order'. In order to achieve this aim, Marx took over the concepts of the 'classical' economists that were still the generally accepted tool of economic analysis, and used them to draw very different conclusions. Ricardo had made a distinction between use-value and exchange-value. The exchange-value of an object was something separate from its price and consisted of the amount of labour embodied in the objects of production, though Ricardo thought that the price in fact tended to approximate to the exchange-value. Thus – in contradistinction to later analyses – the value of an object was determined by the circumstances of production rather than those of demand. Marx took over these concepts, but, in his attempt to show that capitalism was not static but an historically relative system of class exploitation, supplemented Ricardo's views by introducing the idea of surplus-value. Surplus-value was defined as the difference between the value of the products of labour and the cost of producing that labour-power, that is, the labourer's subsistence; for the exchange-value of labour-power was equal to the amount of labour necessary to reproduce that labour-power and this was normally much lower than the exchange-value of the products of that labour-power.

The theoretical part of Volume One divides very easily into three sections. The first section is a rewriting of the *Zur Kritik der politischen Ökonomie* (1859) (*Critique of Political Economy*) and analyses commodities, in the sense of external objects that satisfy human needs, and their value. Marx established two sorts of value – use-value, or the utility of something, and exchange-value which was determined by the amount of labour incorporated in the object. Labour was also of a twofold nature according to whether it created use-values or exchange-values. Because 'the exchange-values of commodities must be capable of being expressed in terms of something common to them all', and the only thing they shared was labour, then labour must be the source of value. But since evidently some people worked faster or more skilfully than others, this labour must be a sort of average 'socially necessary' labour time. There followed a difficult section on the form of value, and the first chapter ended with an account of commodities as exchange-values, which he described as the 'fetishism of commodities' in a passage that recalls the account of alienation in the *Pariser Manuskripte* (1844) (*Paris Manuscripts*) and (even more) the *Note on James Mill*. 'In order,' said Marx here, 'to find an analogy, we must have recourse to the mist-enveloped regions of the religious world.

In that world the productions of the human brain appear as independent beings endowed with life, and entering into relation both with one another and the human race. So it is in the world of commodities with the products of men's hands.' The section ended with a chapter on exchange and an account of money as the means for the circulation of commodities, the material expression for their values and the universal measure of value.

The second section was a small one on the transformation of money into capital. Before the capitalist era, people had sold commodities for money in order to buy more commodities. In the capitalist era, instead of selling to buy, people had bought to sell dearer: they had bought commodities with their money in order, by means of those commodities, to increase their money.

In the third section Marx introduced his key notion of surplus value, the idea that Engels characterized as Marx's principal 'discovery' in economics. Marx made a distinction between *constant* capital which was 'that part of capital which is represented by the means of production, by the raw material, auxiliary material and instruments of labour, and does not, in the process of production, undergo any quantitative alteration of value' and *variable* capital. Of this Marx said: 'That part of capital, represented by labour power, does, in the process of production, undergo an alteration of value. It both reproduces the equivalent of its own value, and also produces an excess, a surplus value, which may itself vary, may be more or less according to the circumstances.' This variation was the rate of surplus value around which the struggle between workers and capitalists centred. The essential point was that the capitalist got the worker to work longer than was merely sufficient to embody in his product the value of his labour power: if the labour power of the worker (roughly what it cost to keep him alive and fit) was £4 a day and the worker could embody £4 of value in the product on which he was working in eight hours, then, if he worked ten hours, the last two hours would yield surplus value – in this case £1.

Thus surplus value could only arise from variable capital,

not from constant capital, as labour alone created value. Put very simply, Marx's reason for thinking that the rate of profit would decrease was that, with the introduction of machinery, labour time would become less and thus yield less surplus value. Of course, machinery would increase production and colonial markets would absorb some of the surplus, but these were only palliatives and an eventual crisis was inevitable. These first nine chapters were complemented by a masterly historical account of the genesis of capitalism which illustrates better than any other writing Marx's approach and method. Marx particularly made pioneering use of official statistical information that came to be available from the middle of the nineteenth century onwards.

Meanwhile, Marx devoted much time and energy to the First International – to whose General Council he was elected on its foundation in 1864. This was one of the reasons he was so delayed in his work on *Das Kapital*. He was particularly active in preparing for the annual congresses of the International and in leading the struggle against the anarchist wing of the International led by Mikhail Bakunin. Although Marx won this contest, the transfer of the seat of the General Council from London to New York in 1872 – a move that Marx supported – led to the swift decline of the International. The most important political event during the existence of the International was the Paris Commune of 1871, when the citizens of Paris, in the aftermath of the Franco-Prussian war, rebelled against their government and held the city for two months. On the bloody suppression of this rebellion, Marx wrote one of his most famous pamphlets – entitled *Address on The Civil War in France* (1871) – which was an enthusiastic defence of the activities and aims of the Commune.

During the last decade of his life Marx's health declined considerably, and he was incapable of the sustained efforts of creative synthesis that had so obviously characterized his previous work. Nevertheless, he managed to comment substantially on contemporary politics in Germany and Russia. In Germany he opposed, in his *Randglossen zum Programm der deutschen Arbeiterpartei* (1875) (*Critique of the Gotha Programme*), the tendency of his followers Wilhelm Leibknecht and August Bebel to compromise with the state socialism of Ferdinand Lassalle in the interest of a united socialist party. In Russia, in correspondence with Vera Sassoulitch, he contemplated the possibility of Russia's bypassing the capitalist stage of development and building communism on the basis of the common ownership of land characteristic of the village council, or *mir*. Marx, however, was increasingly dogged by ill health, and he regularly travelled to European spas and even to Algeria in search of recuperation. The deaths of his eldest daughter and of his wife clouded the last years of his life, and he died in London on 13 March, 1883.

The influence of Marx, so narrow during his lifetime, expanded enormously after his death. This influence was at first evident in the growth of the Social Democratic Party in Germany, but reached world-wide dimensions following the success of the Bolsheviks in Russia in 1917. Paradoxically, although the main thrust of Marx's thought was to anticipate that a proletarian revolution would inaugurate the transition to socialism in advanced industrial countries, Marxism was most successful in developing or Third World countries, such as Russia or China. Since the problems of these countries are primarily agrarian and the initial development of an industrial base, they are necessarily far removed from what were Marx's immediate concerns. On a more general level, over the whole range of the social sciences, Marx's materialist conception of history and his analysis of capitalist society have made him probably the most influential figure of the twentieth century.

David McLellan
University of Kent

Further Reading

Avineri, S. (1968), *The Social and Political Thought of Karl Marx*, Cambridge.

Cohen, G. (1978), *Karl Marx's Theory of History: A Defence*, Oxford.

Marx, K. (1977), *Selected Writings*, ed. D. McLellan, Oxford.

McLellan, D. (1974), *Karl Marx: His Life and Thought*, New York.

Ollman, B. (1971), *Alienation, Marx's Conception of Man in Capitalist Society*, Cambridge.

Plamenatz, J. (1975), *Karl Marx's Philosophy of Man*, Oxford.

Suchting, W. (1983), *Marx: An Introduction*, Brighton.

See also: *Engels*.

Mauss, Marcel (1872–1950)

Marcel Mauss, the French sociologist, trained originally as an academic philosopher at the Universities of Paris and Bordeaux. He never took a doctorate or had a normal teaching career, but was one of the first professional researchers in the social sciences. In 1898, his uncle, Émile Durkheim, founded the journal, *Année Sociologique* and put Mauss in charge of religious studies for the publication. Mauss's focus extended to all religious practices, especially those of ancient and contemporary archaic societies, but he later shifted to problems of comparative social anthropology in general. Although an armchair scholar himself, he is regarded as the founder of the French school of field ethnology whose later members included Marcel Griaule, Louis Dumont and Claude Lévi-Strauss. Mauss was appointed to a lectureship on the 'religions of peoples without a civilization' at the École Pratique des Hautes Études in 1901, and later taught at the Ethnological Institute of Paris University, which he co-founded in 1925. He moved to the Collège de France in 1931.

Mauss's published work included no books but a large variety of essays and critical studies. It can be divided roughly into two periods – before and after World War I. In the first period (when Durkheim was still alive), Mauss's contributions were mainly on comparative religion and included studies (with Hubert) on sacrifice (*Essai sur la nature et la fonction du sacrifice*, 1899; *Sacrifice: Its Nature and Function*, 1964); magic (*Equisse d'une théorie générale de la magie*, 1904; *A General Theory of Magic*, 1972), and an introductory essay on primitive religion (*Mélanges d'histoire des religions*, 1909). He also produced an unfinished doctoral thesis on prayer (*La Prière*, 1909). His most famous studies of this period were (with Durkheim) *De quelques formes primitives de classification: contribution à l'étude des représentations collectives*, 1903 (*Primitive Classification*, 1963), and *Essai sur les variations saisonnières des sociétés Eskimos: étude de morphologie sociale*, 1950 (*Seasonal Variations of the Eskimo: A Study in Social Morphology*, 1979). These two studies foreshadowed major theoretical insights developed in his later work about the functional inter-relations between the material conditions of societies (seasons, climate, physical organization of camps) and the 'collective representations' (as expressed in religious practice and mental categories).

After World War I, Mauss was invested with the dual task of safeguarding Durkheim's scholarly heritage (aiming at the organization of a unified social science) while continuing his own specialized research, which focused on problems of social cohesion in archaic societies. A number of preliminary enquiries culminated in his famous *Essai sur le don*, 1925 (*The Gift*, 1954). In it, he analysed the exchange of gifts, whether utilitarian or symbolic, as a 'total social phenomenon' with economic, religious and moral implications. Systems of reciprocities secure peace among neighbours, maintain the stability of the social structure, and legitimate social hierarchies. Other major statements in his later work stress the dominance of social patterns in the expression of individual feelings. In an article about civilization (1929), he stated clearly the arbitrary nature of collective values and representations, an essay which was markedly prestructural in flavour.

Victor Karady
Centre National de la Recherche Scientifique, Paris

Further Reading

Mauss, M. (1966), *M. Mauss, Sociologie et anthropologie*, 3rd edn, ed. G. Gurevitch and introduction by C. Lévi-Strauss, Paris.

Mauss, M. (1968–9), *Oeuvres*, 3 vols, introduction by V. Karady, Paris.

(These volumes contain the majority of Mauss's work.)

McLuhan, Marshall (1910–80)

McLuhan was for a time one of the most cited authors in the field of study of mass communication, following the publication of his two main books, *The Gutenberg Galaxy* (1962) and *Understanding Media* (1964). Moreover, he was probably as well known outside the circle of academic media specialists as within it. After a fairly conventional career as a teacher of literature, he became a spinner of theory and publicist for his ideas about the consequences for culture and society of changes in communication technology – from writing to print and from print to electronic media. Although his assessment of television happened to be especially topical in the 1960s, he was also continuing a North American (perhaps especially Canadian) tradition of interest in technology, communication and the new. He owed much of his central thesis to a forerunner and colleague at the University of Toronto, the economic historian Harold J. Innis, who had traced the connection between changes in communication technology in the ancient and medieval world and changing forms of political and social power. Innis argued that each medium had a 'bias' towards a certain kind of application, message and effect and thus, eventually, a bias towards a certain kind of society. A similar version of 'communication determinism' was elaborated by McLuhan, with particular stress on the difference between the pictorial medium of television, which involves the spectator imaginatively and sensorily, and the medium of print, with its linear, sequential logic and its bias towards rationalism and individualism.

McLuhan's dicta are often best remembered summarily by his own catch-phrase 'the medium is the message'. He was a controversial figure and it is impossible in a few words to strike an adequate balance in assessing his work. In the positive side were: a lively imagination; a striking and aphoristic turn of phrase; an ability to cross academic boundaries and synthesize his eclectic finds. Furthermore, he seems to have exerted charm as a person and influence as a teacher. The principal entry on the debit side is that he lacked any discernible system of thought or adherence to an established tradition of research method, so that his many ideas are often both questionable and untestable. It is still not clear whether or not he made a valid or original contribution to any precise understanding of media, yet he did call attention to the need to do this, at a good moment and in a way which could not be ignored. This may well remain his most lasting achievement after reality has overtaken his more fanciful predictions about the age of electronic communication. In respect of his own message, the manner of delivery may well have been more significant than the content.

Denis McQuail
University of Amsterdam

Further Reading
Miller, J. (1971), *McLuhan*, London.

Mead, George Herbert (1863–1931)

George Herbert Mead was an American philosopher whose works have had an enduring impact on sociological research and theory. He studied under William James at Harvard, and taught at the Universities of Michigan and Chicago. His posthumously published lectures from the University of Chicago on social psychology, collected in *Mind, Self and Society* (1934), represent his most critical social scientific work. Here, Mead presents a conceptual view of human action, interaction, and organization. This conceptualization represents a blending of general philosophical traditions, including utilitarianism, behaviourism, Darwinism and pragmatism, with specific concepts borrowed from such thinkers as Wilhelm Wundt, William James, Charles Peirce, Charles Horton Cooley, and John Dewey (with whom he founded the 'Chicago School' of pragmatism). In this synthesis, Mead argues that social life is a process of adaptation and adjustment to ongoing patterns of social organization, and that human capacities for symbol use, covert reflection, self-awareness, and self-control are learned responses to environmental pressures for regularized interaction. For Mead, the critical 'conditioned responses' among humans are the behavioural capacities for gesturing, role taking, self and mind. Through conventional gestures, humans signal their course of action; through reading these gestures, humans can mutually assume each others' perspective as well as more 'generalized communities of attitudes' associated with a social context; through minded deliberations, humans can 'imaginatively rehearse' alternative lines of conduct and select the most appropriate response; through the capacities for self, humans can see themselves as objects of evaluation in a situation; and through such self-awareness and self-evaluation, they can control and regulate their responses.

Mead's view of human action, interaction, and organization is the conceptual basis for most modern formulations of interaction in the social sciences, including those in such diverse schools of thought as role theory, ethnomethodology, symbolic interactionism, interactionism, cognitive sociology, action theory, dramaturgy, phenomenology, and ethnoscience.

Jonathan H. Turner
University of California, Riverside

Reference
Mead, G. H. (1932), *Mind, Self, and Society from the Standpoint of a Social Behaviorist*, ed. C. Maris, Chicago.

Further Reading
Mead, G. H. (1938), *The Philosophy of the Act*, Chicago.
Natanson, M. (1956), *The Social Dynamics of George H. Mead*, Washington.

Mead, Margaret (1901–78)

The 'favoured child' and eldest of an academic family, Margaret Mead was born in 1901 near Philadelphia, and was encouraged by her parents to believe that anyone could accomplish whatever he or she set out to do. She did her first degree at Barnard College, New York, and as a graduate student in anthropology at Columbia University was greatly influenced by Franz Boas and Ruth Benedict. In anthropology she discovered the vehicle for critical, optimistic revisions of accepted conventions. From studies of child-rearing in the Pacific, through pioneering discussions of gender, into studies of culture change, cultural pluralism, complex societies, race relations, and 1960s drug culture, Mead regarded disciplinary findings in terms of usefulness to the ordinary individual facing everyday problems.

Mead entered the nature-nurture debate, on the side of nurture, learning and custom (see *Coming of Age in Samoa*, 1925). Recently her work has been criticized for an overemphasis on culture, and a need to prove a point that prevented her from doing effective fieldwork. Derek Freeman (*Margaret Mead and Samoa*, 1983) impugns her methods, her view of Samoa, and her argument for cultural determinism. He fails both to understand her purposes and her position; Mead did not neglect biology and in the nature-nurture debate emphasized the extent to which human beings are tied to 'rhythms of the body'. *Sex and Temperament* (1935) and *Male and Female* (1949) argued against universal sex-role stereotypes, while recalling the significance of gender distinctions.

Her confidence that people could choose alternative individual paths and create wiser sociocultural arrangements remained firm. During return trips to the Pacific, Mead monitored the passage of the Manus into a modern capitalist world; she urged that continuities be part of change (*Growing Up in New Guinea*, 1930; *New Lives for Old*, 1956). Mead's anthropologist was observer, advocate and adviser, and she readily adopted new strategies for each – tape-recorders and film for the field, introspection for the fieldworker (*Blackberry Winter*, 1972; *Letters from the Field*, 1977). World War II forced a concentration on complex nations and international problems. She commented on disarmament, feminism and iconoclastic youth culture. She died in 1978, having altered anthropology, revised the outlook of her country, and affected the fate of people around the world.

Judith Modell
Carnegie-Mellon University, Pittsburgh

Further Reading

American Anthropologist (1980), *In Memoriam Margaret Mead*, 82.

Brady. G. (ed.) (1983), 'Speaking in the name of the real: Freeman and Mead on Samoa', *American Anthropologist*, 85.

Mead, M. (1953), *The Study of Culture at a Distance*, Chicago.

Mead, M. (1959), *An Anthropologist at Work*, Boston.

Merton, Robert King (1910–)

Merton's reputation rests most securely on his having established the sociology of science as a field, with help, of course, from colleagues and students at Columbia (where he has taught since 1941) and elsewhere. His doctoral dissertation at Harvard, first published in 1938, made him famous. He took for granted that scientific theories develop to some extent by exploration of 'immanent' implications and problems, but he showed that science in the great seventeenth century developed in part from technological and economic interests and, beyond that, from the congruence that existed at several points between Puritan *religious* orientation and *positive* interest in science in general. His later work on priority disputes and multiple independent discoveries is also notable. Concerning his functional theory, he stresses that it draws particular attention to the different consequences of social structure for different segments of the population ('multiple manifest and latent functions and dysfunctions'). Some of his other concepts and terms have become widely known (for example, self-fulfilling prophecy, role set). In supposed opposition to the 'general' theory of Parsons, Merton has insisted on what he calls 'theoretical pluralism' – the inevitable and desirable co-existence of many theories in a field. (This misunderstanding is unfortunate.) Parsons was trying to relate to one another, explicitly and systematically, *analytically different types* of empirical system, cultural, social, and so on, as well as he could, of course, but *not* in the only possible way. In any case, Merton has contributed much to 'theories of the middle range' such as reference-group theory. He is the most frequently-cited living sociologist.

Harry M. Johnson
University of Illinois, Champaign-Urbana

Further Reading

Coser, L. A. (ed.) (1975), *The Idea of Social Structure. Essays in Honor of R. K. Merton*, New York.

Merton, R. K. (1935), *Science, Technology and Society in Seventeenth Century England*, reprinted 1970, New York.

Merton, R. K. (1968), *Social Theory and Social Structure*, enlarged edn, New York.

Merton, R. K. (1973), *The Sociology of Science: Theoretical and Empirical Investigations*, edited and with an Introduction by N. W. Storer, Chicago.

Michels, Robert (1876–1936)

Robert Michels made important contributions to the social sciences, especially to the sociology of organizations and political sociology. Born in Cologne in 1876 of a bourgeois-patrician family, Michels studied at the Sorbonne in Paris and at the Universities of Munich, Leipzig, and Halle, where he graduated in 1900 with a dissertation in history. Following his passionate political ideals, he soon joined the German Social Democratic Party and actively participated in the party congresses of 1903, 1904 and 1905. But he later became disillusioned with social democratic policies and leaders and resigned from the party. In the 1920s he showed some sympathy for the Fascist movement. Political activity in socialist quarters excluded Michels from an academic career in Germany, despite the support of influential friends such as Max Weber. In 1914 he thus moved to Basle, where he became professor of political economy; eventually in 1928 he was appointed professor of economics at the University of Perugia in Italy.

Michels wrote a number of books on subjects as different as democracy, socialism, revolution, class conflict, mass society, imperialism, intellectuals, élites, eugenics, sex and morality.

But his most important and long-lasting work is the monograph *Zur Soziologie des Parteiwesens in der modernen Demokratie*, first published in 1911 (English translation, *Political Parties*, New York, 1949). In his classic study of political parties, largely based on firsthand knowledge of the German and Italian socialist parties, Michels formulated his famous 'iron law of oligarchy'. According to it, strong oligarchic tendencies inevitably arise in any political organization, notwithstanding its democratic ideology and commitment. Organizational needs – initially the preservation and growth of the organization – in fact produce selection of leadership and development of specialized knowledge and skills. This in turn leads to the emergence of stable and self-perpetuating leaders, which gives birth to the 'domination of the elected over the electors, of the mandatories over the mandators, of the delegates over the delegators'. Michels's work has inspired and influenced later empirical research on organizations and political parties. The theories and insights of the German sociologist have been generally confirmed, though improved and specified more precisely.

Luisa Leonini
University of Milan

Further Reading

Linz, J. J. (1966), 'Michels e il suo contributo alla sociologia politica', in R. Michels, *La sociologia del partito politico nella democrazia moderna*, Bologna.

May, J. D. (1965), 'Democracy, organization, Michels', *American Political Science Review*, 59.

Mill, John Stuart (1806–73)

John Stuart Mill, the classic exponent of liberalism, was brought up on utilitarian principles by his father, James Mill, a close friend and associate of Bentham. His rigorous childhood education, described in his *Autobiography* (1873), involved a brilliant and precocious mastery of classical languages by the age of seven. For most of his working life he was a clerk at India House in London, though briefly a Member of Parliament.

He married Harriet Taylor whom he always claimed as his inspiration and intellectual partner.

Mill was a many-sided thinker and writer – a philosopher, social scientist and humanist. Amongst the subjects he treated were politics, ethics, logic and scientific method. Particular topics on which he wrote included the position of women (*The Subjection of Women*, 1869), constitutional reform (*Considerations on Representative Government*, 1861), and economics (*Principles of Political Economy*, 1848).

In *Utilitarianism* (1861) Mill expounded and defended the principle that the tendency of actions to promote happiness or its reverse is the standard of right and wrong. His version of utilitarianism was from a logical point of view flawed, and from a moral point of view enhanced, by the notion that some forms of happiness are more worthwhile than others. *On Liberty* (1859) is the classic argument for the claims of the individual against the state, and in it Mill makes an impassioned defence of the principles of liberty and toleration. This is sometimes seen as inconsistent with his basic utilitarianism, but Mill believed that principles like liberty and justice were themselves important social instruments for utility. This follows from his view of human nature, and in particular from his belief that self-determination and the exercise of choice are themselves part of a higher concept of happiness. Regarding toleration, Mill argued in favour of liberty of thought, speech and association, as well as for freedom to cultivate whatever lifestyle one chooses, subject only to the constraint of not harming others. It is often disputed whether there are any actions which do not affect other people in some way, but the distinction between other-regarding and self-regarding actions is an essential element of liberalism.

Mill applied these principles to education, defending a liberal and secular education. He considered compulsory education not an invasion of liberty but essential to it. However, he believed strongly that there should not be a 'state monopoly of education' but that state education should be one amongst a number of competing systems.

In *A System of Logic, Ratiocinative and Deductive* (1843), Mill defended a classical view of induction as empirical generalization and held that this can supply a model for both logical deduction and scientific method. In some respects this may be seen as a classic version of British empiricism, but because Mill was prepared to accept the uniformity of nature as a basic postulate, it is free from the sceptical consequences that this position sometimes seems to involve. Mill extended his discussion of methodology to cover the application of experimental method to social science and set out to provide 'a general science of man in society'. His argument is to be found in Book VI of *A System of Logic*, which has been called the most important contribution to the making of modern sociology until Durkheim's *Rules of Sociological Method*.

Brenda Cohen
University of Surrey

Further Reading
Gray, J. (1983), *Mill on Liberty: A Defence*, London.
Ryan, A. (1974), *J. S. Mill*, London.
Ten, C. L. (1980), *Mill on Liberty*, Oxford.

Montaigne, Michel de (1533–92)

Michel de Montaigne, an independent French thinker on moral and psychological matters and author of *Les Essais* (1580–92), was, until 1571, a minor magistrate in Périgueux near Bordeaux: in that year he retired from public life (although he was still to serve two terms of office as Mayor of Bordeaux, and take an active part in internal diplomatic negotiations during the Religious Wars), and devoted himself to private study. Initially he concentrated on ancient moral philosophy and history, but increasingly was attracted to the study of himself in a way strongly influenced by sceptical doctrines. It is for this self-study and for its political, religious and philosophical consequences that he is best known.

A firm opponent of systematic thought (and especially the still dominant neo-Scholasticism of his day), Montaigne set out to evolve a mode of acquiring knowledge about himself and about the world through an attentive form of introspection and self-examination. This led him to formulate a number of audacious propositions about politics and human psychology: political action, like human action, is seen by him to be a product of chance as well as design; vice and virtue are necessary components in both individuals and in the state (it is significant that Montaigne was one of the few sixteenth-century writers to recognize the acumen of Machiavelli); justice is conventional, not absolute; indeed, as the world consists in mutable beings set in a mutable environment, absolute principles can have no status in human affairs. This thoroughgoing relativism is combined at important points in the *Essais* (notably II,12) with quietism; Montaigne does not himself realize the subversive potential of his own thought, but remains throughout a political conservative and a strong proponent of Roman Catholicism.

Especially in Book III and in late additions to the *Essais*, Montaigne elaborates this relativistic and sceptical stance. Man is conceived of as an individual whose being (*'forme maîtresse'*) is never static and can only be perceived intuitively by others; but all men share the same rational and corporeal nature. A knowledge of one's corporeality is fundamental to self-understanding, and can also provide a means to the understanding of others. The body's functions and states are thus a matter of constant and uninhibited enquiry. Man exists in a world of conventions (*'coutumes'*), to which he attributes a moral or natural character which they do not intrinsically possess; these conventions can be transformed into dogma and lead to repression and tyranny. In two famous chapters of the *Essais* (I,31 and III,6) Montaigne draws attention to the treatment of the Amerindians by the Spaniards as an example of unjustifiable repression in the name of religion. Thus, for both negative and positive reasons, Montaigne comes to stress the need for tolerance in a new version of humanism which transcends education, class, nation and race.

The *Essais* are famous also for their unconstrained form and vigorous style. Montaigne's use of metaphor and free association as an antidote to formal rhetoric and systematic philosophy has left its mark on a number of subsequent thinkers (notably Diderot and Nietzsche); but his relativism, scepticism and project of self-study have also influenced later writers such as Descartes, Pascal and Rousseau.

Ian Maclean
The Queen's College, Oxford

Further Reading
Friedrich, H. (1967), *Montaigne*, 2nd edn, Berne.
Sayce, R. A. (1972), *The Essays of Montaigne. A Critical Exploration*, London.
Starobinski, J. (1982), *Montaigne en mouvement*, Paris.

Montesquieu, Charles Louis de Secondat (1689–1755)

Charles Louis de Secondat, Baron de Montesquieu was one of the major precursors of sociological thought. Born at La Brede near Bordeaux, he inherited the family vineyard estates and was able to use his wealth and training as a lawyer to travel widely both in France and abroad, and to ingratiate himself with the influential Parisian intellectual society of the first half of the eighteenth century. He became a major figure of Enlightenment thought and a perceptive critic of the society of the time.

His major works, the *Lettres Persanes* (1721), the *Considérations sur les causes de la grandeur des Romains et de leur décadence (1734) and the De l'esprit des lois* (1748) ostensibly deal with very different topics, but beneath the surface these can be shown to have a seriousness of purpose and concatenation of subject matter not easily detected. The *Lettres Persanes*, a novel about two Persian princes visiting Paris in the early years of the eighteenth century are, on closer examination, also a critical investigation into the major institutions of *ancien régime* society. The *Considérations*, a study which foreshadows Gibbons's *Decline and Fall of the Roman Empire*, is important in the history of ideas for its revolutionary historical methodology – *histoire raisonnée*, as it was called – making use of an embryonic ideal-type construct.

His third work, and by far his most important, the *De l'esprit des lois* is best known for its contribution to political thought. It continues the critique first developed in the *Lettres Persanes* of the social structure of the *ancien régime*: Montesquieu makes a powerful case for strengthening the role of the nobility and commercial interests as 'intermediate powers' between the absolutist monarchy and the mass of the people. Together with the argument for a 'separation of powers' which Montesquieu adapted from the British constitution, this provided a formula which, if it had been heeded, might have helped save France from the cataclysm that was to occur later in the century.

However, there has been perhaps too great an emphasis on the political aspects of the *Esprit*. Montesquieu, in the Preface to the work, asks the reader to 'approve or condemn the work as a whole', and if one reads beyond the introductory chapters, one finds a wealth of comparative data on all the major institutions of society – economic, belief and value systems, family and kinship systems – with evidence drawn both from his and others' researches on a wide range of societies, plus considerable historical and anthropological material. In this sense, it is true to say that the *De l'esprit des lois* is the first major essay in comparative sociology. Montesquieu brought to the fore the idea that each society, each social system, has its own natural law of development, and it follows that the objective of every student of society is to discover the real nature of that law. By viewing society as a set of interrelated elements, Montesquieu was putting forward an holistic interpretation of social structure akin to contemporary functionalism.

Functionalism is essentially a conservative doctrine, and Montesquieu is remembered as a founder of the conservative tradition in sociological thought. Through the works of Ferguson and Robertson, Bonald and de Maistre, Fustel de Coulanges and Durkheim, his ideas have passed into the mainstream of sociological thought.

John Alan Baum
Middlesex Polytechnic

Further Reading
Baum, J. A. (1979), *Montesquieu and Social Theory*, Oxford.
Shackleton, R. (1961), *Montesquieu: A Critical Biography*,
   Oxford.

Morgan, Lewis Henry (1818–81)

Morgan's reputation rested, in his day, on his contributions to American ethnography. After his death, his conjectural history of the evolution of the family was adopted – and vulgarized – by Engels. In this form it later became part of communist historical dogma.

As a lawyer in upstate New York. Morgan became interested in local Iroquois communities, and he published a useful account of Iroquois culture. The unfamiliar form of Iroquois kinship classification caught his attention, and when he discovered similar systems of classification among Indian tribes speaking different languages, he initiated a broader study, which grew into a world-wide comparison.

Morgan's initial interest in the origin of the Indian groups also gradually gave way to a concern with the development of civil institutions. He came to the conclusion that all kinship systems could be divided into two basic types – those based on monogamous marriage and the family, with appropriate 'descriptive' kinship terminologies; and those based on some form of 'group marriage', with appropriate 'classificatory' terminologies, in which members of the nuclear family were, logically enough, not distinguished from other kin. He developed a 'conjectural history' to account for this development from original promiscuity to modern monogamy. The underlying progressive impulse was, in his view, of a moral nature. This argument was developed at great length and with a wealth of illustrations in his *Systems of Consanguinity and Affinity of the Human Family* (1871).

At this stage Morgan came under the influence of the British school of anthropology, which was concerned especially with the development of political institutions from an original condition of kin-based anarchy to the modern state. In *Ancient Society* (1877) Morgan proposed a series of developments from the one pole to the other, which he linked to his conjectures on the evolution of the family. His notion of progress remained fundamentally moral and idealistic, and, *pace* Engels, he did not greatly emphasize property relations, though (like the writers of the Scottish Enlightenment, from whom he took so much) he believed that the final emergence of private property precipitated the move to a civilized culture, complete with monogamous marriage, the family, and a state organization. His historical conjectures were without foundation, but he collected valuable ethnographic materials, and greatly stimulated research on kinship systems.

Adam Kuper
Brunel University, Uxbridge

Mosca, Gaetano (1858–1941)

Gaetano Mosca, the founding father of Italian political science, was born in 1858 in Palermo, Sicily where he graduated in law in 1881. He met with difficulties in his academic career and for ten years was editor of the proceedings of the Chamber of Deputies in Rome. Eventually, in 1896, he became professor of constitutional law at the University of Turin, and in 1923 he was appointed to the chair of political institutions and doctrines in Rome. Mosca also took an active part in political life: between 1908 and 1919 he was a conservative member of the Chamber of Deputies. From 1914 to 1916 he served as under-secretary for the colonies, and in 1919 he became a Senator of the Kingdom. Already in his first work (*Teorica dei governi e governo parlamentare*, 1884), Mosca, while strongly criticizing the Italian parliamentary system, exposed the myth of democracy and democratic institutions and put forward his rather sombre vision of the process of government. These themes were expanded and elaborated in his major work, the *Elementi di scienza politica* (English translation, *The Ruling Class*, New York, 1939), first published in 1896. In this book he systematically worked out his well-known theory of the ruling class, thus anticipating Pareto's similar (but not identical) theory of élites and their circulation developed a few years later; and influencing Michels's thinking on political parties. According to the theory, in every political regime the rulers are always an organized minority who are able, thanks to the close links among its members, to dominate the unorganized majority. Furthermore, the ruling class tries to justify and legitimate its power on the basis of abstract, moral and legal, principles, the so-called 'political formula', which must be consonant with the values of the community that is governed. In Mosca's view, the theory of the ruling class was intended to make the analysis and classification of political regimes less formalistic, more rigorous and, above all, empirically-grounded, since it based them on the characteristics of such a ruling class, the way it formed and changed.

Luisa Leonini
University of Milan

Further Reading
Meisel, J. H. (1962), *The Myth of the Ruling Class*: *Gaetano Mosca and the Elite*, Ann Arbor.
Sola, G. (1982), 'Introduzione', in G. Mosca, *Scritti politici*, Turin.

Myrdal, Gunnar (1898–)

Born in 1898, Gunnar Myrdal, the Swedish economist and a leading member of the Stockholm School, has held a variety of positions during his long and distinguished career. He was professor of economics at the University of Stockholm (1933–50); general secretary of the United Nations Economic Commission for Europe (1947–57); professor of international economics at the University of Stockholm (1960–7), and director of the Institute for International Economic Studies at the University of Stockholm (1962–7). In 1974 he was awarded the Nobel Memorial Prize in Economics for 'pioneering work in the theory of money and economic fluctuations and penetrating analysis of the interdependence of economic, social and international phenomena'.

Early on in his career, Myrdal concentrated on pure theory.

His doctoral dissertation on price formation and change (1927) constructs a long-run equilibrium model, where anticipations are a datum alongside the given preferences, endowments and techniques. The ideas from his dissertation were applied in his subsequent works on monetary equilibrium where the notions of *ex ante* and *ex post* are used in the analysis of equilibrating factors. Myrdal also contributed to the methodological debates, emphasizing the normative elements implicit in classical and neoclassical theory. His analysis of the government economic policy explored the multiplicative effects of public works within a cumulative process, giving due consideration to leakages through import, and so on.

In the late 1930s, Myrdal embarked on his classic study of the Black minority in the United States (*An American Dilemma*, 1944). In it he argued that the inferior status of Blacks depended not only on economic factors but also on political and socio-logical ones interacting with one another in a cumulative fashion. Then, in the 1950s, he turned his attention to South Asia, the research there culminating in another famous study, *Asian Drama* (1968). Here he criticized the view that an increase in physical capital would inevitably lead to self-sustained growth, and again he argued that it was necessary to examine the interrelated factors of human capital, physical capital and institutions.

Björn Hansson
University of Lund

References

Myrdal, G. (1927), *Prisbildningsproblemet och föränderligheten* (*Price Formation and the Change Factor*), Uppsala.

Myrdal, G. (1944), *An American Dilemma. The Negro Problem and Modern Democracy*, New York.

Myrdal, G. (1953), *The Political Element in the Development of Economic Theory*, London.

Myrdal, G. (1968), *Asian Drama. An Inquiry into the Poverty of Nations*, New York.

Further Reading
Bohrn, H. (1977), *Gunnar Myrdal: A Bibliography*, Stockholm.
Reynolds, L. G. (1977), 'Gunnar Myrdal's contribution to
  economics, 1940–1970', *Scandinavian Journal of Economics*, 74.

Pareto, Vilfredo (1848–1923)

Vilfredo Pareto, born in Paris in 1848, is principally known
today for his work on the theory of élites; but his contribution
to sociology and political science was both more general and
more profound. His approach to the social world was decisively
influenced by his early training as an engineer. Throughout his
career he championed the application of the methods of the
natural sciences to the social studies. The idea of 'equilibrium',
which he originally tackled in relation to mechanics, became
the *idée maîtresse* of his social theories.

Between 1870 and 1893, Pareto devoted himself to business,
politics and journalism. He was a vigorous champion of free
trade. After 1876, with the fall from power of the party of
moderates which originally formed around Cavour (the *destra
storica*), he became progressively more disillusioned with both
the protectionist policies and the general conduct of political
life in Italy. Observing the practice of fashioning governmental
majorities from different facts (*trasformismo*) at close hand
furnished him with some of the materials for his later critique
of parliamentary democracy. He made a name for himself
in these years as an economist, and in 1893 became professor of political economy at Lausanne. He died in Geneva in
1923.

Pareto's first important work, the *Cours d'économie politique*
(1896) (Course of Political Economy), formed the bridge
between his economic and sociological studies. His contention
was that the question of economic utility could not be
considered in isolation from wider social and psychological
forces. Protectionism is roundly condemned as simply a form
of legal spoliation. Stress is upon the degree of social differentiation in a society rather than upon constitutional forms. And
Marx's account of class struggles as an expression of economic
interests is endorsed, though with the proviso that not all strug-

gles between different interests should be reduced to the same schematic form.

In *Les Systèmes socialistes* (1902) [Socialist Systems] Pareto turned the theory of interests against the socialists themselves. The conflict in the modern age should not be seen in terms of a bourgeois élite and the proletariat but between two élites trying to pursue their own advantage through the manipulation of mass support. In parliamentary democracies, no less than in other forms of polity, leadership is by the few at the expense of the many. In the last resort, it is force which sustains a regime. Pareto's comments on 'humanitarians' who forget this sombre truth are scathing.

Pareto's achievement was to shift attention away from the ideological sphere and towards the nonlogical actions which predominate in social life. In his major work, the *Trattato di sociologia generale* (1916) (English translation, *The Mind and Society: Treatise on General Sociology*, 4 Vols, London, 1936), he distinguished two dimensions in nonlogical actions: 'residues' (the uniform tendencies which determine the pattern of conduct) and 'derivations' (the rationalizations which men advance in justification of a particular course of action). Equilibrium in a society is the product of a balance of 'residues'. An élite will always rule; but (contrary to the practice of classical political theory) an explanation of the form which that rule takes (whether force or persuasion predominates) should be sought in the dominant 'residues' and not in the prevalent ideology.

The *Trattato* is a cumbersome and confused work. No one would accept its conclusions today. The shift from a description of the rule of élites to a justification of authoritarian government is especially questionable. But it served to delineate a sphere for sociology which still finds support in some quarters.

B. A. Haddock
University College of Swansea

Further Reading
Borkenau, F. (1936), *Pareto*, London.
Bucolo, P. (ed.) (1980), *The Other Pareto*, London.
Cirillo, R. (1979), *The Economics of Vilfredo Pareto*, London.
Finer, S. E. (ed.) (1966), *Vilfredo Pareto: Sociology Writings*,
    London.

Park, Robert Ezra (1864–1944)

Robert E. Park the sociologist was the son of a businessman,
and was brought up in Red Wing, Minnesota. After studying
with John Dewey at the University of Michigan, he was a
newspaper reporter for ten years. He then studied philosophy
with William James at Harvard, and sociology in Germany,
where he gained a doctorate. From 1905 to 1913 he assisted
Booker T. Washington, the Black leader, at Tuskegee Institute
in Alabama. In 1913 Park began teaching in the department
of sociology at the University of Chicago, where he remained
until his retirement in 1934.

Park was the dominant figure in the Chicago School (of
Sociology) and the most influential American sociologist during
the 1920s. His main writings consist of two studies of the
assimilation of immigrants, a major textbook *Introduction to the
Study of Sociology* (1921) and three posthumously published
volumes of collected essays. His main influence, however, was
exercised upon and through his students, who produced notable
studies of race relations, collective behaviour, urban structure
and urban milieux, and social control. Park sought to adum-
brate a theory of social process, in which public opinion played
a significant role, hence his continuing interest in the role of
the press. He also developed, with Ernest Burgess, an ecological
theory of the city which had a lasting impact upon urban
sociology.

Park's major significance was as the leader of a fruitful school
of empirical sociology and as a scholar whose sociological vision
blended acute observation with the capacity to draw out its
general significance and conceptualize at an abstract level. He
demonstrated the capacity of sociology to grasp and compre-

hend the phenomena of modern urban society in a way which his American sociological predecessors had not.

Martin Bulmer
London School of Economics and Political Science

Further Reading
Matthews, F. H. (1977), *Quest for an American Sociology: Robert E. Park and the Chicago School*, Montreal.

Parsons, Talcott (1902–79)

Talcott Parsons, the son of a Congregational minister in Colorado, became the most important American sociologist. He did an undergraduate degree in biology and philosophy at Amherst College and then did graduate work in social science at The London School of Economics and at Heidelberg. In 1927, he joined the Harvard economics department and in 1931 switched to the sociology department, which had just been created. He became chairman of the sociology department in 1944 and then chairman of the newly formed department of social relations in 1946, a position he retained until 1956. He officially retired in 1973 but continued writing until his death (in Munich) in 1979. His self-image was that of a theoretical synthesizer of social science in general and sociology in particular. Seeing sociocultural forces as the dominant ones shaping human activity, he assigned sociology the role of integrating the analyses of psychology, politics and economics into a science of human action. Sociology also had the role of providing other social sciences with their boundary assumptions (such as specifying what market imperfections exist).

Parsons's first book, *The Structure of Social Action* (1937), assesses the legacy to sociology of Marshall, Pareto, Durkheim and Weber. These thinkers, Parsons argues, converged from different directions on a solution to the problem of why society is not characterized by a Hobbesian war of all against all. According to Parsons, their solution is that people share common values and norms. Parsons's subsequent work, particularly *The Social System* (1951), *Towards a General Theory of Action* (1951), and *Family, Socialization and Interaction Process* (1955), develops the importance of the integration of a shared normative structure into people's need-dispositions for making social order possible. Structure, for Parsons, comprises the elements with greatest permanence in a society. These elements he identifies as the society's values, norms, collectivities and roles. The concern with people being socialized into a society's structure gives a conservative flavour to Parsons's thought.

Parsons argues that for a social structure to persist, four functions must be performed. These are adaptation, goal-attainment, integration and pattern-maintenance or tension-management. Societies tend to differentiate functionally to produce separate institutions specializing in each of these functions. The economy is adaptive, the polity specializes in goal-attainment, the stratification system is integrative, while education and religion are both concerned with pattern-maintenance. The most important social change in human history has been a gradual evolution of more functionally differentiated societies. For the evolution of a more differentiated structure to be successful there must be adaptive upgrading, inclusion and value generalization. The increased specialization produced by functional differentiation makes adaptive upgrading possible. Inclusion refers to processes (such as extension of the franchise) that produce commitment by people to the new more specialized structures. Finally, values must be generalized or stated more abstractly in order to legitimize a wider range of activities.

Parsons sees money, power, influence and commitment as generalized symbolic media that mediate the interchanges among the differentiated sectors of society. Power is defined as the capacity to achieve results. He develops an analysis of power based on its being the political system's equivalent of money. Force is the equivalent of the gold backing of a currency – it provides a back-up to power, but if it has to be resorted to frequently then the political system is breaking down. Inflation can ruin power just as it may destroy a currency.

Parsons's substantive concerns have ranged from Nazi Germany to Ancient Greece to modern school classes. Many of his specific analyses have proved highly influential. Particularly noteworthy are: his analysis of illness as legitimated deviance; of McCarthyism as a response to strains in American society resulting from the American assumption of the responsibilities of being a world power; of the pressures in American society pushing towards full citizenship for Black Americans; and of secularization as a result of increasing functional differentiation. Parsons's analysis of business and the professions involves the use of one of his best-known classifications, the pattern variables. The four pattern variables which can be used to describe any role relationship are affectivity v. neutrality, specificity v. diffuseness, universalism v. particularism, and quality v. performance. The relationship of business people to their clients is identical to professionals to their clients when this relationship is classified using the pattern variables. Each group relates neutrally, specifically, universalistically and in terms of the expected performance of the client. Understood this way, business people and professionals are similar, and their roles mesh easily together. Thus this analysis is better than one that sees professionals as altruistic and radically different from egotistical business people.

Parsons's influence on American sociology is immense. His *The Structure of Social Action* was the first major English-language presentation of the works of Weber and Durkheim and helped make their ideas central to American sociology's heritage. Many of Parsons's specific analyses and concepts are widely accepted, though few people accept his overall position. In the 1940s and 1950s, he was the dominant American theorist. In the 1960s his ideas came under increasing attack for being incapable of dealing with change. Since then, this criticism has come to be seen as simplistic. His work is increasingly being examined in terms of the solutions it offers to various dilemmas about how to theorize about society.

Kenneth Menzies
University of Guelph, Ontario

Further Reading
Bourricaud, F. (1981 [1977]), *The Sociology of Talcott Parsons*, Chicago. (Original French, *L'Individualisme institutionel: essai sur la sociologie de Talcott Parsons*, Paris.)
Menzies, K. (1977), *Talcott Parsons and the Social Image of Man*, London.

Pavlov, Ivan Petrovich (1849–1936)

The great Russian physiologist and founder of the study of conditioned reflexes, I. P. Pavlov, was the great-grandson of a freed serf and son and grandson of village priests. His sixty-two years of continuous and active research on what he came to call 'Higher Nervous Activity' profoundly and immutably altered the course of scientific study and conceptualization of the behaviour of living organisms, and for the first time established appropriate contact between philosophical empiricism and associationism and laboratory science. The young Pavlov won a gold medal for his second experiment ('The nerve supply of the pancreas'), one of eleven publications before his graduation in 1879 from the Imperial Medico-Surgical Academy in St Petersburg. After completing his doctoral dissertation ('Efferent nerves of the heart') in 1883, he was appointed lecturer in physiology, spent two years in postdoctoral research with Ludwig in Leipzig and Haidenhain in Breslau, became professor of pharmacology in the Academy and director of the Physiological Laboratory of the new St Petersburg Institute of Experimental Medicine in 1890, and, in 1895, professor of physiology in the Academy. In 1924 he was appointed director of a new Institute of Physiology, created by the Soviet Academy of Sciences especially for his burgeoning research enterprise. He remained in this post until his death, in Leningrad, in 1936.

Pavlov was fifty-five when in 1904 he won the Nobel Prize for his work on neural regulation of digestive secretion – the first given to a Russian and to a physiologist. A special surgical technique he developed during this period, the Pavlov Pouch, is still used. This technique exemplifies a cardinal principle in his work – he disdained the artificiality of 'acute' preparations used by his contemporaries in their stimulation and extirpation research, preferring to study an intact and physiologically 'normal' animal whose life need not be 'sacrificed' after the experiment. Not long after receiving the Nobel award, Pavlov abruptly shifted to the topic for which we remember him, conditioning. Here, too, he emphasized the chronic preparation, studying some dogs for many years, yet always maintaining sound physiological standards (Rule 1. Control of all stimulation, experimental as well as surrounding; Rule 2. Reliable quantitative measures).

Then, already over seventy and famous, he again shifted his emphasis, this time to the study of psychopathology, beginning with laboratory-produced experimental neurosis but also including work with actual patients in mental hospitals and psychiatric clinics.

The basic terminology and research strategies employed today in research on animal conditioning and human behaviour modification originated mainly in Pavlov's laboratory. Modern psychiatry and clinical psychology depend substantially upon ideas and methods, not to mention the myriad of facts, growing out of his work. From behaviour therapy to biofeedback, from the study of how worms and fish learn to the theory and treatment of neurotic anxiety, Pavlov's stubbornly objective and pervasively materialistic application of the scientific method in the study of the nervous system's control of all of the functions of life, including its most adaptive feature – its plasticity – have continued to prove fruitful if not essential.

H. D. Kimmel
University of South Florida

Further Reading
Babkin, B. P. (1949), *Pavlov: A Biography*, Chicago.
Gray, J. A. (1979), *Pavlov*, London.
Pavlov, I. P. (1960 [1927]), *Conditioned Reflexes: An Investigation of the Physiological Activity of the Cerebral Cortex*, New York.

Pavlov, I. P. (1940–9), *Polnoe Sobranie Trudov [Complete Works]*, Moscow.

Peirce, Charles Sanders (1839–1914)

Although considered by many as the founder of serious philosophical study in the United States, and America's greatest philosopher, Peirce thought of himself as a 'man of science' and a student of logic, conceived broadly as the science of scientific method. The son of Benjamin Peirce, then the leading American mathematician, and Sarah Mills Peirce, daughter of US Senator Mills (founder of a law school in Northampton), he was raised in a circle of physicists, naturalists, and lawyers, the intellectual élite of mid-century Boston. His father trained him in mathematics and in intellectual discipline. After study at Harvard, in order to deepen his understanding of 'logic', he resolved to acquire firsthand experience in methods of physical science. He became a senior staff scientist with the US Coast and Geodetic Survey, then the premier government scientific bureau, and by 1880 was an internationally recognized expert in gravity measurement, having travelled widely in Europe on scientific duties. In 1891 he resigned his government post, and retired to a quiet region of rural Pennsylvania in order to study logic. There he developed and wrote his mature works. He left a tremendous *nachlass* which is just now being edited and published (Fisch, Ketner, Kloesel, 1979).

The range of his interests, in each of which he invariably made original research contributions, reads like that of Da Vinci, if one omits art. Here is a description of them he prepared for Cattell's *Men of Science*: 'Logic, especially logic of relations, probabilities, theory of inductive and retroductive validity and of definition, epistemology; metrology; history of science; multiple algebra; doctrine of the nature and constitution of numbers; gravity; wave-lengths; phonetics of Elizabethan English; great men; ethics; phaneroscopy; speculative cosmology; experimental psychology; physical geometry; foundations of mathematics; classification of science; code of terminology; topical geometry.'

In order to grasp his thought, the fundament of which is methodology, one must remember that he was basically a scientist and a mathematician, thoroughly imbued with the lore and method of laboratories. He described his work as 'the attempt of a physicist to make such conjecture as to the constitution of the universe as the methods of science may permit, with the aid of all that has been done by previous philosophers'. His classification of the sciences is the key for following his thinking. He regarded Mathematics as the most fundamental science. Below that is the science of Philosophy, including Phaneroscopy (phenomenology), Aesthetics, Ethics, and Logic. Logic, which is equivalent to Semiotic, the science of signs, was composed of Speculative Grammar (definitions), Critic (logic in the present-day sense), and Methodeutic (methodology). The last branch of philosophy is Metaphysics. Then comes Special Sciences – Physics and Psychics with their various subdivisions. The informing idea of this classification, and of Peirce's system of scientific philosophy, is that each science requires principles and methods from that which is prior to it.

His work is a rich intellectual legacy which is attracting widespread interest from a number of disciplines. His influence, both acknowledged and unacknowledged, upon contemporary thought is strong and is increasing.

Kenneth Laine Ketner
Texas Tech University

Reference
Fisch, M. H., Ketner, K. L. and Kloesel, C. J. W. (1979), 'The new tools of Peirce scholarship, with particular reference to semiotic', *Peirce Studies*, No. 1, Institute for Studies in Pragmaticism, Lubbock.

Further Reading
Eisele, C. (1979), *Studies in the Scientific and Mathematical Philosophy of Charles S. Peirce: Essays by Carolyn Eisele* (ed. R. M. Martin), The Hague.

Fisch, M. H. *et al.* (eds) (1982–), *Writings of Charles S. Peirce: A Chronological Edition*, Vols 1–, Bloomington.

Ketner, K. L. *et al.* (eds) (1981), *Proceedings of the C. S. Peirce Bicentennial International Congress*, Lubbock.

Ketner, K. L. (ed.) (1983), 'Peirce's semiotic and its audiences', special issue of *American Journal of Semiotics*.

Piaget, Jean (1896–1980)

Jean Piaget, the Swiss psychologist, biologist and philosopher, was professor of experimental psychology at the University of Geneva (1940–1971) and of developmental psychology at the Sorbonne in Paris (1952–1963). As a psychologist, Piaget was influenced by Freud, Janet, J. M. Baldwin and Claparède. Piaget's theories and experiments, which he published in innumerable books and articles, place him among the foremost psychologists of the century.

Piaget's lifelong quest was for the origins of knowledge. Trained as a biologist, and initially influenced by Bergson's evolutionary philosophy, he sought to explain the conditions of knowledge by studying its genesis. Evolutionary theory, the developmental psychology of children's intelligence and the history of science were to provide the scientific underpinnings of this epistemological project.

In his early work (1923–36), Piaget tried to gain insight into children's logic by studying their verbally expressed thought. Using a free method of interrogation, the 'clinical method', Piaget investigated children's reasoning about everyday phenomena, causality and moral problems. A leading idea expressed in Piaget's early books is that of egocentrism in early childhood and its gradual replacement by socialized, and therefore logical, thinking. Young children's egocentrism is revealed in their incapacity to differentiate between their own point of view and that of another. Neither experience nor the influence of adults are sufficient grounds for the attainment of logical thinking. Instead, Piaget explained the abandonment of egocentrism by the child's desire and need to communicate with children of the same age.

In the late 1920s and early 1930s Piaget made extensive

observations of his own children as babies and elaborated his theory of sensorimotor intelligence in infancy. Contrary to contemporary conceptions, he considered babies as actively and spontaneously oriented towards their environment. As they 'assimilate' things to their action patterns, they at the same time have to 'accommodate' these patterns to the exigencies of the external world. In this process of interaction with the environment the child's innate reflexes and patterns of behaviour are altered, differentiated and mutually co-ordinated. The organization of action patterns gives rise to a 'logic of actions'. In his account of the development of the object concept, Piaget states that initially children do not appear to recognize a world existing independently of their actions upon it. A baby playing with a toy does not search for it when it is covered; according to Piaget, it ceases to exist for the baby. The concept of an independently existing world is gradually constructed during infancy and is attained only at about 18 months when the child becomes capable of representing things mentally.

The existence of a logic in action, demonstrated in the baby studies, made Piaget revise his earlier theories of the origins of logical thinking in early and middle childhood. Logical operations are prepared in sensorimotor intelligence and the former are the result of internalization of the latter. The attainment of logical thinking, therefore, is not the result of verbal interactions with other children, but of the child's reconstruction of the action logic on a new, mental plane. Piaget now viewed cognitive development as resulting in stages, characterized by a dynamic equilibrium between the child's cognitive structures and the environment. Development is the result of a process of equilibration, in which equilibria of a progressively more stable kind are sought and attained. Piaget distinguished three stages: the sensorimotor stage (0–about 18 months), the stage of concrete operations (about 7–11 years) and the stage of formal operations (from about 11 years). In each of these three stages children's thinking is characterized by its own kind of logic: an action logic in the sensorimotor stage, a logic applied to concrete situations in the concrete operational stage, and a logic applied to statements of a symbolic or verbal kind in the formal operational stage.

In the period between the sensorimotor and the concrete operational stage (which Piaget called the preoperational period) the child's thinking lacks the possibility to carry out operations, that is, reversible mental actions. Piaget and his collaborators demonstrated in many simple yet elegant experiments the transition from preoperational to concrete thinking about concepts such as number, velocity, space, and physical causality. In these experiments they no longer restricted themselves to verbal interaction, but introduced materials which the child could manipulate. In the famous conservation task, the child must judge whether the amount of fluid poured into a glass of different proportions changes or does not change. Preoperational children are characteristically misled by the perceptual appearance of the situation. Only concrete operational children can reverse the transfer in thought and give the correct answer.

From 1950 onward Piaget wrote his great epistemological studies, in which he rejected empiricism and rationalism. Consequently he opposed behaviourism, maturational theories of development and nativist ideas in Gestalt psychology. The newborn child is neither a *tabula rasa*, ready to receive the impression of the environment, nor endowed with a priori knowledge about the world. Piaget showed himself a pupil of Kant by assuming that our knowledge of the world is mediated by cognitive structures. But, unlike Kant, he did not consider these as fundamental ideas given at birth: he showed them to be the products of a lengthy process of construction in the interaction of subject and environment. He therefore coined his epistemology a *genetic* epistemology.

The aim of genetic epistemology is to reconstruct the development of knowledge from its most elementary biological forms up to its highest achievements, scientific thinking included. Psychology has a place in this project, in so far as it studies the development of biological structures in the human baby into sensorimotor and operational intelligence. But the enterprise is essentially a biological one, as the development of intelligence is conceived of as an extension of biological adaptation. Intelligence is the specific product in humans of the same biological principles applying to all living nature: adaptation resulting in structural reorganizations and in equilibria of increasing stability.

Piaget saw psychology as a necessary but limited part of his epistemology, and he always regretted the exclusive interest for the psychological component of his work. In the International Centre for Genetic Epistemology, which he founded at the University of Geneva in 1955 and to which he attracted specialists in all fields of study, he stimulated the interdisciplinary study of epistemology. But the acclaim for his epistemological ideas was never more than a shadow of the universal enthusiasm for the *psychologist* Piaget.

Piaget's influence on developmental psychology can hardly be overestimated. His ideas were seen as a help in supplanting behaviouristic and psychoanalytic theories in psychology. He set the margins for discussions in cognitive developmental psychology from the 1960s up to the present time. But his ideas and methods have always been the object of sharp criticism. Many developmental psychologists think that Piaget underrated the cognitive capacities of young children, and he is reproached for neglecting in his later studies the social context of development in favour of an isolated epistemic subject. Therefore, many now go beyond the mature Piaget and find inspiration in his early works.

Ed Elbers
University of Utrecht

Further Reading
(A) Works by Piaget
Piaget, J. (1923), *Le Langage et la pensée chez l'enfant*, Neuchâtel. (*The Language and Thought of the Child*, London, 1926.)
Piaget, J. (1932), *Le Jugement moral chez l'enfant*, Paris. (*The Moral Judgment of the Child*, London, 1932.)
Piaget, J. (1936), *La Naissance de l'intelligence chez l'enfant*,

Neuchâtel. (*The Origin of Intelligence in the Child*, London, 1952.)

Piaget, J. and Inhelder, B. (1948), *La Représentation de l'espace chez l'enfant*, Paris. (*The Child's Conception of Space*, London, 1956.)

Piaget, J. (1950), *Introduction à l'épistémologie génétique*, Vols 1–3, Paris.

Piaget, J. and Inhelder, B, (1959), *La Génèse des structures logiques élémentaires*, Neuchâtel. (*The Early Growth of Logic in the Child*, London, 1964.)

Piaget, J. and Inhelder, B. (1966), *La Psychologie de l'enfant*, Paris. (*The Psychology of the Child*, London, 1969.)

Piaget, J. (1967), *Biologie et connaissance*, Paris. (*Biology and Knowledge*, London, 1971.)

Piaget, J. (1974), *La Prise de conscience*, Paris. (*The Grasp of Consciousness*, London, 1976.)

Piaget, J. (1975), *L'Equilibration des structures cognitives*, Paris. (*The Development of Thought: Equilibration of Cognitive Structures*, Oxford, 1977.)

(B) General

Boden, M. (1979), *Piaget*, London.

Flavell, J. H. (1963), *The Developmental Psychology of Jean Piaget*, Princeton.

Gruber, H. E. and Vonèche, J. J. (eds) (1977), *The Essential Piaget: An Interpretive Reference and Guide*, London.

Rotman, B. (1977), *Jean Piaget: Psychologist of the Real*, Hassocks.

Plato (428/7–348/7 B.C.)

Plato was born into a wealthy, well-connected family of the old Athenian aristocracy (Davies, 1971). He and his elder brothers Adeimantos and Glaukon (both of whom figure in the *Republic*) belonged to the circle of young men attached to Socrates, as did his cousins Kritias and Charmides, who played a leading part in the oligarchic junta of the Thirty which seized power at the end of the Peloponnesian War in 404/3. In the seventh

Letter (a sort of *apologia pro vita sua* by Plato himself or a disciple) Plato claims to have been quickly shocked by the tyrannous behaviour of the Thirty, and equally disgusted with the restored democracy when it condemned Socrates to death in 399; but his chances of playing any prominent part in Athenian politics had in any case been fatally compromised by his close connections with the junta. He settled down to the 'theoretical life' of a philosopher and teacher which he praises (for example, *Theaetetus* 172–6) as the highest form of human activity. In 367, however, after thirty years of highly productive theoretical activity, he attempted to put some of the political ideas of the *Republic* into practice by training the young ruler of Syracuse, Dionysius II, for the role of philosopher-king. Not surprisingly, he failed; one of Plato's most obvious weaknesses as a political analyst was his neglect of external factors and relations with other powers, which in the fourth century B.C. constituted in fact the main problem for the Greek cities. While there are problems of detail in dating Plato's dialogues, one can perhaps say that in his work before the Sicilian episode he is still engaged in a vivacious debate with ideas current in the Athens of his youth, whereas in his later works (*Sophist, Statesman, Philebus, Timaeus, Critias, Laws*) he is addressing himself more specifically to fellow-philosophers, present and future. The philosophical centre he founded in the Academy – a sort of Institute for Advanced Studies in rural surroundings – continued after his death.

The influences which shaped Plato's thought are thus the aristocratic milieu in which he grew up and the political events of his lifetime, the personality of Socrates, and the standards of systematic reasoning associated with the role of philosopher. His contributions to social thought as we would now define it lie mainly in the fields of political and moral philosophy, psychology and education; but these aspects of his thought cannot be detached from his epistemology and cosmology.

Part of the fascination of reading Plato comes from the dialogue form in which he presented his ideas. He was no doubt influenced in this choice by Socrates, who communicated his own ideas solely through argument and left no written works.

More generally, the Athenians were used to hearing different points of view upheld by opposing speakers in political assemblies, in law courts and in drama. Socrates takes the leading part in Plato's earlier dialogues, and this enabled the author both to acknowledge his debt to his teacher and, perhaps, to avoid taking full responsibility for the ideas he was putting forward. Plato never figures in his own dialogues. The dialogue form also suited his gifts as a brilliantly natural and graceful writer, a skilful parodist and master of characterization and light-hearted conversation. The introductory scenes of his dialogues provide the historian with lively sketches of upper-class manners and mores in the late fifth century B.C.

The key element in Plato's thought as it concerned social life was a widening of the gap between body and spirit. This enabled him to preserve an essential core of religious belief from the criticisms which had been directed against traditional religion, to ground Socrates' argument that virtue is a kind of knowledge in a general theory of epistemology which offered solutions to logical problems raised by earlier philosophers, and to provide a foundation for belief in the immortality of the soul; at the same time it formalized a psychological split between lower and higher elements in the personality, and linked this to a justification of social hierarchy, and to a theory of education in which censorship played an essential part.

Plato's early dialogues show Socrates attacking a traditional, unreflective upper-class practice of virtue as a routine response of the gentleman to predictable situations. When asked to define courage (*Laches*), piety (*Euthyphro*), or moderation (*Charmides*), his interlocutors give specific examples of brave, pious or self-controlled behaviour, and Socrates then proves to them that such acts would not in all circumstances be considered virtuous. Echoes of the same attitude can be found in Xenophon and Euripides.

Some of Plato's contemporaries went on from this criticism of traditional conceptions of virtue to deny its existence altogether: in the *Republic*, Thrasymachus argues that values and virtues are defined by the ruling class to suit their own interests, and Glaukon argues that they represent the interests of the majority. Plato therefore needed a concept of virtue which was flexible and abstract enough to satisfy Socratic criticism but nevertheless safe against relativist attack. His response was the theory of Forms or Ideas, existing at a level of ultimate, abstract reality which was only imperfectly reflected in the material world but of which the human mind could gradually acquire better knowledge through philosophical training.

Coming closer to the world of Ideas thus becomes both the highest aim of human life and the standard by which all kinds of knowledge are judged; it follows that human societies should be directed by philosophers or by laws formulated by philosophers. The human personality is divided into three elements: intelligence, *amour-propre* (*Thumos*) and the physical appetites. Education aims to train the first to dominate the other two.

Thumos refers to a set of qualities regarded somewhat ambiguously in Plato's culture (Dover, 1974). It was the basis of man's pursuit of prestige and honour and thus – like the appetites – beneficial when exercised in moderation but dangerous when obsessive. Too eager a pursuit of honour led to tyranny or to a tendency to take offence for no reason. Thus there was a popular basis for the view that even ambition for what the ordinary man in the street considered the supreme good had to be controlled. This point was particularly important for Plato, because his belief that the good society was a society ruled by good and wise men meant that the essential problem of political organization was to prevent the ruling élite from becoming corrupted. This led him to formulate the idea of the 'mixed constitution', later to influence Polybius, Montesquieu and the Constitution of the United States.

Because a philosophical education involved training in subjects like astronomy and mathematics for which not all had equal interest or aptitude, and because the philosopher had to detach himself from activities and preoccupations likely to strengthen the influence of his *Thumos* and bodily appetites, the hierarchy of faculties in the psyche led to a hierarchy of groups in the ideal city. Philosophers would have supreme authority, semi-educated 'watch-dogs' would act as a military and police force on their behalf, and those who supplied the economic needs of the city would have the lowest status of all. Education was to be carefully adjusted to the reproduction of the system; the lower class were to be trained to obedience and persuaded by a political 'myth' that their status was due to natural causes; poets should only represent socially commendable behaviour; knowledge of alternative forms of society was to be carefully suppressed, except in the case of selected members of the ruling élite.

Such views have in our century led to attacks on Plato as a proto-Fascist or -Stalinist (Crossman, 1937; Popper, 1945). In the *Laws* the more extreme proposals of the *Republic* (in particular, the abolition of private property and the family) were dropped; it is interesting to see Plato grappling here with detailed problems of law-drafting, and the text is a key piece of evidence on Greek legal thought. Return to law as a source of authority was a capitulation to the rigid type of definition of virtue which Socrates had attacked (see the *Statesman*); but the argument which had seemed valid when applied to individuals would not work for collectivities. There was something wrong with the analogy between parts of the city and parts of the human psyche.

S. C. Humphreys
University of Michigan

References
Crossman, R. H. (1937), *Plato Today*, London.
Davies, J. K. (1971), *Athenian Propertied Families*, Oxford.
Dover, K. J. (1974), *Greek Popular Morality in the Time of Plato and Aristotle*, Oxford.
Popper, K. (1945), *The Open Society and its Enemies*, London.

Further Reading
Gouldner, A. W. (1966), *Enter Plato: Classical Greece and the Origins of Social Theory*, New York.
Guthrie, W. K. C. (1975–8), *A History of Greek Philosophy*, vols IV–V, Cambridge.
Ryle, G. (1966), *Plato's Progress*, Cambridge.

Shorey, P. (1933), *What Plato Said*, Chicago.

Taylor, A. E. (1926), *Plato. The Man and his Work*, London.

Wood, E. M. and Wood, N. (1978), *Class Ideology and Ancient Political Theory: Socrates, Plato and Aristotle in Social Context*, Oxford.

See also: *Aristotle*.

Popper, Karl Raimund (1902–)

Sir Karl Popper is one of the most creative, wide-ranging and controversial philosophers of the twentieth century. Sir Peter Medawar, Nobel laureate in physiology and medicine, has called Popper 'incomparably the greatest philosopher of science that has ever been'. Yet virtually every one of Popper's many contributions – to logic, probability theory, methodology, evolutionary epistemology, quantum physics, social and political philosophy, and intellectual history – is heatedly disputed by professional philosophers.

Popper was born in Vienna in 1902, studied physics, philosophy and music at the University of Vienna, and left Vienna in January 1937 to become senior lecturer in philosophy at Canterbury University College in Christchurch, New Zealand. He was appointed to the staff of The London School of Economics and Political Science in 1945, and became professor of logic and scientific method there in 1949, and remained there until his retirement in 1969. He was knighted in 1965 and made a Companion of Honour in 1982.

His first and most important work is *Logik der Forschung* (1934), published in English translation as *The Logic of Scientific Discovery* (1959), which challenged the main tenets of the positivist philosophers of Popper's native Vienna. An ardent advocate of reason and the scientific spirit, Popper nonetheless denied the very existence of scientific induction, argued that probability (in the sense of the probability calculus) could not be used to evaluate universal scientific theories, disputed the importance of the verification (as opposed to falsification) of hypotheses, denied the importance of meaning analysis in most branches of philosophy and in science, and introduced his famous falsifiability criterion of demarcation to distinguish science from ideology and metaphysics.

This early clash with positivism has set the tone and the underlying themes for much of the later controversy over Popper's ideas: at a time when most physicists and philosophers of physics are inductivist, subjectivist, positivist, instrumentalist, Popper remains deductivist, realist, anti-positivist, anti-instrumentalist.

The chief ideas of Popper's philosophy all relate to the basic anti-reductionist theme – first announced explicitly in *The Self and Its Brain* (1977) (written with Sir John Eccles) – that 'something can come from nothing'. Scientific theories introduce new forms into the universe and cannot be reduced to observations, contrary to proponents of induction. The future is not contained in the present or the past. There is indeterminism in physics, and also in history – not only because of physical indeterminism, but also because new scientific ideas affect history and thus the course of the physical universe. There is genuine emergence in biology. Value cannot be reduced to fact; mind cannot be reduced to matter. Descriptive and argumentative levels of language cannot be reduced to expressive and signal levels. Consciousness is the spearhead of evolution, and the products of consciousness are not determined. Nonetheless, the Copenhagen interpretation of quantum mechanics – which is often used to introduce consciousness or the 'observer' into the heart of physics – is rejected by Popper, who maintains that quantum physics is just as objective as classical physics.

Although Popper is first and foremost a physicist, all of his thought is nonetheless permeated by an evolutionary, Darwinian outlook; and biology has come to dominate his later thinking, particularly his *Objective Knowledge* (1972). His most important contributions to social and political philosophy are *The Open Society and Its Enemies* (1945) and *The Poverty of Historicism* (1957), works both in intellectual history and in the methodology of the social sciences, which dispute the main themes of Marxism and of social planning. The idea of 'piecemeal social engineering' which Popper introduced in these works has had an important influence on practical politicians in the West, particularly in England, Germany, and Italy.

W. W. Bartley, III
The Hoover Institution, Stanford University

Further Reading
Other Works by Popper:
Conjectures and Refutations, 1963.
Unended Quest, 1974.
The Open Universe, 1982.
Quantum Theory and the Schism in Physics, 1982.
Realism and the Aim of Science, 1983.

Works about Popper:
Bartley, W. W. III (1976–82), 'The Philosophy of Karl Popper' (3 parts), *Philosophia*.
Bunge, M. (ed.) (1964), *The Critical Approach to Science and Philosophy*, Chicago.
Schilpp, P. A. (ed.) (1974), *The Philosophy of Karl Popper*, la Salle, Ill.

Radcliffe-Brown, Alfred Reginald (1881–1955)

Radcliffe-Brown was the first social anthropologist in Britain to have a full professional training, being Rivers's first undergraduate anthropology student at Cambridge. Later he carried out field research in the Andaman Islands (1906–8) where he initially interested himself in historical, ethnological questions, in the manner of Rivers. However, around 1909 he was converted to the sociology of Durkheim, and he eventually published a Durkheimian analysis of Andaman beliefs and rituals (1922). For the rest of his career he developed an essentially Durkheimian anthropology, parallel with Durkheim's nephew Mauss in Paris, and opposed the entrenched ethnological tradition. The version of Durkheimian theory which he propagated was orthodox, and less interesting than the subtler variant developed by Mauss, but he made an enduring contribution at the level of ethnographic analysis.

Radcliffe-Brown also made field studies in Australia (1910–11), and while his own ethnographic contribution was not remarkable, he was able to bring new order to the rich but confused and scattered reports on Australian social organization, demonstrating the structural uniformities which could be discerned despite various local divergences (Radcliffe-Brown, 1931). These Australian studies dealt particularly with kinship systems, and Radcliffe-Brown greatly influenced the development of kinship theory, breaking with the pseudo-historical explanations which Rivers and his predecessors had favoured, and establishing structural-functional explanations of kinship institutions.

Radcliffe-Brown held foundation chairs in social anthopology in the Universities of Cape Town and Sydney, and, from 1937 to 1946, in Oxford, and he taught also at the University of Chicago and a number of other universities in several continents. His body of publications was not large, but he became the leading influence in British social anthropology in the mid-twentieth century.

Adam Kuper
Brunel University, Uxbridge

References
Radcliffe-Brown, A. R. (1922), *The Andaman Islanders*, Cambridge.
Radcliffe-Brown, A. R. (1931), *The Social Organization of Australian Tribes*, Sydney.

Further Reading
Kuper, A. (ed.) (1977), *The Social Anthropology of Radcliffe-Brown*, London.

Ricardo, David (1772–1823)

David Ricardo, political economist and politician, was born in London on 18 April 1772, the third son of a Dutch Jew who had moved to England around 1760 and worked on the London Stock Exchange. Ricardo's education reflected his father's wish that he join him in business, which he did at the age of 14; he is reported by his brother not to have had a 'classical education', but one 'usually allotted to those who are destined for a mercantile way of life'. At the age of 21, following a period of waning attachment to Judaism, he married a Quaker, became a Unitarian and was estranged from his father. Thrown back on his own resources, he pursued a brilliant career as a jobber, within a few years amassing considerable wealth. At this time, his leisure hours were spent studying mathematics, chemistry, geology and minerology.

In 1799, Ricardo happened to peruse Adam Smith's *Wealth of Nations*. The subject matter interested him, although it was ten years before he published anything himself on it. His first article appeared anonymously in the *Morning Chronicle*, addressed to the 'Bullion Controversy'. Briefly, he argued that the low value of the pound on the foreign exchanges and the premium quoted on bullion over paper resulted from an over-issue of paper currency. His views were elaborated in published letters and pamphlets.

The 'Bullion Controversy' brought Ricardo into contact with, among others, James Mill, Jeremy Bentham and Thomas Malthus. Mill remained a close friend, encouraging the reticent Ricardo to publish, giving advice on style, and eventually persuading him to enter Parliament, which he did in 1819 as the independent member for the pocket borough of Portarlington in Ireland; with Bentham, Mill was also responsible for tutoring Ricardo in Utilitarianism. As for Malthus, he too became an enduring friend, although his intellectual role was mainly adversarial: something which provided Ricardo with a mental stimulus which, in the sphere of political economy, his more admiring friends were largely incapable of supplying.

In 1814, Ricardo began a gradual retirement from business, taking up residence in Gatcombe Park, Gloucestershire. One year later he published *An Essay on the Influence of a Low Price of Corn on the Profits of Stock*, one of many pamphlets spawned during the 'Corn Law Controversy'. Borrowing Malthus's theory of rent – that rent is an intra-'marginal' surplus and not a component of price, itself determined at the agricultural 'margin' – Ricardo inveighed against protection, claiming it would result in a rise of money wages, a reduced rate of profit, and a consequent slackening in the pace of capital accumulation. This was predicated on a theory of profitability at variance with Adam Smith's 'competition of capitals' thesis; taking the social propensity to save as given, Ricardo argued that 'permanent' movements in general profitability would uniquely result from changes in the (real) prices of wage-goods.

These views were developed in *On the Principles of Political Economy and Taxation* (first edition, 1817). In particular, Ricardo wanted to disseminate a single proposition, that the only serious threat to the unconstrained expansion of free-market capitalism came from the less productive cultivation of domestic land.

To illustrate this proposition Ricardo had developed a 'pure' labour theory of value, with 'permanent' changes in exchange relationships between competitively produced, freely reproducible commodities, the sole consequence of altered direct or indirect labour inputs (always assuming uniform profitability). He had also discovered limitations, eventually reduced to one of differences in the time structures of labour inputs. Pressed by Malthus to justify his use of the theory in the face of problems which he had himself unearthed, Ricardo departed on his celebrated quest for an 'invariable measure of value' which, if 'perfect', would magically obviate all variations in exchange relationships not the result of 'labour-embodied' changes, and this *without* assuming identical time-labour profiles. This futile search found expression in a new chapter 'On Value' in the third edition of the *Principles* (1821). Ironically, the impossibility of finding a 'perfect' measure of value was only recognized in a paper Ricardo was finalizing immediately before his sudden death on 11 September 1823.

Adumbration of a theory of comparative advantage in international trade (*Principles*, all editions) and of the possibility of net labour displacing accumulation (*Principles*, third edition) constitute further distinctive Ricardian contributions. Generally, he was a vigorous and fairly uncompromising advocate of *laissez-faire* capitalism: relief works schemes would be abolished, since they involved taking capital from those who knew best how to allocate it; taxation should be minimal, with the National Debt speedily paid off; the Poor Laws should be scrapped, because they distorted the labour market; and monopolies were *necessarily* mismanaged.

These views were promulgated from the floor of the House of Commons, where Ricardo also campaigned against religious discrimination and in favour of a meritocratic society. His guiding legislative principle was that it be for the public benefit and not in the interest of any particular class, with the 'public benefit' rigidly identified with the outcome of a private property, *laissez-faire* system. To this end, he favoured a gradual extension of the electoral franchise, immediately in order to weaken the legislative power of the landed aristocracy.

In his lifetime, Ricardo's political economy reigned supreme. But after his death, perhaps owing to the inability of followers such as James Mill and J.R. McCulloch to work to the same high level of abstraction, 'Ricardian' economics was rendered platitudinous and diluted to little more than free-trade sloganizing. At the same time, Ricardo's labour theory of value was used by 'Ricardian Socialists' (such as Piercy Ravenstone and Thomas Hodgskin) to justify labour's claim to the whole product — a view Ricardo would have abhorred. Later, his writings exerted a powerful influence on Karl Marx which, if only by association, had the effect of placing Ricardo outside the mainstream of economic thought: a view which Alfred Marshall (and, more recently, Samuel Hollander) attempted to rebut. Following publication of Piero Sraffa's *Production of Commodities by Means of Commodities* (1960) Ricardo again achieved prominence as primogenitor of a 'Neo-Ricardian' school of thought, this identification resting on Sraffa's interpretation of Ricardo in his Introduction to *The Works and Correspondence of David Ricardo*. Sraffa's interpretation has increasingly been challenged, and a consensus has not yet been reached. It is, however, a tribute to Ricardo's complex genius that he should still evoke controversy.

Terry Peach
University of Manchester

Further Reading
Blaug, M. (1958), *Ricardian Economics: A Historical Study*, New Haven, Conn.
Hollander, J. H. (1910), *David Ricardo: A Centenary Estimate*, Baltimore.
Hollander, S. (1979), *The Economics of David Ricardo*, Toronto.
Ricardo, D. (1951–73), *The Works and Correspondence of David Ricardo*, edited by P. Sraffa with the collaboration of M. H. Dobb, Cambridge.

Rogers, Carl R. (1902–1987)

Founder of client-centred or non-directive psychotherapy, Carl Rogers is considered part of the 'third force' in psychotherapy, a force which is characterized in opposition to psychoanalytic approaches on the one hand and behaviourist approaches on the other. Rogers himself thinks of his therapy as a 'person-centred approach' to human relationships, which can be extended to education, marriage and family relationships, intensive groups and even international relations.

Like other members of the third force, Rogers's basic premise is that every human being has an 'actualizing tendency' towards complete growth that can be mobilized in the correct therapeutic setting. Rogers's theory and therapy emphasize the actual here and now relationship between therapist and patient or client rather than the transference. The therapist is encouraged: (1) to be genuine (congruence between his or her feelings and their expression to the client); (2) to show unconditional positive regard for the client; and (3) to demonstrate empathic understanding of the client. The goal is 'to free the client to become an independent, self-directing person'. This method is in contrast to a behaviourist approach, where the therapist selects particular reinforcement techniques to modify particular behaviours.

Beginning his studies at the Union Theological Seminary in New York City, Rogers soon crossed the street to Columbia University's Teachers College (Ph.D. 1931). His early work with children, as Director of the Society for the Prevention of Cruelty to Children in Rochester, New York, led to his 1939 book, *Clinical Treatment of the Problem Child*. Challenging the medical model of psychiatric diagnosis and psychoanalysis, he chronicled the development of his client-centred approach through several books, beginning with *Counselling and Psychotherapy* in 1942. As professor of clinical psychology at the University of Chicago, he published *Client-Centered Therapy* (1951), a statement of his technique which included applications in education – as student-centred teaching – as well as group therapy, and play therapy for children.

On Becoming a Person (1961) brought together Rogers's writings from the 1950s, in which he emphasized that the therapist must be personally present to infuse the therapeutic relationship with an 'I-Thou' quality, a theme taken from the works of the philosopher Martin Buber. Carl Rogers's treatment method has had a profound effect on the practice of psychotherapy, particularly among nonpsychiatrists in their counselling of 'clients' without serious mental illness. Although Rogers himself spent several years attempting to treat patients with serious mental illness, this work was less successful. In the early 1970s, Rogers examined the encounter group movement and the changing institution of marriage. His 1980 collection, *A Way of Being*, highlights autobiographical material about his half-century as a 'practising psychologist'.

Louisa B. Tarullo
Harvard University

Further Reading
Rogers, C. R. (1967), 'C. R. Rogers', in E. Boring and G.
    Lindzey (eds), *A History of Psychology in Autobiography*, vol.
    5, New York.

Rostow, Walt Whitman (1916–)

Few contemporary economists present us with broad vistas on the scale of their classical predecessors. One such, both economist and historian, is Walt W. Rostow whose grand vision of the evolutionary process, whether right or wrong, can be compared with that of Marx. In fact, Rostow describes his *magnum opus* as a non-Communist Manifesto. Very early in his development, Rostow set himself the tasks of applying neoclassical economics to economic history analysis and relating economic forces to social and political ones.

Rostow offers a sweeping generalization of economic growth universally relevant to most societies and periods. This grand design was subject to much criticism for being empty of content, tautological, and historically wrong. However, as M. M. Postan, a benevolent critic, remarked, it does not matter that historical experience of various countries diverges from the sequential order of stages postulated by Rostow, nor that the relevant quantities did not always move as Rostow postulated. Rostow's contribution should be evaluated as a treatise on the morphology of economic development (Kindleberger and di Tella, 1982). And Fishlow (1965), a not so friendly critic, suggests that though we cannot accept the whole of Rostow's explanation of economic growth, 'There is good cause to pursue his many suggestions concerning the process by which industrialization becomes rooted. Rostow, paradoxically, is at his best read as a prospectus rather than as a treatise.' Though to Fishlow the manifesto is nothing but a partial hypothesis, 'it is a rare occasion when operational, albeit partial, theories pregnant with potential are put forward. The conception of take-off is just such an event'. Rostow's pioneering work on British business cycles is regarded by many as the first breakthrough of rigorous application of economic theory to history, anticipating cliometrics.

Born in 1916, Rostow was educated at Yale University. He was a Rhodes scholar in the 1930s, beginning a life-long and fruitful on-and-off association with Oxbridge. His public service career, begun during the war, continued in the post-war years at the UN. In 1951 he joined the Massachusetts Institute of Technology faculty where he remained until 1961, when he became involved in various advisory capacities with the Kennedy-Johnson administrations. His controversial position during the Vietnam war earned him much animosity. In 1969 he returned to the academic world, to the University of Texas at Austin – an association that has proven very fruitful.

George R. Feiwel
University of Tennessee

References
Fishlow, A. (1965), 'Empty economic stages?', *Economic Journal*, 75.
Kindleberger, C. P. and di Tella, G. (eds) (1982), *Economics in the Long View: Essays in Honor of W. W. Rostow*, 3 vols, New York.

Further Reading
Rostow, W. W. (1960), *The Stages of Economic Growth*, Cambridge.
Rostow, W. W. (1978), *The World Economy: History and Prospect*, Austin, Texas.
Rostow, W. W. (1980), *Why the Poor Get Richer and the Rich Slow Down*, Austin, Texas.

Rousseau, Jean-Jacques (1712–78)

Rousseau's contribution to the social sciences has been a paradoxical one. In his first *Discours* (Discours sur les sciences et les arts, 1964 [1750]) ['On science and art'], Rousseau argued that scientific inquiry in general tends rather to corrupt than to enlighten, and that public virtue would be better served by ignorance than by systematic knowledge. On the other hand, in his second *Discours* ('Sur l'origine et les fondements de l'inégalité parmi les hommes', 1964 [1775]) ['On the origins of inequality'], Rousseau himself offered a pioneering work in social theory that generations of social scientists have considered crucial to the founding of such disciplines as sociology and social anthropology – the very sorts of theoretical inquiry that Rousseau had virtually ruled out in his first *Discours* as inimical to the public good (See Derathé, 1970; Durkheim, 1965; Lévi-Strauss, 1962.)

Furthermore, whereas Rousseau argued in the second *Discours* that man is not originally a social being and that sociability is fundamentally alien to man's nature, his argument in *Du contrat social* (1762) [*The Social Contract*, 1978], his main work of political philosophy, is that one can only conceive of a legitimate state where the members are wholeheartedly devoted to the good of the community and are able to identify their own interests with those of the whole society. It would seem that an author whose work is rooted in such basic contradictions would be incapable of producing a cogent and consistent social philosophy, and indeed many critics would dismiss Rousseau's achievement on just these grounds. However, one of the central claims of Rousseau's thought is that society itself is founded on irresolvable contradiction, and that therefore paradox may be the most appropriate medium in which to understand the essence of social life.

It is in his magnificent treatise on education, *Émile, ou de l'education* (1762) [*Émile*, 1979], that Rousseau states the basic insight of his social theory – the impossibility of reconciling the contradiction between nature and society: 'He who would preserve the supremacy of natural feelings in social life knows not what he asks. Ever at war with himself, hesitating between his wishes and his duties, he will be neither a man nor a citizen. He will be of no use to himself nor to others. He will be a man of our day, a Frenchman, an Englishman, one of the great middle class.' This insight is further developed in *The Social Contract* (published in the same year as *Émile*).

The core idea of *The Social Contract* is a very simple one: it is that no polity can be considered legitimate except in so far as its laws issue from the will of its members; that citizens are only entitled to renounce natural liberty for the sake of a superior freedom; and that the touchstones of politics based on right are law, democratic will and popular sovereignty. Rousseau managed to articulate a vision of politics as a moral community, even though he remained suspicious of all social relationships and held to the view that society as such is inevitably corrupting. His solution to the problem lay in substituting the power of law for the power of men, thus making men independent of one another by making them all equally dependent on the laws of the republic.

Although Rousseau categorically repudiated the conditions of political life in modernity, many of the fundamental ideas of liberal democracy are owed to him: the idea that the overarching function of government is legislation; the idea that political legitimacy flows from the will of the people; and the idea that formal equality and the rule of law are essential to democratic liberty.

From the first *Discours* onwards, Rousseau's work represented a lifelong battle against the assumptions and aspirations of the Enlightenment. Although Rousseau knew, and had been personally close to, many of the leading members of the French Enlightenment, his ideas led him into increasingly heated and passionate controversies with the champions of Enlightenment. Of these, the most significant product was Rousseau's *Lettre à d'Alembert sur les spectacles* (1758) [*Letter to D'Alembert*, 1968], debating the issue of whether the theatre should be introduced into Rousseau's native city of Geneva. In general, the spokesmen of the Enlightenment sought to refashion the nature of man and society by constructing scientific principles of social existence. Rousseau, by contrast, thought that man is best as he is by nature, that human nature is invariably deformed by life in society, and that such a science of society could only deepen the corruption and debasement of man. This was, in fact, the central insight of his social and moral philosophy, the foundation upon which all his political principles and psychological analyses are built.

Despite recurrent attempts to expose 'totalitarian' traits within Rousseau's political thought, the ever-present concern throughout his political writings was with republican liberty. Rousseau feared that without the sustaining nourishment of genuine citizenship and civic virtue, men in society would become slaves to social conformity, that they would (in the words of the second *Discours*) always live outside of themselves rather than within themselves, and that they would forfeit their natural liberty without attaining the higher condition of civil freedom, thus being worse off rather than better for having left nature to enter social existence. Notwithstanding the supposed romanticism attributed to Rousseau's thought, he possessed a sober and clear-headed insight into the possibility that post-Enlightenment science and technological civilization would pose an ever-greater threat to freedom and civic solidarity.

Even though Rousseau's literary and autobiographical writings have established the image of him as an unworldly and misanthropic dreamer, his political discernment is testified to by his acute diagnosis of the crumbling social order in Europe: In *Considérations sur le gouvernement de la Pologne* (1782) [*The Government of Poland*, 1972] Rousseau writes, 'I see all the states of Europe hastening to their doom'; in *Émile*, he predicts, 'The crisis is approaching, and we are on the edge of a revolution'; 'In my opinion it is impossible that the great kingdoms of Europe should last much longer'.

There remains, of course, the predictable complaint that Rousseau's social theory is irretrievably utopian, and cannot in any sense be applied to modern conditions. For Rousseau himself, given the conception of political philosophy that he adheres to, and steeped as he is in the classical utopianism of Plato, this does not necessarily count as a very telling objection. As he remarks in *Émile*, 'We dream and the dreams of a bad night are given to us as philosophy. You will say I too am a dreamer; I admit this, but I do what the others fail to do. I give my dreams as dreams, and leave the reader to discover whether there is anything in them which may prove useful to those who are awake.'

Ronald Beiner
University of Southampton
and Queen's University, Kingston, Ontario

References

Derathé, R. (1970), *Jean-Jacques Rousseau et la science politique de son temps*, Paris.

Durkheim, E. (1965 [1953]), *Montesquieu and Rousseau: Forerunners of Sociology*, trans. R. Manheim, Ann Arbor, Mich. (French edn, *Montesquieu et Rousseau, précursors de la sociologie*, Paris.)

Lévi-Strauss, C. (1962), 'Jean-Jacques Rousseau, fondateur des sciences de l'homme', in S. Baud-Bovy *et al.*, *Jean-Jacques Rousseau*, Neuchâtel.

Further Reading
Texts by Rousseau:
(1979), *Emile, or On Education*, trans. A. Bloom, New York.
(1964), *The First and Second Discourses*, ed. R. D. Masters, trans. R. D. and J. R. Masters, New York.
(1972), *The Government of Poland*, trans. W. Kendall, Indianapolis.
(1978) *On the Social Contract*, ed. R. D. Masters, trans. J. R. Masters, New York.
(1968), *Politics and the Arts*, trans. A. Bloom, Ithaca, New York.
Other:
Masters, R. D. (1968), *The Political Philosophy of Rousseau*, Princeton, New Jersey.
Shklar, J. N. (1969), *Men and Citizens: A Study of Rousseau's Social Theory*, Cambridge.

Saint-Simon, Claude-Henri De (1700–1825)

Born into the nobility but an advocate of doing away with hereditary privileges, Saint-Simon was a true entrepreneur of social ideas and an early visionary of major features and trends of the modern industrial social order. Paradoxically, he later formulated principles of socialism and corporatism. Though it was his secretary Auguste Comte who coined the term 'sociology', Saint-Simon merits credit for having conceptualized a science of social organization, which he called 'social physiology' to emphasize that historical change is at the heart of human society. Saint-Simon's analyses of social classes, social stratification, and the relation between dominant ideas and social organization were taken over by later Marxism. Saint-Simon viewed conflict between classes and revolutions as explosions of social contradictions to be recurrent features of Western history, which he saw as alternating between 'organic periods' and 'periods of crises'. Still, he saw the progress of a new age, anticipated by Condorcet, as realizable through increased productivity of all sectors of society. What was needed was a new political system, based on scientific knowledge and led by a meritocracy of scientists, artists, and industrialists. The science of society would synthesize the knowledge necessary for reorganizing the polity and ending a period of crises. Saint-Simon proposed (*De la réorganisation de la société européene*, 1814; *The Reorganization of European Society*) that to facilitate the productive forces of an industrial age, a new European Parliament should replace present national bodies. A common body politic had existed in the Middle Ages, and a new one, cemented by the social teachings of a 'new Christianity', could be founded having as its mission the uplift or socialization (in the sense of full social participation) of the impoverished proletariat, the most numerous class. Thus, for Saint-Simon, economic and spiritual development would lead to the end of the exploitation of man by man.

Edward A. Tiryakian
Duke University, North Carolina

Further Reading

Manuel, F. E. (1956), *The New World of Henri Saint-Simon*, Cambridge, Mass.
Taylor, K. (ed.) (1975), *Henri Saint-Simon (1760–1825): Selected Writings*, New York.
See also: *Comte*.

Sartre, Jean-Paul (1905–80)

Although not the originator of the term existentialism (Gabriel Marcel was), Jean-Paul Sartre is undoubtedly the figure who made existential philosophy one of the most powerful intellectual currents over a twenty-year period from the early 1940s onwards. A philosopher by training, he extended the existential phenomenology of Husserl and Heidegger in a landmark treatise, *L'être et le néant* (1943) (*Being and Nothingness*, 1956), and in a famous conference which marked post-war France (*Existentialism and Humanism*, 1948). Sartre was a man of letters par excellence, but for the purpose of this volume, we will gloss over his considerable contributions as a novelist, playwright, and literary critic, as well as editor of a major review (*Les Temps Modernes*). However, there is a unity and totality to his writings, the many-sided search and affirmation of freedom as the basic aspect of the human condition.

Man, for Sartre, does not have an essential or objective nature; he is what he chooses to be; he is foremost a project, or in the famous Sartrian formula, 'Existence precedes essence'. Men do not exist in the abstract but in situations. There is a duality of being in all human situations, a being 'in-itself' (*en soi*), that of fixed objects, and a transcending being which is consciousness (*pour soi*), subjectivity. Where Marx talked of 'commodification', Sartre talked of 'objectification' or the reduction of conscious being to inert, object being. The theme of alienation common to both Marxists and Sartrian analysis derives ultimately from Hegel (who influenced both Marx and Kierkegaard, the forerunner of existential thought). In Sartre's early analyses, *La nausée* (1938) (*Nausea*, 1948); *Huis clos* (1945) (*No Exit*, 1946) and other works, social relationships are sources of self-alienation (quite in contrast to G. H. Mead who viewed them as sources of self-development). Both the person and others can equate or identify the role one plays with the being of the self, that is, self is reduced to a given social role defined by others. For Sartre, this reduction of being *qua* social object is to live inauthentically, in 'bad faith'. Sartre viewed organized, institutionalized society – at least the bourgeois society that he, like his surrealist predecessors, never ceased to inveigh against – as a set of oppressive objectification of practices, what he termed 'pratico-inert'.

As a 'man of the left', Sartre was convinced that intellectual writers should be 'engaged' in causes, that thoughts and social action are one. His classroom was the Café Flore and the Café des Deux Magots on the Left Bank more than the university. He had deep involvements with Marxism (reflected in *Critique de la raison dialectique*, 1960 [*Critique of Dialectical Reason*, 1976]), with the French Communist Party and the Soviet Union (manifest in his refusal to accept the Nobel Prize), and he was in the vanguard of various protest movements: bitterly opposed to French colonialism (Indochina, and particularly Algeria) and American imperialism in Vietnam, as well as the Soviet intervention in Czechoslovakia in 1968. His existential perspective made him the champion of all whose liberty he saw as deprived by inauthentic society, whether the oppressed were homosexuals (*Saint Genet, comédien et martyr*, 1952) (*Saint Genet, Actor and Martyr*, 1964), or Jews (*Anti-Semite and Jew*, 1948), or Blacks ('Black Orpheus' in an anthology of poems edited by Senghor), or colonial victims (introduction to F. Fanon's *Wretched of the Earth*). He sided with revolutionary and protest movements (China, Cuba, the May 1968 student movement), because in their projects he saw the possibility of human freedom being realized for all. His direct influence on the social sciences was meagre, but his moral influence on a great many social scientists and on a wider public was immense. As Marcuse said of him, Sartre was 'the conscience of the world'.

Edward A. Tiryakian
Duke University, North Carolina

Further Reading

Craib, I. (1976), *Existentialism and Sociology: A Study of Jean-Paul Sartre*, Cambridge.

Hayim, G. J. (1980), *The Existential Sociology of Jean-Paul Sartre*, Amherst, Mass.

Stack, G. J. (1977), *Sartre's Philosophy of Social Existence*, St Louis.

Tiryakian, E. A. (1979), *Sociologism and Existentialism*, New York.

Saussure, Ferdinand de (1857–1913)

Although linguistics existed as a science as early as the beginning of the nineteenth century, Ferdinand de Saussure, born in 1857 in Geneva, son of an eminent Swiss naturalist, is generally regarded as the founder of modern linguistics. Saussure's *Cours de linguistique générale*, 1916 (*Course in General Linguistics*, New

York, 1959) is the most important of all linguistic works written in Western Europe in the twentieth century. Yet it was first published only after his death and was an edited version of notes taken by his students of lectures he gave in Geneva between 1907 and 1911. After having spent ten productive years (1881–91) teaching in Paris (before returning to a chair at Geneva, where he remained until his death), Saussure became increasingly perfectionist, and this prevented him from presenting any treatment of linguistics in the form of a book, since he found it impossible to write anything at all, on such a difficult subject, which he regarded as worthy of publication. This combination of modesty and painful consciousness may explain why he only produced two books in his lifetime, both of them when he was still young, and both in comparative and Indo-European grammar, and not in theoretical linguistics. His first book, published in 1879, when he was only twenty-one, was written in Leipzig while he was attending the lectures of two important Neo-grammarians, Leskien and Curtius. His brilliant insights into the vexed question of the Indo-European resonants brought him immediate fame. The second book was his doctoral dissertation (1880), and was concerned with the absolute genitive in Sanskrit.

Saussure's major contribution is to theoretical linguistics. Yet his writings on the subject are confined to the *Cours*, and then only in the introduction, in Part One 'Principes généraux', and in Part Two, 'Linguistique synchronique', the remainder of the book, albeit suggestive, not having enjoyed equivalent fame. His theory is characterized by the famous distinctions he introduced, which were adopted later by all linguists, and by his conception of the linguistic sign.

After distinguishing the study of all social institutions from semiology, as the study of sign systems, then semiology itself from linguistics, and finally the study of language in general from the study of specific human languages, Saussure arrives at the distinctions which have deeply influenced all linguistic thinking and practice in this century. These are:

(1) *Langue* versus *parole*, that is, a distinction between, on the

one hand, language as a social resource and inherited system made up of units and rules combining them at all levels, and, on the other hand, speech as the concrete activity by which language is manifested and put to use by individuals in specific circumstances. Saussure states that linguistics proper is linguistics of *langue*, even though we may speak of a linguistics of *parole* and despite the fact that the use of speech alters language systems themselves in the course of history. In fact, he only considers linguistics of *langue* in the *Cours*.

(2) *Synchrony* versus *diachrony*: Saussure repeatedly emphasizes that linguistics, like any other science dealing with values (see below), must embrace two perspectives. A synchronic study is conducted without consideration of the past and it deals with the system of relationships which is reflected in a language as a collective construct. A diachronic study deals mostly with unconscious historical change from one state to another.

(3) *Syntagmatic* versus *associative* relationships: a syntagm is defined as a combination of words in the speech chain, and it ties together elements that are effectively present, whereas the relationships called *associative* by Saussure (and, later, 'paradigmatic' by Hjelmslev) unite absent terms belonging to a virtual mnemonic series. Thus, the word *teaching* has an associative relationship with the words *education, training, instruction*, and so on, but a syntagmatic relationship with the word *his* in the syntagm *his teaching*. Saussure adds that the very best type of syntagm is the sentence, but he says that sentences belong to *parole* and not to *langue*, so that they are excluded from consideration. This attitude, although consistent, was to have serious consequences for structural linguistics, as it is the reason for its almost total neglect of syntax.

Saussure defines the linguistic sign as a double-faced psychic entity which comprises the concept and the acoustical image. These he calls the *signifié* and the *signifiant*. The sign has two fundamental material characteristics. First, it is arbitrary. There is no internal and necessary relationship between the signifié and the signifiant; if there were any, then, to take an example [ks] would be the only possible signifiant for the meaning 'ox'. Thus different languages would not exist in the world. Second, the signifiant is linear: it is uttered along the time dimension, which is a line, and it is not possible to utter more than one sign at the same time. Saussure adds that the whole mechanism of language relies on this essential principle.

Saussure then goes on to treat the notion of *'value' (valeur)*, which is the status of a linguistic unit in relation to other units, from the very existence of which it draws its definition, so that value and identity are two notions that can be equated. Therefore, in language, as Saussure says in a formula that was to become very famous, 'there are only differences'. For example, since English *sheep* coexists, in the language, with *mutton*, whereas there is nothing comparable as far as the French *mouton* is concerned, *sheep*, although meaning *mouton*, has a different value.

Saussure's theory, despite its uncompleted form, has been very influential. The phonology of the Prague School and Hjelmslevian glossomatics, to mention only two examples, owe much to it. Even some of the gaps have been indirectly useful. Thus, the absence of the sentence has been compensated for by transformational syntax, and the nontreatment of the linguistics of *parole* by the development of pragmatics.

Claude Hagège
École Pratique des Hautes Études
University of Paris

References
Saussure, F. de (1879), *Mémoire sur le système primitif des voyelles dans les langues indo-européennes*, Leipzig.
Saussure, F. de (1880), *De l'emploi du génitif absolu en sanscrit*, Geneva.
Saussure, F. de (1916), *Cours de linguistique générale*, Paris.

Further Reading
Amacker, R. (1975), *Linguistique saussurienne*, Paris and Geneva.
Culler, J. (1976), *Saussure*, Glasgow.
Engler, R. (ed.) (1968–74), *Ferdinand de Saussure, Cours de linguistique générale*, Wiesbaden.

Schumpeter, Joseph Alois (1883–1950)

Schumpeter, who belongs to the top layer of eminent twentieth-century economists, cannot be easily assigned to a definite school or branch of economics. His outstanding characteristics were his broad erudition, his interdisciplinary thinking, combining economic theory with sociology and history, and his immense capacity for mastering plentiful and difficult materials.

Throughout his life he was attracted by the problem which dominated the thinking of the classical economists and of Marx: the long-term dynamics of the capitalist system. He saw one of the main sources of growth (and profits) in the existence of 'risk-loving' entrepreneurs who, by pioneering new products, new production methods and so on, are destroying old structures and inducing change. This idea was already propounded in his early *Theorie der wirtschaftlichen Entwicklung* (1912) (*Theory of Economic Development*, 1951), and then came up repeatedly, particularly in his monumental two-volume study on all aspects of the business-cycle – theoretical, statistical, historical (*Business Cycles*, 1939). The intertwining of economic, sociological and political factors and their influence on long-term trends was treated in a more popular fashion in *Capitalism, Socialism and Democracy* (1942), which became an outstanding success. After Schumpeter's death, his widow. Elizabeth Boody, edited the unfinished *History of Economic Analysis* (1954), an enormous and unique tableau of economic thought from earliest times till today.

The numerous economic and sociological publications by Schumpeter, which included seventeen books, were produced in his academic career which led him from provincial universities in the Habsburg Empire (Czernowitz, Graz) to the University of Bonn (1925), and finally to Harvard University

(1932). In between he had an unlucky spell as Minister of Finance and private banker in inflation-ridden Austria just after World War I.

Kurt W. Rothschild
Johannes Kepler University, Linz

Further Reading
Frisch, H. (ed.) (1981), *Schumpeterian Economics*, Eastbourne.
Harris, S. E. (ed.) (1951), *Schumpeter: Social Scientist*,
   Cambridge, Mass.

Simmel, Georg (1858–1918)

Lukács, a student and early admirer, who later became an important Marxist theorist and an outspoken critic of social scientists, once called Simmel the greatest 'philosopher of transition' of his day. Simmel was the only one among his academic contemporaries in Germany who was able to draw upon the conflicting schools of philosophy of the time (neo-Kantianism, neo-Hegelianism, Marxism, and Philosophy of Life) to define the starting point for analyses of a kind that probably only he was capable of carrying out. Simmel could exploit a variety of theoretical idioms, and he could also combine different disciplinary and methodological perspectives. He studied important cultural phenomena such as religion, the money economy, the rise of morality, the self-preservation of groups, using modes of analysis drawn from philosophy, psychology, sociology, economics and theology, each of which yielded specific insights. This pluralism, however, made him suspect among his colleagues, most of whom were preoccupied with gaining academic recognition, building up a following, and establishing the special claims of their disciplines. Yet today, long after his more limited critics have been forgotten, it is precisely this synthesizing approach which is Simmel's attraction for those who wish to break through the traditional disciplinary boundaries within the social sciences.

Simmel once described his work, with deliberate ambiguity,

as a 'struggle for life'. He referred to the mental and physical struggle for individual survival in a sociocultural environment increasingly dominated by an expanding technology, economy, and bureaucracy, and, also, to the struggle of the educated bourgeoisie against growing 'proletarianization' of spiritual and material life, a development which was equally the consequence of industrialization, mass consumption, and modern conditions of living and communication.

This critical and conservative argument was pursued in so many domains, although at times his methodology was insufficiently developed so that his interpreters could not easily comprehend the underlying logic. Simmel himself recognized that the fate of his legacy was in doubt. His most enduring contributions have proved to be his works on Kant (including *Kant*, 1904; *Kant und Goethe*, 1906; and *Hauptprobleme der Philosophie*, 1910), his writings on the philosophy of art and culture (including *Philosophische Kultur*, 1911; *Rembrandt*, 1916; and *Zur Philosophie der Kunst*, 1922), and above all, his analyses of capitalism and his attempt to define a distinctive sociology with its own methods, themes and theories.

Simmel was born a Jew, but he was baptised and received a Christian education. He spent most of his life in Berlin and was a thoroughly metropolitan and urban figure. As he showed in a study which is still worth reading, the metropolis provided the point of reference for his critical analyses of modern culture (*Die Grosstadte und das Geistesleben*, 1903). When his father, a businessman, died, a friend of the family supported him while he completed his studies, and enabled him to live without financial anxieties as a *Privat-dozent*, whose only income would otherwise have come from lecture fees.

Simmel had a considerable reputation in Germany and abroad, yet his academic career was not smooth. In fact, he was a victim of discrimination because of his Jewish origins and his unorthodox life and views. He was repeatedly passed over for positions in the University of Berlin, and in both 1908 and 1915 he was rejected by the University of Heidelberg, with which he had philosophical affinities, despite the support of such famous colleagues and friends as Max Weber, Rickert and Husserl.

But the failure, in conventional terms, of Simmel's career was above all a consequence of his individualistic intellectual development. Initially, he was mainly concerned with problems of natural science, social philosophy and evolution (*Über soziale Differenzierung*, 1890). He later took up a critique of idealism, reconstructing the origins and meaning of morality, on the basis of novel psychological, sociological and historical insights (*Einleitung in die Moralwissenschaften*, 1892–3). Then, for several years, he was concerned with aspects of the Kantian theory of knowledge and with problems in the philosophy of history (*Die Probleme der Geschichtsphilosophie*, 1892) (*The Problems of the Philosophy of History*, 1977). In the process he developed a typological and interpretive approach which he then employed in a 'Marx-completing' (as he himself put it) study of the impact of a money economy on human life (*Philosophie des Geldes*, 1900) (*The Philosophy of Money*, 1978), and in other topical studies.

Simmel's analysis of capitalism and his *Soziologie: Untersuchungen über die Formen der Vergesellschaftung* (1908), which includes most of his contributions to pure sociology in this period, are now generally regarded as his main contributions to the establishment of sociology as a science. There has been particular interest in his concept of a 'formal' or 'pure' sociology, in which the forms of social life are abstracted from their historical-material context. In this way he treated topics such as power, conflict, group structure, individuality and social differentiation. These exercises have also been the object of strong, sometimes one-sided, and uninformed, criticism.

At about the same time, Simmel engaged in an extensive discussion of Marxist theories of value and of alienation. Politically, he was for a while attracted by the ideology of the Social Democrats. He was a founder member of the German sociological association, served on its board, and delivered the opening lecture at its inaugural meeting in 1910, but he resigned from the organization two years later because of conflicts concerning the theory and politics of science, although giving as his reason his desire to concentrate on philosophical interests.

He now turned to philosophical questions of life and culture, under the influence of Hegelian thinking (*Lebensanchaungen*, 1918; *Der Konflikt der modernen Kultur*, 1918). These works earned him a name as a metaphysician and as an apologist for capitalism, but in a later work, *Grundfragen der Soziologie* (1917), he argued that his entire œuvre was engaged with one basic question: the limits of individuality in modern society. He died before he was able to develop the projected new social science, which was to encompass psychological, philosophical and epistemological aspects, and which would amount to a 'general' or 'philosophical' sociology. For those who share this ambition, his work remains a rewarding resource.

Peter-Ernst Schnabel
University of Bielefeld

Further Reading
A.
Works of Simmel in English translation include:
The Sociology of Religion, 1959.
Fundamental Problems of Sociology, 1950.
The Philosophy of Money, 1937.
Two valuable anthologies are:
Levine, D. N. (ed.) (1971), *Georg Simmel on Individuality and Social Forms, Selected Writings*, Chicago.
Wolff, K. H. (1950), *The Sociology of Georg Simmel*, Glencoe, Ill.
B.
Coser, L. A. (ed.) (1965), *Georg Simmel*, Englewood Cliffs, NJ.
Frisby, D. P. (1981), *Sociological Impressionism: A Reassessment of Georg Simmel's Social Theory*, London.

Simon, Herbert A. (1916–)

Herbert A. Simon is a social scientist for all seasons. He has made signal contributions to economics, psychology, political science, sociology, philosophy, computer science and business administration, but with a common theme of inquiry running throughout his work: the study of human (organizational) decision making for which he was awarded the 1978 Nobel

Memorial Prize in Economics. But unlike the economic imperialists, Simon addresses his works in various disciplines in the languages of those disciplines. In 1976, Simon was nominated Distinguished Fellow of the American Economics Association and was cited, *inter alia*, for showing that a unified social science is still possible and for going far in demonstrating how to build it.

Born in 1916 in Milwaukee, Wisconsin, Simon obtained a Ph.D. in political science from the University of Chicago. After a few years of field research in municipal administration and on the faculty of the Illinois Institute of Technology, in 1949 Simon became one of the founding fathers of the Graduate School of Industrial Administration at Carnegie where he has remained a guiding light in the development of the business and psychology programmes.

Within the unifying theme of decision making, Simon's professional career can be divided into two major categories: (1) decisions in organizations and modelling of behaviour, and (2) artificial intelligence. (1) He developed two closely inter-related concepts: bounded rationality and satisficing – two ideas which he admits form the core of his entire intellectual activity (Simon, 1980). In a nutshell these concepts focus on the limits of human and organizational gathering and processing of information. These ideas challenged the dominant notion of rational economic man and gave rise to the behavioural study of organizations, but did not quite penetrate mainstream economics. His contributions to economics also include the relations between causal ordering and identifiability, the theorem on the conditions for the existence of positive solution vectors for input-output matrices, theorems on near-decomposability and aggregation, and a number of applied econometric studies. Simon is also one of the pioneers of operations research. (2) In the mid-1950s Simon and Allen Newell (1972) approached the study of problem-solving through computer simulation. They opened up and have since concentrated on the entire spectrum of artificial intelligence and human cognition.

In his autobiography Simon (1980) notes that early in his career he perceived the need to infuse into the social sciences the kind of rigour, mathematical underpinnings, and techniques of experimentation that had contributed to the success of the natural sciences and that he aims at closer relations between the natural and social scientists.

George R. Feiwel
University of Tennessee

References
Newell, A. and Simon, H. A. (1972), *Human Problem Solving*, Englewood Cliffs, NJ.
Simon, H. A. (1980), 'Herbert A. Simon', in G. Lindzey (ed.), *A History of Psychology in Autobiography*, Vol. VII, San Francisco.

Further Reading
Ando, A. (1979), 'On the contributions of Herbert A. Simon to economics', *Scandinavian Journal of Economics*, 81.
Baumol, W. J. (1979), 'On the contributions of Herbert A. Simon to economics', *Scandinavian Journal of Economics*, 81.
March, J. G. (1978), 'The 1978 Nobel Prize in Economics', *Science*, 202.
Simon, H. A. (1976 [1947]), *Administrative Behavior*, 3rd edn, New York.
Simon, H. A. (1982), *Models of Bounded Rationality*, 2 Vols, Cambridge, Mass.

Skinner, Burrhus F. (1904–)

A behaviourist and the most prominent figure in contemporary American psychology, Skinner has devoted most of his professional career to studying the effects of the consequences of behaviour on behaviour. He received his Ph.D. from Harvard in 1931, and from 1948 to 1975 was a professor there. His approach is descriptive and inductive; he is unconcerned with the physiological, mental, or affective processes taking place within organisms (see *The Behavior of Organisms*, 1938). The prototypic environment for Skinnerian (operant) conditioning is the Skinner Box, a chamber designed to give the animal being conditioned little room to move around in; it is equipped with a lever or other manipulandum which when activated produces a specific consequence (for example, food, water, avoidance of electric shock) according to a predetermined schedule. A consequence which, over trials, leads to an increase in the frequency of the response producing the consequence is referred to as a reinforcing stimulus. One of Skinner's major contributions has been to demonstrate that various schedules of reinforcement are characterized by unique response-frequency patterns. The ability to generate predictable response patterns has, in turn, found useful application in almost all areas of psychological research. Operant conditioning techniques also comprise the primary procedural foundation of behaviour modification, a set of intervention strategies which have been effectively employed in all major institutional settings, particularly in schools, mental hospitals, and care facilities for the psychologically retarded. Skinner was one of the pioneers of programmed learning. As a social critic, he has throughout his professional life advocated the reorganization of societies so that positive reinforcement (rewarding desired behaviours) rather than punishment or the threat of punishment be used to control human actions. His philosophy is detailed in two widely read books, *Walden Two* (1948), a novel about an entire society being controlled by operant techniques, and *Beyond Freedom and Dignity* (1971). Skinner's most important general contribution to the social and behavioural sciences may be to inspire methodological precision and accountability.

Albert R. Gilgen
University of Northern Iowa

Further Reading
Gilgen, A. R. (1982), *American Psychology since World War II: A Profile of the Discipline*, Westport, Connecticut.

Smith, Adam (1723–90)

Adam Smith was born in Kirkcaldy, on the East Coast of Scotland, in 1723. After attending the Burgh School Smith proceeded to Glasgow University (1737–40) where he studied under Francis Hutcheson. Thereafter he took up a Snell Exhibition in Balliol College, Oxford (1740–6). In 1748 Henry Home (Lord Kames) sponsored a course of public lectures on rhetoric and Smith was appointed to deliver them. The course was successful and led, in 175l, to Smith's election to the chair of logic in Glasgow University where he lectured on language and on the communication of ideas. In 1752 Smith was transferred to the chair of moral philosophy where he continued his teaching in logic, but extended the range to include natural theology, ethics, jurisprudence and economics.

Smith's most important publications in this period, apart from two contributions to the *Edinburgh Review* (1755–6), were the *Theory of Moral Sentiments* (1759, later editions, 176l, 1767, 1774, 1781, 1790) and the *Considerations Concerning the First Formation of Languages* (1761).

The *Theory of Moral Sentiments* served to draw Smith to the attention of Charles Townsend and was to lead to his appointment as tutor to the Duke of Buccleuch in 1764, whereupon he resigned his chair. The years 1764–6 were spent in France, first in Bordeaux and later in Paris where Smith arrived after a tour of Geneva and a meeting with Voltaire. The party settled in Paris late in 1765 where Smith met the leading *philosophes*. Of especial significance were his contacts with the French economists or Physiocrats, notably Quesnay and Turgot, who had already developed a sophisticated macroeconomic model for a capital using system.

Smith returned to London in 1766, and to Kirkcaldy in the following year. The next six years were spent at home working on his major book, which was completed after a further three years in London (1773–6). The basis of Smith's continuing fame, *An Inquiry into the Nature and Causes of the Wealth of Nations*, was published on 9 March 1776. It was an immediate success and later editions (of which the third is the most important) appeared in 1778, 1784, 1786 and 1789.

In 1778 Smith was appointed Commissioner of Customs and of the Salt Duties, posts which brought an additional income of £600 per annum (to be added to the continuing pension of

£300 from Buccleuch) and which caused Smith to remove his household to Edinburgh (where his mother died in 1784). Adam Smith himself died, unmarried, on 17 July 1790 after ensuring that his literary executors, Joseph Black and James Hutton, had burned all his manuscripts with the exception of those which were published under the title of *Essays on Philosophical Subjects* (1795). He did not complete his intended account of 'the general principles of law and government', although generous traces of the argument survive in the lecture notes.

The broad structure of the argument on which Smith based his system of social sciences may be established by following the order of Smith's lectures from the chair of moral philosophy. The ethical argument is contained in *Theory of Moral Sentiments* and stands in the broad tradition of Hutcheson and Hume. Smith was concerned, in large measure, to explain the way in which the mind forms judgements as to what is fit and proper to be done or to be avoided. He argued that men form such judgements by visualizing how they would behave in the circumstances confronting another person or how an imagined or 'ideal' spectator might react to their actions or expressions of feeling in a given situation. A capacity to form judgements on *particular* occasions leads in turn to the **emergence** of *general rules* of conduct which correct the natural partiality for self. In particular Smith argued that those rules of behaviour which related to justice constitute the 'main pillar which upholds the whole edifice' of society.

Smith recognized that rules of behaviour would vary in different communities at the same point in time as well as over time, and addressed himself to this problem in the lectures on jurisprudence. In dealing with 'private law' such as that which relates to life, liberty or property, Smith deployed the analysis of the *Theory of Moral Sentiments* in explaining the origin of particular rules in the context of four socioeconomic stages – those of hunting, pasture, agriculture and commerce. In the lectures on 'public' jurisprudence he paid particular attention to the transition from the feudal-agrarian state to that of commerce; that is, to the emergence of the exchange economy and the substitution of a cash for a service nexus.

The economic analysis which completed the sequence and which culminated in the *Wealth of Nations* is predicated upon a system of justice and takes as given the point that self-regarding actions have a social reference. In fact the most complete statement of the psychology on which the *Wealth of Nations* relies is to be found in Part VI of *The Theory of Moral Sentiments* which was added in 1790.

The formal analysis of the *Wealth of Nations* begins with an account of the division of labour and of the phenomenon of economic interdependence before proceeding to the analysis of price, the allocation of resources and the treatment of distribution. Building on the equilibrium analysis of Book I, the second book develops a version of the Physiocratic *model* of the circular flow of income and output before proceeding to the analysis of the main theme of economic growth. Here, as throughout Smith's work, the emphasis is upon the unintended consequences of individual activity and leads directly to the policy prescriptions with which Smith is most commonly associated: namely, the call for economic liberty and the dismantling of all impediments, especially mercantilist impediments, to individual effort.

Yet Smith's liberalism can be exaggerated. In addition to such necessary functions as the provision of defence, justice and public works, Jacob Viner (1928) has shown that Smith saw a wide and elastic range of governmental activity.

The generally 'optimistic' tone which Smith uses in discussing the performance of the modern economy has also to be qualified by reference to further links with the ethical and historical analyses. Smith gave a great deal of attention to the social consequences of the division of labour, emphasizing the problem of isolation, the breakdown of the family unit, and that mental mutilation (affecting the capacity for moral judgement) which follows from concentrating the mind on a restricted range of activities. If government has to act in this, as in other spheres, Smith noted that it would be constrained by the habits and prejudices of the governed. He observed further that the type of government often found in conjuction with the exchange or commercial economy would be subject to pressure from particular economic interests, thus limiting its efficiency, and, also, that the political sphere, like the economic, was a focus for the competitive pursuit of power and status.

A. S. Skinner
Glasgow University

References
Works by Adam Smith:

I *Theory of Moral Sentiments*, ed. D. D. Raphael and A. L. Macfie (1976).
II *Wealth of Nations*, ed. R. H. Campbell, A. S. Skinner and W. B. Todd (1976).
III *Essays on Philosophical Subjects*, ed. W. P. D. Wightman (1980) consisting of:
  'The History of Astronomy'; 'The History of the Ancient Physics'; 'History of the Ancient Logics and Metaphysics';
'Of the External Senses'; 'Of the Imitative Arts';
'Of the Affinity between Music, Dancing and Poetry'.
The volume also includes:
'Contributions to the *Edinburgh Review*' (1755–6) and
'Of the Affinity between certain English and Italian Verses', edited by J. C. Bryce.
Dugald Stewart, *Account of the Life and Writings of Adam Smith*, edited by I. S. Ross.
IV *Lectures on Rhetoric and Belles Lettres*, ed. J. C. Bryce (1983). This volume includes the *Considerations Concerning the First Formation of Languages*.
V *Lectures on Jurisprudence*, ed. R. L. Meek, D. D. Raphael and P. G. Stein (1978). This volume includes two sets of students notes.
VI *Correspondence of Adam Smith*, edited by E. C. Mossner and I. S. Ross (1977). This volume includes:
A Letter from Governor Pownall to Adam Smith (1776);

Smith's *Thoughts on the State of the Contest with America* (1778);
and
Jeremy Bentham's *Letters to Adam Smith on Usury* (1787, 1790).

Further Reading

Campbell, T. D. (1971), *Adam Smith's Science of Morals*, London.

Haakonssen, K. (1981), *The Science of the Legislator: The Natural Jurisprudence of David Hume and Adam Smith*, Cambridge.

Hollander, S. (1973), *The Economics of Adam Smith*, Toronto.

Lindgren, R. (1975), *The Social Philosophy of Adam Smith*, The Hague.

Macfie, A. L. (1967), *The Individual in Society: Papers on Adam Smith*, London.

O'Driscoll, G. P. (ed.) (1979), *Adam Smith and Modern Political Economy*, Iowa.

Rae, J. (1965 [1895]), *Life of Adam Smith*, London. (Reprinted with an introduction by J. Viner, New York.)

Reisman, D. A. (1976), *Adam Smith's Sociological Economics*, London.

Scott, W. R. (1937), *Adam Smith as Student and Professor*, Glasgow.

Skinner, A. S. and Wilson, T. (1975), *Essays on Adam Smith*, Oxford.

Viner, J. (1928), 'Adam Smith and laissez faire', in J. Hollander *et al.*, *Adam Smith, 1776–1926*, Chicago.

Winch, D. (1965), *Classical Political Economy and the Colonies*, London.

Winch, D. (1978), *Adam Smith's Politics*, Cambridge.

Sombart, Werner (1863–1941)

Werner Sombart, a German sociologist, economist and economic historian, first taught at the University of Breslau (1890–1906) and then at a *Hochschule* in Berlin (1906–17). From 1917 to 1931 he was professor at the University of Berlin, and he died in Berlin on 19 May 1941. Sombart's most famous work is his three-volume study on the development of capitalism (*Der moderne Kapitalismus*, 1902–28) in which he presented a survey of the historical phases that capitalism could go through before being replaced by socialism: *Prae-kapitalismus* (see Rostow's traditional society) which is characterized by *das Nährungsprinzip* (food principle), *Frühkapitalismus* (or early capitalism) from the fifteenth century until 1760, *Hochkapitalismus* (or high capitalism) from 1760 until 1913, and *Spätkapitalismus* (or late capitalism) from 1914 on. The last three phases are characterized by the *Erwerbsprinzip*: a restless and rational striving after capital accumulation and profits. Sombart's theory resembles the well-known stage theories of List, Hildebrand, Knies, Bücher, and others, but his different phases are not necessarily determined by chronological succession. Sombart explicitly states that other successions, mixed forms, and even parallel forms appeared in the course of history. Initially strongly influenced by Marx, Sombart later became a pronounced anti-Marxist. He shared with Max Weber the conviction that sociology and economics must be free of value judgements. In his book *Sozialismus und soziale Bewegung im 19 Jahrhundert* (1896) (*Socialism and the Social Movement*, 1909), Sombart revealed himself to be an advocate of profound social reforms for the benefit of the working class. Although he formed no school in the strict sense of the word, he had a great influence on traditional economic history up to 1950.

Erik Aerts
Archives Générales du Royaume, Brussels

Sorel, Georges Eugène (1847–1922)

Often associated with the sociologists Mosca and Pareto, Georges Sorel, the French social philosopher, is more properly seen as an innovator in Marxist theory and the methodology of the social sciences. By temperament a *moraliste*, by training and profession an engineer in government employment (until 1892) and scientist, Sorel's work falls into two broad categories: his writings on politics (including ethics), and his examination of the philosophical problems posed by explanation in general and, more specifically, by science and religion.

Despite frequent changes in political position, the morality advocated by Sorel remained throughout a conservative one, emphasizing the values of work, the family, self-denial and heroism. His earliest writings gave little hint of radicalism, but by 1893 Sorel had espoused Marxism. From 1896 he began a reinterpretation of Marxism, which was initially perceived as a science which had discovered the 'laws' that 'determined' the development of capitalism. This culminated in 1908 in his *Réflexions sur la violence* (*Reflections on Violence*, New York, 1914). Taking the class war as the 'alpha and omega' of socialism, Sorel described the central tenets of Marxism as 'myths', as images capable of inspiring the working class to action. The most powerful of these myths was that of the general strike, which, Sorel hoped, would lead the working class to eschew the practices of parliamentary democracy, adopt the use of violence, and in the process create the ethical and material bases of socialism.

At a philosophical level Sorel sought to discredit the positivist designation of science as the sole legitimate mode of explanation. Defending science as a progressive, experimental activity, Sorel's rejection of its universalistic claims was counterbalanced by a recognition of the distinctiveness of our different forms of consciousness and by an advocacy of both an intellectual and methodological pluralism. These issues were dealt with at length in his defence of William James, *De l'utilité du pragmatisme* (1921).

Jeremy Jennings
University College of Swansea

Further Reading

Roth, J. J. (1980), *The Cult of Violence: Sorel and the Sorelians*, Berkeley and Los Angeles.

Sorel, G. (1969 [1908]), *The Illusions of Progress*, Berkeley and Los Angeles. (Original French edn, *Les illusions du progrès*.)

Sorel, G. (1972 [1914]), *Reflections on Violence*, New York.

Sorel, G. (1976), *From Georges Sorel: Essays in Socialism and Philosophy*, New York.

Stanley, J. L. (1982), *The Sociology of Virtue: The Political and Social Theories of Georges Sorel*, Berkeley and Los Angeles.

Sorokin, Pitirim A. (1889–1968)

One of this century's foremost sociologists, Pitirim A. Sorokin led a very active life: involved in radical politics in his youth in Russia, banished by the Bolshevik government, he became a controversial academic at Harvard. His stress on social dynamics in his *magnum opus*, *Social and Cultural Dynamics* (4 vols, 1937–41, abridged edn, 1957) reflects the social and historical changes he experienced. Social reality for Sorokin is ever-changing, with recurrent discernible features; this entails knowledge of the historical process and of cultures other than our own Western. While Sorokin's study of the rise and fall of cultural systems may liken him to his contemporary Arnold Toynbee, he may also be viewed as a descendant of the first sociological prophet of modern society, Henri Saint-Simon. Both used their experiences of revolutions (the American and the French in the case of Saint-Simon) as stimulants for creative writing about social organization, social discontinuities, and the need for social reconstruction. Both also came to propose altruism as a necessary social force in the 'reconstruction of humanity' (the title of a work of Sorokin published in 1948).

Sorokin's career (presented in the autobiographical *A Long Journey*, 1963) may be divided into three periods. The first reads like a Dostoevsky saga. Born in a poor peasant milieu, never enjoying the care of parents, Sorokin experienced physical as much as intellectual hunger, but his exceptional intellect permitted him to complete graduate training in sociology and criminology. Politically a populist seeking major reforms for the peasantry and the working class, he later became secretary to Kerensky in the provisional government of 1917, which lost out to the Bolsheviks. Sentenced to death for anti-state activities by both the Tzarist and Leninist regimes, he was exiled in 1922. His experiences of the Russian Revolution and of the great Russian famine of 1921 provided him with many observations for materials on social behaviour in extreme situations (*Sociology of Revolution*, 1925; *Man and Society in Calamity*, 1942; *Hunger as a Factor in Human Affairs*, 1975).

The social cataclysms of World War I and the Russian Revolution led him to renounce an earlier optimistic positivism that combined with a general orientation of evolutionary progress. Coming to America in 1924 and moving from the University of Minnesota to establish a department of sociology at Harvard in 1930, Sorokin entered a period of sociological maturity marked by a spate of landmark studies in the areas of social stratification, sociological theory, rural sociology, and social change. His *Social Mobility* (1927) is still an important background work in the area of stratification and mobility, a primary field of investigation for sociology in the United States and Great Britain.

Sorokin suffered a second 'banishment' in the late 1930s, when he found himself eclipsed by a younger colleague, Talcott Parsons, who, unlike Sorokin, succeeded in establishing a major school of sociology, sometimes called the 'structural-functional' school, that drew various of Sorokin's earlier students. Parsons became head of a new department, Social Relations, and after World War II Sorokin was cut off from graduate teaching. Yet he entered a third period of creativity, publishing several works concerning altruistic behaviour (a topic rediscovered twenty years later by sociobiology), as well as critiques of both contemporary sociology (*Fads and Foibles*, 1956) and American society (*The American Sex Revolution*, 1957; *Power and Morality*, 1959). The latter anticipated by a decade the writings of 'humanistic', 'critical' sociology associated with such names as Gouldner, Birnbaum, and Friedrichs, among others. From the 1940s to the mid 1960s, Sorokin's place in American sociology was similar to that of C. Wright Mills at Columbia, both mavericks and gadflies in the profession, both critics of the concentration of military-industrial power. Fortunately, grassroots support provided vindication: Sorokin won the presidency of the American Sociological Association (ASA) in a write-in campaign at age seventy-five, and the year following his death, at the annual meetings of ASA, he was the object of a thronged testimonial session organized by students in recognition of his bitter opposition to the Vietnam war.

Given his enormous productivity, to summarize his writings is necessarily to oversimplify, and the reader should consult major volumes devoted to him (Allen, 1963; Tiryakian, 1963; Hall and Prasad, 1972). A few key emphases, however, may be useful for an initial orientation. Sorokin's 'integralist' sociology is an alternative to the two major sociological paradigms of the contemporary period, namely the 'structural-functional', on the one hand (sometimes identified with a 'consensus' view of society) and the Marxist, on the other (sometimes identified with a 'conflict' model). Unlike both, Sorokin rejected an evolutionary perspective. His major macro-unit of analysis is a *civilization*, a cluster of societies sharing similar paramount cultural orientations, which are reflected in major social institutions. Cultural orientations, or fundamental social values, have three major channels of perceiving and relating to reality: a *sensate* orientation sees truth as contained or expressing the reality of a material, physical universe, hence, stressing the value of the senses; an *ideational* orientation, in contrast, views reality as beyond the senses, transcending the physical world, and being given by faith and revelation; an *idealistic* orientation sees truth as being both in this world and beyond it, hence requiring an enriched reason, somewhat in the mode of Aristotle and Thomas Aquinas. Sorokin's comparative study of civilizations led him to find cycles of fluctuations in the cultural dominance of a given orientation, cycles of ascendancy, maturity and decline which take several centuries to complete. The twentieth century is characterized in the West by advanced industrial societies in the phase of a late sensate culture which rose to hegemony in the sixteenth century and is now marked by increasing hedonism and violence. Change is immanent to all large-scale social groupings but there are limits to the extent that a given cultural orientation can go, akin to the limits of a pendulum swing. In its decadent or declining phase, a civilization frequently experiences calamities or crises which tend to manifest a polarization of behaviour: many persons will come to behave in a rapacious, brutal, hedonistic and even criminal manner, while others will also engage in acts of altruism, charity, self-sacrifice, not found with the same frequency in 'normal times'. Sorokin, like Saint-Simon, saw the present age as one of crisis (*S.O.S. The Meaning of our Crisis*, 1951), one involving the concentration of irresponsible power and the decadence of sensate values. His denunciations of materialism, hedonism and totalitarianism are strikingly similar in tone and content to that of a later Russian exile to America, Aleksandr Solzhenitsyn. Indeed, the latter's famous Harvard address of 1978 (*A World Split Apart*) could well have been pronounced by Sorokin while he was at Harvard.

Edward A. Tiryakian
Duke University
North Carolina

References

Allen, P. J. (ed.) (1963), *Pitirim A. Sorokin in Review*, Durham, N.C.

Hall, G. C. and Prasad, R. (eds) (1972), *Sorokin and Sociology*, New York.

Tiryakian, E. A. (ed.) (1963), *Sociological Theory, Values and Sociocultural Change*, New York.

Further Reading

Coser, L. A. (1977), *Masters of Sociological Thought*, 2nd edn, New York.

Cowell, F. R. (1967), *Values in Human Society – The Sociology of P. A. Sorokin*, Boston.

Spencer, Herbert (1820–1903)

Herbert Spencer was the major theorist of social evolutionism and made important and lasting contributions to sociology's methods and concepts. Born at Derby in the English Midlands, his education was haphazard and strongly inclined to scientific subjects. He never attended secondary school or university and, after some years' employment as a railway engineer and political journalist, he supported himself by his writing.

Strongly marked by his provincial, nonconformist background, Spencer was active in the 1840s in radical middle-class politics and his first book, *Social Statics* (1850), attempts to justify his libertarian social ideals as the necessary outcome of a process of natural development. In the 1850s a series of essays (especially 'The development hypothesis' and 'Progress: its law and cause') drew from biology the elements of a general evolutionary *Naturphilosophie*. This was the basis of his life-work, the multi-volume *System of Synthetic Philosophy* (1862–96) which first set forth a set of general evolutionary principles and then applied them to biology, psychology, sociology and ethics. In sociology in particular Spencer broke new ground in comparative data collection and synthesis. Several other works appeared alongside the *System*: his influential essay *Education* (1860), strongly utilitarian and anti-classical; *The Study of Sociology* (1873), an original exposition of sociological method; and *The Man Versus the State* (1884), a vigorous defence of his *laissez-faire* views.

Spencer was an evolutionist before Darwin – it was even he who coined the phrase 'survival of the fittest' – and always upheld certain pre-Darwinian views, notably the inheritance of acquired characteristics. His evolutionary sociology has a number of distinct strands. From the organic analogy came a functionalist language of societal description and a characterization of progressive or evolutionary change as a process of differentiation in social structures and functions, accompanied by higher levels of integration. Change was also represented as a movement between two distinct types of society: 'militant', where integration derives from a controlling centre (as in an army), and 'industrial', where order is the spontaneous product of individuals co-operating (as in a market). In his later writings Spencer abandoned militant/industrial as a description of process and used it purely as a typological contrast. Finally, Spencer also explained evolution as the product of a steady adaptation of the individual character to 'the social state'. In this respect his sociology rests on definite psychological foundations, despite a strain between this methodological individualism and the holism implied in the organic model of society.

Spencer's reputation reached its apogee in the 1870s and 1880s. As *the* major expression of so-called 'Social Darwinism', Spencer's work was taken up by positivist Marxists and Asian modernizers as well as by apologists for *laissez-faire* capitalism. American social science was cast in a Spencerian mould for a generation or more. However, his political ideals were coming to seem anachronistic by the 1880s, and the evolutionary paradigm, with its optimistic naturalism, lost much of its appeal after 1900. But Spencer exerted influence even on writers like L. T. Hobhouse, who rejected much of his politics, or Durkheim, who pitched his methodology against Spencer but still adapted his typology of societies from Spencer. After long neglect, a wheel came full circle when Parsons, the chief modern exponent of functionalism, revived an essentially Spencerian form of social evolutionary theory in the 1960s.

J. D. Y. Peel
University of Liverpool

Further Reading
Burrow, J. W. (1966), *Evolution and Society*, Cambridge.
Peel, J. D. Y. (1971), *Herbert Spencer: The Evolution of a Sociologist*, London.
Herbert Spencer on Social Evolution (1972), selected writings edited and with an introduction by J. D. Y. Peel, Chicago.

Sullivan, Harry Stack (1892–1949)

Harry Stack Sullivan was born in Norwich, New York on 21 February 1892 and died on 14 January 1949 in Paris. Helen Swick Perry's excellent biography of Sullivan records in detail the events of his life, certain aspects of which profoundly influenced his highly original and creative contributions to psychiatry.

The first and foremost is the effect upon Sullivan's view of the world of his rural, Irish, Roman-Catholic background, and growing up socially isolated because of the then current religious prejudices, as virulent as racial prejudice. It is the fact of his having been a Roman Catholic, rather than his practising the religion itself, that is of central importance in understanding some of his points of view.

The second important biographical fact is that his formal education was limited to one semester at Cornell in 1908 and his receiving his medical degree from the Chicago School of Medicine and Surgery in 1917, a school which Sullivan himself described as 'a diploma mill'. His formal academic work in both institutions can only be described at best as marginal, at worst abysmal. Obviously Sullivan, who in his prime was an intellectual of the highest versatility, was largely self-educated.

Between 1918 and 1922, the years before he began work at Sheppard-Pratt Hospital, Sullivan served in various capacities in the Army Medical Corps and in a number of federal agencies dealing with veterans' matters. This experience in the army gave structure to his life and probably saved him from a mental breakdown. But more importantly, it gave him the chance clinically, in his various roles, to become certified by the government as a neuropsychiatrist. Thus, the loose ends of his cursory medical education were brought into synthesis. He finally had clear and formal medical status in psychiatry.

These themes of social isolation stemming from his Roman-Catholic background, his avid interest in self-education and innovation, and his profound sense not only of American patriotism but of world patriotism marked his life's work.

Sullivan began to formulate his own theoretical ideas, which were stimulated and elaborated by two close friendships: with Clara Thompson, whom he met in 1923, and Edward Sapir, whom he met in 1926. To Thompson he owed the debt of being exposed to psychoanalysis in a formal sense and to Sapir, the anthropologist, he owed support for his convictions about the importance of the interaction between individuals and their cultural and family environments. Although there is no doubt that Sapir was a brilliant intellectual foil to Sullivan through their mutual interest in culture and personality, there was a common bond which probably intensified their friendship: Sullivan as a Roman Catholic and Sapir as a Jew had both suffered religious and ethnic prejudice.

It is interesting that in formulating his theoretical propositions concerning the human condition, be it normal or pathological, Sullivan never abandoned the original intellectual stance he had hoped to realize as a student at Cornell, where he had intended to become either a mathematician or a physicist. To a degree that is equalled by no other psychiatrist before or since, Sullivan was extremely aware of when he was speaking as a scientist, profoundly influenced by the operationalism of Percy Bridgeman and other scientific thinkers and philosophers, and when he was speaking as an artist in the domain of interpersonal relationships. In his own language, Sullivan, depending on the particular situation, was the 'personification' of the natural scientist, the interpersonal artist, or the poetic, imaginative, Irish, lyric thinker. It was his ability to speak in different tongues that gave Sullivan credence in academic circles as well as in the medical domain of science. Given this basic tenet of the operational, to Sullivan what went on between people was the only data admissible to psychiatry. He largely ignored dreams and what he called reverie processes, because they could not be observed. They could create behaviour which could be observed and was thus admissible as clinical data.

A second aspect of Sullivan's theory is that it is *species specific*: human beings are not part of an evolutionary chain as seen by Freud, but are to be seen in their own right. Their primate heritage gives them a capacity no other species possesses: a symbol system and a capacity to interchange symbol systems. This conceptualization was no doubt profoundly reinforced by his friendship with Sapir, whose expertise in anthropology was linguistic relativity. Thus, as Perry has remarked, the capacity to communicate or the inability to communicate is the key to the human condition. Closely related to this idea is Sullivan's assertion that our particular primate status requires us to be in interpersonal contact at all times with significant others. If that contact cannot be maintained, deterioration and mental illness are inevitable.

Corollary to these two basic ideas was Sullivan's postulation that anxiety early in life was induced by the anxious mother and thus anxiety as what he called a 'dysjunctive state' was an inevitable part of the human condition. Sullivan can thus be seen not only as an interpersonal theorist, but as an extremely provocative expositor of the place of anxiety in human affairs. Possibly one of the most interesting aspects of Sullivan's work – given the realities of his personal history – are his highly sophisticated and value-free essays on human sexuality.

One of his most important clinical contributions was the development of milieu therapy in the treatment of schizophrenics. A natural outgrowth of his emphasis on the interpersonal, it is a standard approach in modern psychiatry.

Sullivan's theoretical creativity, for practical purposes, stopped with the onset of World War II, where he became engaged, once again, in various capacities with the military. He was one of the first to see the implications of Hiroshima and, having full knowledge that to undertake a crusade on behalf of peace was to cost him his life, with implacable will he forged ahead. His attempt to set up various foundations bridging psychiatry and the social sciences, his enlisting psychiatrists and social scientists in the cause of peace, all marked the turbulent last years of his life. It can be said that he died serving the cause of humanity.

George W. Goethals
Harvard University

Further Reading
Sullivan, H. S. (1953), *The Interpersonal Theory of Psychiatry*, London.

Tawney, Richard Henry (1880–1962)

R. H. Tawney, distinguished economic historian, social philosopher and passionate enemy of privilege, was born in Calcutta in 1880, the son of an Oriental scholar in the Indian Educational Service, and was educated at Rugby School and Balliol College, Oxford. The most formative experience of his early life was his work as first tutor of the Workers' Educational Association (WEA), a movement in adult education for working people; here his egalitarian Anglican beliefs found their most complete expression.

Largely through his teaching in this organization, and, after 1921, at the London School of Economics (his lifelong academic home), Tawney developed a concept of economic history as a branch of moral philosophy. In his view, the subject entailed the retrieval of the resistance of groups and individuals in the past to the imposition on them of capitalist thought and behaviour. No one could miss the presentmindedness of his history or his commitment to the British Labour movement, expressed both in his important scholarly works, such as *The Agrarian Problem in the Sixteenth Century* (1912) and in *Religion and the Rise of Capitalism* (1926), and in his role as adviser to the Labour party on educational policy over a period of fifty years.

In effect, Tawney was the epitome of the engaged scholar in British academic life in the first half of the twentieth century. Indeed it was this very quality which made his work so attractive to a generation of students, who learned from him that the study of economic history could raise fundamental questions concerning human behaviour and moral values. The same desire to speak to major social issues and to avoid the desiccation of academic specialism can be seen in his more speculative essays in social philosophy, *The Acquisitive Society* (1920) and *Equality* (1931).

As a spokesman for Christian socialism and humane scholarship, he has had no peer in Britain, either in his lifetime or since his death in 1962.

J. M. Winter
Pembroke College, Cambridge

Further Reading

Terrill, R. (1973), *R. H. Tawney and his Times*, London.

Tawney, R. H. (1978), *History and Society*, London.

Tawney, R. H. (1979), *The American Labour Movement*, Brighton.

Winter, J. M. (ed.) (1972), *R. H. Tawney's Commonplace Book*, Cambridge.

Winter, J. M. (1974), *Socialism and the Challenge of War*, London.

Tocqueville, Alexis de (1805–59)

Alexis de Tocqueville, French statesman and political writer, may be considered the founder of comparative historical sociology. He was one of the first to undertake the rigorous comparison of social systems, studying France, England, America and Algeria, and collecting information also on India – his aim being to specify similarities and differences.

An aristocrat by birth, and a committed political animal, he was also a nonpositivist sociologist: his approach was closer to that of Weber than of Marx or Durkheim. 'Liberty,' he remarked, 'is the foremost of my passions.' In the hope of furthering the cause of liberty in France, he undertook the study of democracy in America, where the role of the 'equality of status' as the 'generating factor' attracted him. In America, equality could be reconciled with liberty because democracy preceded equalization and structured it. Men who enjoyed identical civil rights rejected all pressures, and the importance of associations and of local elections frustrated the development of administrative centralization – which, like the threat of social atomization, fostered despotism. In France, in contrast, the Revolution of 1789 reduced the aristocratic society to rubble. The extremely centralized state, rather than the society itself as in the US, did try to foster the equality of civil status, but the resistance to the aristocracy stimulated the development of universalistic and radical theories, unknown in the US, which legitimated the revolutionary process. From that point democracy became inceasingly vulnerable, and it confronted a state, which, while supporting its development, nevertheless remained external to the society. Moreover, both in the US and in France, democracy was threatened by a new authoritarianism, that of industrial power, whose growth it fostered.

Tocqueville's two major works, *De la démocratie en Amérique*, vol. I–IV, (1835–40) (*Democracy in America*, 1945) and *L'Ancien régime et la révolution* (1856) (*The Ancient Regime*, 1952), form a logical unity. In his prolific correspondence with Beaumont, Gobineau, and Mill, as in his *Souvenirs*, Tocqueville was always careful to distinguish the multiple variables which organize different social systems: avoiding deterministic approaches, he always emphasized the essential significance of the values specific to the actors who fashioned consensus or turned revolutionary as a consequence of disappointed hopes.

Pierre Birnbaum
University of Paris

Further Reading
Birnbaum, P. (1970), *Sociologie de Tocqueville*, Paris.
Drescher, S. (1968), *Dilemmas of Democracy: Tocqueville and Modernization*, Pittsburgh.
Lively, J. (1965), *The Social and Political Thoughts of Alexis de Tocqueville*, London.

Tönnies, Ferdinand (1855–1936).

Tönnies, German social theorist and philosopher, was born into an old North German farming family and raised in a small-town environment. He studied philology, philosophy, theology, archaeology and art history at several universities, taking his doctorate at Tübingen in 1875. In 1881 he was granted his *habilitation* for a study of Hobbes which drew on newly-discovered papers of the philosopher. This stimulated his interest in the history and philosophy of law. In the course of his study he introduced the categories of *Gemeinschaft* and *Gesellschaft* (which were to find their way into the title of his magnum opus).

Tönnies served on the staff of the Prussian statistical bureau in Berlin, and began to publish on social and political themes. His commitment to reform delayed his academic career, and he was only appointed to a chair in economics and political science in 1913, when he was nearly fifty. He retired from this post three years later, but returned to the University of Kiel as lecturer in sociology in 1920. He was one of the founders of the German Sociological Association (as was Simmel) and became its president in 1922. But he disbanded the association in 1933 in protest against National Socialism and the already obvious trend towards a 'German National' sociology.

In his principal work, *Gemeinschaft und Gesellschaft* (1887)

(*Community and Association*, London, 1957), one of the classics of sociology, Tönnies adopted a position somewhere between the then dominant schools of natural law and historical jurists. *Gemeinschaft*, motivated by a 'natural will' (*Wessenwille*), was a social form characterized by an intense emotional spirit. It was constituted by co-operation, custom and religion, and its typical expressions were the family, village and small-town community. By contrast, *Gesellschaft* was a large-scale organization, such as the city, state or nation, based on convention, law and public opinion. This dualistic frame of reference resembled Durkheim's contrast between 'organic' and 'mechanical' solidarity, and Weber's distinction between *Vergemeinschaftung* and *Vergesellschaftung*, which were parallel attempts to define the social changes that followed industrialization. Using this contrast, Tönnies built up a system of pure, applied and empirical sociology, but his ambitious attempt to link psychological processes and social structure have largely been forgotten.

Peter-Ernst Schnabel
University of Bielefeld

Further Reading

Cahnman, W. J. (ed.) (1973), *Ferdinand Tönnies: A New Evaluation*, Leiden.

Jacoby, E. G. (1971), *Die moderne Gesellschaft in sozialwissenschaftlichen Denken von Ferdinand Tönnies. Eine biographische Einführung*, Stuttgart.

Mühlmann, E. W. (1957), 'Sociology in Germany: shift in alignment', in H. Becker and A. Boskoff (eds), *Modern Sociological Theory in Continuity and Change*, New York.

Tylor, Edward Burnett (1832–1917)

Born into a well-to-do Quaker industrial family, Tylor did not attend a university. He became interested in 'primitive cultures' by chance, a casual meeting with an English archaeologist leading him to spend several months in Mexico.

Partly under the influence of Darwinian evolutionary thinking, some archaeologists had begun to argue that the remains of ancient cultures exhibited a serial progression, like the fossil varieties of contemporary animal species. German philologists claimed to have discovered a similar progression in man's intellectual productions, notably language. Tylor developed these themes in his *Researches into the Early History of Mankind and the Development of Civilization* (1865). In his second major book, *Primitive Culture* (1871), he extended the argument to the development of religion, suggesting that all religions had advanced from an original form, 'animism', which attributed the possession of spirits to inanimate natural objects. His arguments were based on world-wide comparisons, and were informed by a search for 'survivals': fossilized forms of behaviour which carried over from earlier stages of development and persisted especially in ceremonial contexts. In an important late paper (Tylor, 1889), he introduced a statistical method for the comparative study of cultural traits.

Tylor also introduced a novel German idea of culture into English-speaking discourse. Culture, in this usage, included not only the products of élite civilization, but the whole gamut of learnt skills, habits, modes of communication and beliefs which went to make up a particular way of life, and it was the proper object of anthropological study. Cultures progressed along uniform lines, either as a result of borrowing or by independent inventions which took similar forms at particular levels of development.

Due in part to his longevity, Tylor was the most authoritative figure in anthropology by the turn of the century, and some talked simply of 'Mr Tylor's science'. Oxford created a readership in anthropology for him in 1884, and he later became a professor by personal title. He was elected a Fellow of the Royal Society, and towards the end of his career he was knighted.

Adam Kuper
Brunel University, Uxbridge

Reference

Tylor, E. (1889), 'On a method of investigating the development of institutions', *Journal of the Anthropological Institute*, 18.

Further Reading
Leopold, J. (1980), *Culture in Comparative and Evolutionary Perspective: E. B. Tylor and the Making of Primitive Culture*, Berlin.

Van Gennep, Arnold (1873–1957)

Arnold Van Gennep, the creator of modern French folklore studies, was born in Germany but educated mostly in France. He took a degree at the École Pratique des Hautes Études in Paris, applied (without success) for a chair at the Collège de France, and actually held the first professorship in Swiss ethnography at the University of Neuchâtel (1913–15), yet he remained all his life an academic outsider, if not an outcast. His relationship with the academic ethnology of Durkheimian allegiance, then on the upsurge, was aloof. This did not prevent him from becoming a tireless and methodical collector of information on French popular culture, an efficient organizer of local data-gathering through questionnaires, the founder and publisher of several journals and book collections specializing in folklore, the compiler of a comprehensive bibliography of French folk traditions (1932–3; 1935) and, above all, a prolific author of studies on customs, beliefs and rituals in traditional France and in several European and overseas societies. Because he was linguistically so gifted and enormously well read, he was able to make a powerful contribution – through translations (of Frazer, Havelock Ellis, Westermarck and others) and scientific journalism – to the popularization of the ethnographic knowledge then available.

Van Gennep secured a measure of intellectual legitimacy for the scientific study of folklore, which had been totally neglected in Republican France. His approach was essentially empirical with limited theoretical underpinning, but with a bias towards the comparative method. *Les Rites de passage* (1909) (*The Rites of Passage*, 1960) is a classical illustration of his approach. Rituals marking various stages in the life cycle (pregnancy, birth, childhood, initiation, engagement, marriage, burial) regularly include three sequences: separation, transition, and aggregation or incorporation. Van Gennep stresses the sequential unity of all rituals, as well as their formal patterns, and suggests that rites of passage are indispensable elements of folk culture since they consecrate stages of the physical reproduction of every society.

Victor Karady
Centre National de la Recherche Scientifique, Paris

References
Van Gennep, A. (1908–14), *Essais d'ethnographie et de linguistique*, 5 vols, Paris.
Van Gennep, A. (1932–3), *Le Folklore du Dauphiné. Étude descriptive et comparée de psychologie populaire*, 2 vols, Paris.
Van Gennep, A. (1935), *Le folklore de la Flandre et du Hainaut français (département du Nord)*, 2 vols, Paris.

Further Reading
Belmont, N. (1979), *Arnold Van Gennep, The Creator of French Ethnography*, Chicago.

Veblen, Thorstein Bunde (1857–1929)

Thorstein Veblen, the son of immigrants to the United States, was brought up in isolated farming communities in Wisconsin and Minnesota. He received his doctorate in philosophy from Yale in 1884, but his agnosticism prevented his gaining an academic appointment until 1896 when he received a fellowship in economics at Chicago where he remained until 1906. Subsequently he taught at the Universities of Stanford and Missouri, and in 1918 he moved to New York where he was, for a year, an editor of *The Dial* and taught briefly at the New School for Social Research. The last years of his life were spent in self-imposed, relative isolation in California. Veblen was a true interdisciplinary scholar who possessed a wealth of economic, anthropological, sociological and linguistic knowledge, but his rejection of academic boosterism and his undisguised extra-marital affairs prevented him from gaining an academic rank commensurate with his abilities.

Veblen was a Darwinist in so far as he felt that biological and social evolution were characterized by blind, purposeless drift. In consequence, he rejected Marxism as teleological, utopian and unscientific, and condemned mainstream, orthodox economics for dealing in neat abstractions while avoiding examination of the real, and sometimes unsavoury, factors which affected the working of the economy. In Veblen's view, the metaphysical conceptions of classical economics were anachronistic in the era of machine production and served only to sanctify the economic dominance of businessmen and especially of financier-tycoons – the captains of industry – who, Veblen felt, produced little but waste, industrial disruption and paper profits for themselves.

Veblen's first two books, *The Theory of the Leisure Class* (1899) and, more specialized, *Theory of Business Enterprise* (1904), provided a mordant and ironic examination of these processes. Veblen drew a sharp distinction between socially useful 'industrial' occupations and nonproductive, socially deleterious 'pecuniary' ones and depicted American society as being permeated by the spirit of business enterprise which was manifested in fraud, chicanery, self-aggrandisement and predation. *The Higher Learning in America* (1918) further documented the implications of this spirit in the 'business-like' conduct of American universities.

After 1914, Veblen's writings became more overtly political as he cast aside the guise of academic objectivity which had lightly veiled the condemnations contained in his earlier writings. In *Imperial Germany and the Industrial Revolution* (1915) and *An Inquiry Into the Nature of Peace* (1917) he analysed the emergence of Germany as an industrial and military power and pessimistically concluded that a lasting peace was unlikely, as the newly industrialized, militaristic and dynastic nations of Germany and Japan would eventually join forces and provoke a renewed and perhaps more devastating world conflict. The Russian Revolution encouraged Veblen to think that the 'vested interests' in America might similarly be overthrown, but the optimistic materialism of the 1920s dashed his hopes, and his last major work, *Absentee Ownership* (1923), represents the bitter and splenetic outpourings of a disappointed man.

Veblen's writings, which included a large number of important articles and several books in addition to those cited above, constituted an excoriating critique of capitalistic institutions and documented the dominance of 'imbecile institutions' over reason in human affairs. Personally, Veblen was taciturn, uncommunicative and resolutely unconventional. He made disciples almost inadvertently, greatly influencing the school of institutional economists who insisted on studying the sordid realities of the working of the economic system and indirectly influencing, among many others, such unconventional theorists as the economist J. K. Galbraith and the radical sociologist C. W. Mills. Veblen's reputation has declined in recent years, at least in part and rather ironically, as many of his ideas and concepts have passed into common academic parlance. In this respect Veblen has 'paid the penalty of taking the lead', a phrase he coined in the context of a discussion of Britain's failure to maintain its earlier industrial and commercial dominance.

John Whitworth
Simon Fraser University

Further Reading
Diggins, J. P. (1978), *The Bard of Savagery: Thorstein Veblen and Modern Social Theory*, New York.
Dorfman, J. (1934), *Thorstein Veblen and His America*, New York.

Watson, John Broadus (1878–1958)

As the founder of behaviourism and as a publicist and popularizer of psychology, John B. Watson was perhaps the most influential American psychologist of his generation. Born in 1878 near Greenville, South Carolina, Watson grew up in a large and poor rural family. He attended Furman University, a small Baptist college near Greenville, and graduated with a Master of Arts Degree in 1899. Watson entered the University of Chicago in 1900, where he studied with John Dewey, psychologist James Rowland Angell, neurophysiologist H. H. Donaldson and biologist Jacques Loeb.

At Chicago, Angell had been instrumental in founding the functional school of psychology. Influenced by Darwin, William James and Dewey, the functionalists opposed the elementistic psychology developed by Wilhelm Wundt in Germany and espoused in America as structuralism by British-trained psychologist E. B. Titchener. Whereas structuralism attempted to discover the structure of mind by first isolating the basic elements of consciousness, functionalism was concerned with the mind in use and held that the function of consciousness was its capacity to enable an organism to adapt to its environment.

Although a protégé of Angell, Watson was later to reject both functionalism and structuralism. Even as a student he was particularly influenced by Loeb's insistence that all life processes could be explained in physiochemical terms. Watson's own interests lay in comparative or animal psychology. He was uncomfortable with human subjects and what he considered to be the artificiality of introspective methods, which required subjects to observe and record the sensations and perceptions of their own conscious experience. His dissertation, completed under H. H. Donaldson, was a study of the correlation between the learned behaviour and the neurophysiology of the white rat. In 1903, Watson received the first Ph.D. granted in psychology from the University of Chicago. With the recommendation of Angell and Dewey, he was invited to stay at Chicago as lecturer and director of the psychological laboratory and quickly gained a reputation as a leading figure in the relatively new field of comparative psychology.

In 1908, Watson was invited by James Mark Baldwin to develop a programme in experimental psychology at Johns Hopkins University. Less than a year later, Baldwin was forced to resign, leaving Watson as chairman of the department and editor of the *Psychological Review*. At Johns Hopkins, Watson became increasingly dissatisfied with the assumptions of both structuralism and functionalism. As long as psychology considered its subject matter to be the investigation of consciousness, he argued, it perpetuated a mind-body dualism that kept it beyond the pale of current scientific assumptions. Watson believed that he could resolve this issue by simply denying the existence of mind as a distinct entity. For years he had been investigating animals without referring to purely mental categories or functions. As early as 1910, he had become convinced that psychological investigations could be conducted exclusively through the observation of behaviour without any reference to consciousness. By 1913, he was ready to make his position public. In a lecture entitled 'Psychology as the Behaviourist Views It', Watson issued an open challenge to the established preconceptions of psychological method and theory.

Watson's behaviourism not only offered a new methodological approach to psychological investigation, but attempted to redefine fundamental assumptions of the profession itself. Claiming that psychology had 'failed signally' to take its place as 'an undisputed natural science', Watson placed the blame on the use of the introspective method and its underlying assumption of the existence of states of consciousness. Watson considered 'mind' and 'consciousness' to be as unverifiable as 'soul' and refused to make any assumption that could not be observed and verified from overt behaviour. Behaviourism, Watson argued, would at once enable psychology to become a 'purely objective natural science', with its 'theoretical goal' being nothing less than the 'prediction and control of behavior'. Watson hoped to ally psychology with the positivist trend in the natural and social sciences. He also sought to bridge the gap between experimental and applied psychology by claiming that behaviourism would enable psychologists to develop techniques that would be of direct use to 'the educator, the physician, the jurist and the business man'.

In 1914, Watson was elected president of the American Psychological Association. In his presidential address the following year, he consolidated his behaviourist theory by offering the conditioned motor reflex (as described by Russian neurologist, V. M. Bechterev) as an objective methodology that could be used to measure and control sensory responses. Watson then began experiments on human subjects which culminated in 1919 which his famous 'Little Albert' experiment, by which Watson claimed to have developed techniques to condition, at will, specific emotional reactions in infants. In the midst of conducting this experiment, Watson became romantically involved with his graduate assistant, and as a result, was forced to resign from Johns Hopkins in 1920 under the cloud of a widely publicized divorce scandal.

Watson then moved to New York, where he became a successful advertising executive until his retirement in 1945. During this period, he was a tireless promoter of the use of psychological techniques in business and industry. He also continued to teach at the New School for Social Research and sponsored psychological research on infants at Columbia University. During the 1920s and 1930s, Watson promoted behaviourism to a mass audience. His widely read *Behaviorism* (1924) was followed by an enormous output of popular magazine and newspaper articles. In *The Psychological Care of Infant and Child* (1928), Watson advised parents to raise children according to a strict regimen that discouraged displays of affection. Later writings included his utopian vision of a society ordered on behaviouristic principles and governed by a hierarchy of technicians.

Although few psychologists were willing to accept Watson's abandonment of consciousness wholeheartedly and came to reject the more radical aspects of his extreme materialism, behaviourism's objective methodology had a powerful impact on the direction of American experimental psychology. Moreover, the popular reception of behaviourism in America was not only a tribute to Watson's skill as a propagandist, but reflected a national preoccupation with order and efficiency in a society that was in the process of rapid urban and industrial expansion.

Kerry W. Buckley

Further Reading
Boakes, R. A. (1984), *From Darwin to Behaviorism*, Cambridge.
Buckley, K. W. (1986), *Mechanical Man: John B. Watson and the Beginnings of Behaviorism*, New York.

Watson, J. B. (1913), 'Psychology as the behaviorist views it', *Psychological Review*, 20.

Watson, J. B. (1924), *Behaviorism*, New York.

Watson, J. B. and Watson, R. R. (1928), *The Psychological Care of Infant and Child*, New York.

Weber, Max (1864–1920)

Max Weber, the son of a member of the Reichstag and an activist Protestant mother, grew up in Berlin in an intellectually lively home frequently visited by the Bismarckian era's leading politicians and intellectuals. After receiving an outstanding secondary education in languages, history, and the classics, he studied law, economics, history, and philosophy at the Universities of Heidelberg, Strasbourg, Göttingen, and Berlin. Although his first appointments, at the Universities of Freiburg (1894) and Heidelberg (1897), were in the faculty of economics, he is best known today as one of the major founders of modern sociology and as one of the intellectual giants of interdisciplinary scholarship. As strange as it may sound, he ranged freely across the entire palette of written history, from the ancient Greeks to the early Hindus, from the Old Testament prophets to the Confucian literati, from the economic organization of early Near-Eastern civilizations to the trading companies of the Medieval West, and from the origins of Continental law to comparative analyses of the rise of the modern state.

The diversity of these themes – only a small sampling – should not lead us to view Weber as a scholar of unlimited energies frantically leaping about for its own sake. Rather, when looked at closely, a grand design becomes visible in his writings, yet one that remained incomplete and whose inner coherence can be plotted only against the inner torments of their author. Weber and others of his generation in Germany viewed the dawning of rapid industrialization and the modern age itself with profound ambivalence rather than as a first step toward a new era of progress. While welcoming the possibilities it offered for a burgeoning of individualism and an escape from the feudal chains of the past, he saw few firm guidelines in reference to which modern man might be able to establish a comprehensive meaning for his life or even his everyday action (1946). Moreover, the overtowering bureaucracies indispensable to the organization of industrial societies were endowed with the capacity to render persons politically powerless as well as to replace creative potential with stifling routine and merely functional relationships. These developments threatened to curtail the flowering of individualism.

Just such quandries stood behind all of Weber's sociological writings, particularly those undertaken after 1903. In these studies he wished to define precisely the uniqueness of his own civilization and to understand on a universal scale the manner in which persons, influenced by social constellations, formulate *meaning* for their lives that guides action. A curiosity founded in such questions instilled in him an amazing capacity to place himself, once he had constructed a 'mental image' of another era and civilization, into the minds of persons quite unlike himself. This aim to understand how values and actions made sense to their beholders, however foreign they were to the social scientist investigating them, formed the foundation for Weber's *verstehende* sociology.

Perhaps it was this sensitivity, as well as a sheer respect for meanings formulated over centuries, that prompted Weber to construct one of his most famous axioms, one debated heatedly to this day. To him, all scientific judgements must be 'value-free': once researchers have selected their themes of inquiry, then personal values, preferences, and prejudices must not be allowed to interfere with the collection of empirical data and its 'objective' evaluation (1949). Everyone involved in scientific work should avoid an inadvertent intermixture of his values with those of the actors being studied. To Weber, even the scientist who happened to be a Calvinist was duty-bound – as long as he wished to pursue science – to describe, for example, tribal sexual practices accurately and to interpret them in reference to their indigenous 'cultural significance', however repugnant they seemed to him personally. This postulate also implied a strict division between that which *exists* (the question for scientific analysis) and that which *should be* (the realm of personal values).

In explicitly circumscribing the legitimate domain of science and denying it the right to produce norms, ideals, and values, Weber had a larger purpose in mind. He hoped to establish an inviolable realm within which individuals would be forced to confront themselves and autonomously formulate a set of personal values capable of guiding their actions and endowing them with meaning. Nothing less was required as a counter-force in an age in which bureaucratization and the scientific world view threatened to encroach upon decision making, thus upsetting the already tenuous character of individualism. Weber's own adherence to a value-free science, particularly in his studies of pre-modern and non-Western societies, the penetration of his insight into the diverse ways in which meaning could be formed and patterned action ensued, and the universal-historical scope of his investigations enabled him to write – however fragmented, incomplete, and poorly organized – a comparative historical sociology of civilizations unique in the history of sociology.

Even though his interest focused upon comparisons between civilizations, Weber's emphasis upon individual meaning prevented him from taking the Hegelian Absolute Spirit, the Marxian organization of production and class struggle, or the 'social facts' of Durkheim as his point of departure. Nor was he inclined, due to his continuous accentuation of the conflicts between diverse 'spheres of life' (religious, political, economic, legal, aesthetic) and the centrality of power and domination, to view societies, like Parsons, as basically integrated wholes. In fact, Weber's orientation to the individual and the meaning he attaches to his action would seem to carry him dangerously close to a radical subjectivism. Two procedures guarded against this possibility:

First, in his substantive studies, it was the patterned actions of individuals in groups, and not individuals acting alone, that captured his attention. It was only this regular action that, according to Weber, proved to be culturally significant and historically powerful. Individuals tended to become knit together into collectivities primarily in five ways: acknowledgement of common material interests (as occurred when classes were formed), recognition of common 'ideal interests' (as took place when status groups arose), adherence to a single world view (as occurred in religious groups), acknowledgement of affectual feelings (as found in person-oriented groups, such as the household, the clan, and the neighbourhood), and awareness of relations of domination (as took place in the charismatic, patriarchal, feudal, patrimonial, and bureaucratic forms of domination). However massive and enduring an institution might appear, it must not, according to Weber, be understood as more than the orientations of individuals acting in common.

The second means employed by Weber to avoid lapsing into a radical subjectivism involves his major methodological tool, one that reveals his indebtedness to Kant: the 'ideal type' (1949). Indeed, this heuristic construct so effectively guarded against this possibility that a number of commentators have accused Weber – particularly in his later work – of moving away from a *verstehende* sociology and of reifying the social phenomena he studies. In part, Weber himself is to blame. Instead of discussing, for example, 'bureaucratically-oriented action', he uses the term 'bureaucracy', and rather than using 'class-oriented action', he speaks of 'classes'.

Perhaps the ideal type can be best understood against the backdrop of Weber's view of social reality. For him, when examined at its basic level, social reality presents a ceaseless flow of occurrences and events, very few of which, although repeatedly interwoven, seem to fall together coherently. Due to its infinite complexity, no investigator can expect to capture reality exhaustively, nor even to render accurately all its contours.

Weber took over a nominalistic position to confront this conundrum and propounded the use of the ideal type. This purely analytic tool enables us to acquire a purchase upon reality through its 'simplification'. Far from arbitrary, however, the procedures for doing so involve a deliberate *exaggeration of the essence* of the phenomenon under study and its reconstruction in a form with greater internal unity than ever appeared in empirical reality. Thus, Weber's conceptualization, for example, of the bureaucracy or the Calvinist does not aim to portray accurately all bureaucracies or Calvinists, but to call attention only to essential aspects. As an artificial construct, the ideal type abstracts from reality and fails to define *any* particular phenomenon. Nonetheless, it serves two crucial purposes: it allows us, once an entire series of ideal types appropriate for a theme under investigation have been formed, to undertake comparisons across civilizations and epochs; and, when used as a heuristic yardstick in comparison to which a given bureaucracy or Calvinist church can be defined and its deviation assessed, it enables an isolation and clear conceptualization of distinctive attributes. Only after a number of idealtypical 'experiments' have been conducted can we move on to questions regarding the purely empirical *causes* for the uniqueness of the particular case. For Weber, these questions were more interesting than ones of definition alone.

Although he outlined a methodology – only hinted at above – that would allow him to investigate the manner in which individuals formulated meaning in different civilizations and epochs as well as to define precisely the uniqueness of the modern West, it must be concluded that, when viewed in reference to these broad aims, his various writings constitute mere fragments. Most, including his comparative studies on the *Economic Ethics of the World Religions* (*EEWR*) (these include *The Religion of China* [1951], *The Religion of India* [1958] and *Ancient Judaism* [1952]), and *Economy and Society* (*E&S*), were published in incomplete form. Nonetheless, the discrete elements of the whole have stood on their own and become classics in their own right. Broadly speaking, Weber's works divide into more empirical investigations on the one hand and analytical models on the other.

By far his most famous, debated, and readable book, *The Protestant Ethic and the Spirit of Capitalism* (1930 [1922]), falls into the former category. In this classic, Weber sought to understand certain origins of modern capitalism. For him, this form of capitalism was distinguished by a systematic organization of work, the replacement of a 'traditional economic ethic' among workers as well as entrepreneurs by methodical labour, and a systematic search for profit. Thus, Weber saw an attitude toward work and profit – a 'spirit of capitalism' – as important, and denied that the influx of precious metals, technological advances, population increases, the universal desire for riches, or the Herculean efforts of 'economic supermen' (Carnegie, Rockefeller, Fugger) were adequate to explain the origin of modern capitalism.

Religious roots, according to Weber, anchored this 'spirit', namely the doctrines of the Protestant sects and churches, particularly the seventeenth-century pastoral exhortations of Calvinism. The deep anxiety introduced by this religion's predestination doctrine in respect to the overriding question of one's personal salvation proved more than believers could reasonably bear. Gradually, worldly success came to be viewed as a *sign* that God had bestowed his favour and, thus, as evidence of membership among the predestined elect. In this way, since it allowed the devout *to believe* they belonged among the chosen few and thereby alleviated intense anxiety, worldly success itself became endowed with a religious – indeed, a salvation – incentive, or 'psychological premium'. Methodical labour in a calling (*Beruf*) proved the surest pathway toward worldly success, as did the continuous reinvestment of one's wealth – an unintended consequence of this attitude – rather than its squandering on worldly pleasures. To Weber, the medieval monk's 'other-worldly asceticism' became, with Calvinism, transformed into an 'inner-worldly asceticism'.

In calling attention to this religiously-based cause of modern capitalism, Weber in no way sought to substitute an 'idealist' for a 'materialist' explanation (1930 [1922]). Rather, he aimed only to point out the heretofore neglected idealist side in order to emphasize that a comprehensive explanation of modern capitalism's origins must include consideration of the 'economic ethic' as well as the 'economic form'. Far from claiming that Calvinism led to modern capitalism in a monocausal fashion, Weber asserted that the rise of this type of capitalism can be explained adequately only through multidimensional models (1961 [1927]; Collins, 1980; Cohen, 1981; Kalberg, 1983).

Indeed, as Weber noted in his discussion of 'backwoods Pennsylvania' (1930 [1922]), and as Gordon Marshall has demonstrated in the case of Scotland (1980, 1982), a constellation of material factors must exist in a manner such that a conducive context is formulated, for without this context the 'spirit of capitalism' is powerless to introduce modern capitalism. On the other hand, once firmly entrenched, modern capitalism perpetuates itself on the basis of secularized socialization processes as well as coercive mechanisms and no longer requires its original 'spirit'.

While addressing the rise of modern capitalism in a novel manner, *The Protestant Ethic* failed to grapple with the larger, comparative issue: the distinctiveness of the Occident, Weber knew well, could be defined only through a series of comparisons with non-Western civilizations. In turning to China and India, he again took the issue of modern capitalism as his focus, though here he posed the negative question of why, in these civilizations, this type of capitalism had failed to develop. Moreover, far from attempting to assess only whether Confucian, Taoist, Hindu, and Buddhist teachings introduced or inhibited methodical economic action, these studies turned as well to the 'materialist' side and sought to discuss the economic ethics of non-Western world religions in the context of a whole series of social structural and organizational variables. This comparative procedure enabled Weber also to delineate the array of 'material' factors in the West that proved unique and conducive to the development of modern capitalism. These empirical studies, in addition to his investigations of ancient Judaism, carried him a giant step further as well in his attempt to understand the manner in which sociological configurations influence the formation of meaning.

Yet these studies remained, as Weber himself repeatedly emphasized (1972 [1920]; 1930 [1922]), drastically incomplete, especially if examined in reference to his overall goals. They are, furthermore, too poorly organized to provide us with a distinctly Weberian approach for an unlocking of the elusive relationship between ideas and interests. These empirical investigations must be read through the lens of the analytical categories and models Weber develops for the analysis of social action on a universal-historical scale in one of the genuine classics of modern social science, *E&S* (1968 [1922]).

At first glance, this tome seems to conceal thoroughly Weber's larger aims. Part One is concerned primarily with the articulation of a broad series of sociological concepts. Although empirically-based, each of these, since formulated on a universal-historical scale, remains at a high level of abstraction. Nonetheless, each one can be utilized as a heuristic yardstick that serves as a point of reference for the definition of particular cases. The ideal types in Part Two are less all-encompassing and relate generally to specific epochs and civilizations (Mommsen, 1974). This section reveals on every page how its author, in considering historical examples, extracted their essence and constructed ideal types. Just this perpetual movement between the historical and ideal-typical levels, as well as Weber's unwillingness to formulate an ideal type before scrutinizing innumerable cases, accounts for its exceedingly disjointed character. His failure to discuss his overriding themes in a synoptic fashion has also decreased the readability of *E&S*.

These problems have blinded most Weber specialists to the comprehensive 'analytic' of social action buried between the lines of this treatise and utilizable for the comparative and historical study even of entire civilizations (Kalberg, 1980, 1985). Consequently, each chapter has been read and debated apart from its broader purposes in the Weberian corpus and in an ahistorical fashion. Nonetheless, standing on their own, the separate chapters have attained classical status in a wide variety of sociology's subfields, such as the sociology of religion, urban sociology, stratification, economic sociology, modernization and development, the sociology of law, and political sociology. In each chapter, Weber lays out, in light of the specific problematic involved, a universal-historical analytic that includes a differentiated discussion of the ways in which, at each stage in each analytic, social action becomes patterned by diverse internal and external constraints and acquires its *locus* in specific status groups and organizations.

Only the typology of rulership (*Herrschaft*) can be given special attention here. (This translation has been suggested by Benjamin Nelson and appears to me preferable to either 'domination', which captures the element of force yet weakens the notion of legitimacy, or 'authority', which conveys legitimacy but downplays the component of force.) In this voluminous section Weber wished to define the major bases conceivable for the legitimation of rulership and to articulate, for each, the typical relationships between rulers, administrative bodies, and the ruled. Charismatic personalities derived a right to rule from their extraordinary personal qualities and the belief of the ruled in their transcendent inspiration; traditional rulership (patriarchal, feudal, and patrimonial) rested upon custom and the belief that 'time immemorial' itself provided a justification for continued rule; and rational-legal (bureaucratic) rulership was legitimated through laws, statutes, and regulations. Crucial for the endurance of all types is at least a minimum belief on the part of the ruled that the rulership is justified. While many interpreters have reified these concepts, Weber designed them exclusively as heuristic yardsticks.

Throughout *E&S*, as well as the *EEWR*, a subtle and dialectical view of the relationships between value-oriented, interest-oriented, and tradition-oriented action prevails. As opposed to the more empirically-based *EEWR* studies, these relationships in the *E&S* are dealt with more as models which, on the one hand, combine ideal types in relationships of 'elective affinities' and, on the other hand, chart the patterned 'relations of antagonisms' between discrete concepts and even differentiated spheres of life. At this point, Weber's sociology goes far beyond mere concept-formation and classification and moves to the level of the dynamic interaction of constellations. At this 'contextual' level, he shifts repeatedly back and forth between ideal types of varying range, all of which aim to articulate 'developmental sequences': entire series of ideal types that, on the basis of a developmental dimension as well as a focus upon spheres of life and types of rulership, seek to conceptualize epochal change. Whether the change hypothesized by these research instruments in fact took place in the history of a particular epoch and civilization remained for Weber an empirical question, one that involved, above all, the strength of 'carrier' strata, the success of new groups and organizations in establishing their rulership, and sheer power. Despite his awareness of the inflexibility of tradition and the manner in which millennia-long histories remained within civilizational 'tracks', or world views, Weber's conviction that power and unexpected historical 'accidents' could always introduce a chain-reaction realignment of configurations prevented him from constructing global formulas that promised to forecast the unfolding of societies. To Weber, the materialist interpretation of history, for example, provided a useful hypothesis rather than a scientific explanation.

This sketch of Weber's sociology has touched upon only a few of its major contours. The intensity of Weber's persistent struggle with the immense complexity, unresolved paradoxes, and even contradictory drifts of social reality, and his refusal to simplify on behalf of doctrinal or ideological positions, can be appreciated only by those who directly confront his writings. Fortunately, in turning toward systematic analyses of the major underlying themes in his corpus as a whole, the ongoing Weber renaissance in the Federal Republic of Germany (Kalberg, 1979), Great Britain, and the United States (Glassman, 1983) promises to knit together its fragments and to reveal the concerns that literally possessed one of our century's most remarkable scholars.

Stephen Kalberg
Harvard University

References

Cohen, I. J. (1981), 'Introduction to the Transaction Edition', in M. Weber, *General Economic History*, New Brunswick.

Collins, R. (1980), 'Weber's last theory of capitalism', *American Sociological Review*, 56.

Glassman, R. (1983), 'The Weber renaissance', in S. G. McNall (ed.), *Current Perspectives in Social Theory*, Greenwood, Connecticut.

Kalberg, S. (1979), 'The search for thematic orientations in a fragmented œuvre: the discussion of Max Weber in recent German sociological literature', *Sociology*, 13.

Kalberg, S. (1980), 'Max Weber's types of rationality: cornerstones for the analysis of rationalization processes in history', *American Journal of Sociology*, 85.

Kalberg, S. (1983), 'Max Weber's universal-historical architectonic of economically-oriented action: a preliminary reconstruction', in S. G. McNall (ed.), *Current Perspectives in Social Theory*, Greenwood, Connecticut.

Kalberg, S. (1986), *Max Weber's Comparative Historical Sociology of Reconstruction*, London.

Marshall, G. (1980), *Presbyteries and Profits: Calvinism and the Development of Capitalism in Scotland, 1560–1707*, Oxford.

Marshall, G. (1982), *In Search of the Spirit of Capitalism*, London.

Mommsen, W. (1974), *Max Weber: Gesellschaft, Politik und Geschichte*, Frankfurt.

Weber, M. (1972 [1920]), *Collected Papers on the Sociology of Religion*, London. (Original German edn, *Gesammelte Aufsatze zur Religionssoziologie*, vol. 1, Tübingen.)

Weber, M. (1961 [1927]), *General Economic History*, London. (Original German edn, *Wirtschaftsgeschichte*, Munich.)

Weber, M. (1930 [1922]), *The Protestant Ethic and the Spirit of Capitalism*, London. (Original German edn, *Die protestantische Ethik und der 'Geist' des Kapitalismus*, Tübingen.)

Weber, M. (1946), *From Max Weber*, eds H. H. Gerth and C. W. Mills, New York.

Weber, M. (1949), *The Methodology of the Social Sciences*, selection and translation of essays by E. Shils, New York.

Weber, M. (1951), *The Religion of China*, New York.

Weber, M. (1952), *Ancient Judaism*, New York.

Weber, M. (1958), *The Religion of India*, New York.

Weber, M. (1968 [1922]), *Economy and Society*, New York. (Original German edn, *Wirtschaft und Gesellschaft*, Tübingen.)

Further Reading
Bendix, R. (1960), *Max Weber: An Intellectual Portrait*, London.
Bendix, R. and Roth, G. (1971), *Scholarship and Partisanship:*
  Essays on Max Weber, Berkeley and Los Angeles.
Löwith, K. (1982), *Max Weber and Karl Marx*, London.
Nelson, B. (1981), *On the Roads to Modernity: Conscience, Science*
  and Civilizations, Totowa, NJ.

Wittgenstein, Ludwig Josef Johann (1889–1951)

Wittgenstein was born in Vienna and though originally trained
as an engineer became a pupil of Bertrand Russell at
Cambridge. He returned to Austria to serve in the First World
War, and in 1921 published the German edition of the *Tractatus
Logico-Philosophicus*. He then became a school teacher in Lower
Austria. In this, as in everything else, he was an intense and
demanding man, and soon resigned his post. After that, he
became involved in the design of a house which still stands in
Vienna, a monument to the aesthetic austerity that he championed. Around this time he rejected the *Tractatus* and began
to articulate his later philosophy. He returned to Cambridge in
1929 and held the chair of philosophy from 1939 to 1947.

In the *Tractatus* the essence of language is assumed to reside
in its fact-stating function. This is said to rest on the capacity
of sentences to 'picture' facts. Pictures consist of parts which
correspond to the parts of the thing pictured. The parts of a
picture stand to one another in a certain relation, and this says
how the corresponding objects are arranged if the picture is
true. In language the parts are names, and elementary sentences
are arrangements of names. More complicated sentences can
then be built up by using the rules of Russell's logic. Wittgenstein may have based his picture theory on the way in which
systems of material points have a symbolic representation in
sophisticated versions of theoretical mechanics. Certainly the
conclusion he drew was that the only meaningful language was
the language of science. All attempts to transcend this and
express what is 'higher' – namely, ethics, aesthetics and the
meaning of life – are doomed. Even the attempt to state the
relation of language to the world tries to go beyond these limits,

so the doctrines of the *Tractatus* itself are meaningless. Those who understand my propositions correctly, said Wittgenstein, will surmount them like a ladder, and then throw them away.

Is this an attack on everything nonscientific? Wittgenstein's friend, Paul Engelmann, tells us that it is the exact opposite. The aim is not to dismiss what cannot be said, the 'higher', but to *protect* it. The *Tractatus* is an ethical document which must be understood in terms of Wittgenstein's involvement with the great Viennese critic Karl Kraus and the influential architect Adolf Loos. Kraus exposed moral corruption which shows itself in the corruption of language. Loos conducted a campaign against aesthetic corruption which shows itself in the confusion of art with utility and the pollution of functional simplicity by needless decoration. The *Tractatus* likewise expressed the ethics of purity, separation, simplicity and the integrity of silence.

Why Wittgenstein became dissatisfied with this position is unclear, but some light may be shed by relating his shift of opinion to a broad cultural change in which he participated. If the *Tractatus* addressed the issues that exercised pre-war Viennese intellectuals, the late philosophy addressed the problems that confronted them in the post-war years. We know that the military defeats and economic and constitutional problems in Europe were accompanied by an acute sense of cultural crisis. One symptom of this was the enormous popularity of Spengler's irrational life-philosophy with its conservative pessimism. Wittgenstein is known to have been impressed by Spengler, and the later work can be seen as a brilliant expression of this form of conservative irrationalism. All the features of this style – the priority of the concrete over the abstract, of practice over norms, life over reason and being over thought – are prominently displayed.

In his later work Wittgenstein rejected the idea that language has a single essential function. It is not structured by correspondence with objects but by its role in the stream of life. There are as many ways for words to carry meaning as there are ways of organizing action. The picture theory gave way to the idea of 'language-games'. We must not theorize about language but observe its diversity as we name, count, instruct, question, promise, pray and so on. The real heart of the late philosophy, however, is the analysis of rule following. It is tempting to explain human behaviour in terms of our capacity to follow rules. In § 201 of the *Investigations* Wittgenstein argued that no course of action can be determined by rules because any course of action could be said to accord with the rule. Any non-standard interpretation of a rule could be justified by a non-standard interpretation of the rules for following the rule. Ultimately it must be said of all rules that they are obeyed 'blindly'. At every point, rules, and the application of the concepts in them, depend on taken for granted practices or customs. Wittgenstein used this insight to bring out the conventional character of all knowledge and discourse, whether it was an introspective report or a mathematical truth.

For the later Wittgenstein, then, the notion of meaning is explained in terms of *use*. Meaningless or metaphysical discourse is language 'on holiday', that is, not employed in a language game that has a genuine role in a form of life. The job of the philosopher is to inhibit our tendency to detach words from their real use. In this the philosopher is like a doctor who must bring language back to its healthy everyday life. What had to be accepted as given, said Wittgenstein, was the 'form of life'. Other than this all belief is groundless: this is the end-point of all justification. Nothing could be a clearer expression of the conservative thinker's belief in the priority of life over reason.

It is only now that this European dimension of Wittgenstein's thinking, both in its early and late phase, is beginning to emerge. This offsets the somewhat narrow readings that have been given them as forms of logical and linguistic 'analysis'. Nevertheless the full potential of the late philosophy, as the basis of a social theory of knowledge, still awaits exploitation.

David Bloor
University of Edinburgh

Further Reading

As Wittgenstein's unpublished writings gradually appear in print, the corpus of his work now stands at over a dozen volumes. Nevertheless, the main texts of the early and late philosophy, respectively, are still:

Tractatus Logico-Philosophicus, trans. D. F. Pears and B. F. McGuinness, London, 1961; and *Philosophical Investigations*, trans. G. E. M. Anscombe, Oxford, 1953.

Bloor, D. (1983), *Wittgenstein: A Social Theory of Knowledge*, London.

Engelman, P. (1967), *Letters from Ludwig Wittgenstein with a Memoir*, Oxford.

Janik, A. and Toulmin, S. (1973), *Wittgenstein's Vienna*, London.

Specht, E. K. (1963), *The Foundations Of Wittgenstein's Late Philosophy*, Manchester.

Winch, P. (1958), *The Idea of a Social Science and its Relation to Philosophy*, London.